# UNIFIED FITNESS

**Also by John Alton:**
*Living Qigong: The Chinese Way*
*to Good Health and Long Life*

A 35-Day Exercise Program for
*Sustainable Health*

# UNIFIED FITNESS

# *John Alton*

HAMPTON ROADS
PUBLISHING COMPANY, INC.

Cover design by Grace Pedalino
Cover graphic by Eyewire
Cover photographs by Norman Carter

Interior photography by Norman Carter and Mike Cundiff
Interior art by Anne L. Dunn, John Hughes,
Rebecca Parrish, and Rosalie Day White

Hampton Roads Publishing Company, Inc.
1125 Stoney Ridge Road
Charlottesville, VA 22902

434-296-2772
fax: 434-296-5096
e-mail: hrpc@hrpub.com
www.hrpub.com

If you are unable to order this book from your local
bookseller, you may order directly from the publisher.
Call 1-800-766-8009, toll-free.

Library of Congress Catalog Card Number: 2001094967
ISBN 1-57174-224-7
10 9 8 7 6 5 4 3 2 1
Printed on acid-free paper in Canada

This book is dedicated
to the memory
of William Andrew Alton,
1957-1972.

# Table of Contents

## Phase 4: Troubleshooting Unified Fitness

# Case Studies Guide

# Case Studies Guide

# Chronic Health Problems and Unified Fitness Solutions

# Chronic Health Problems and Unified Fitness Solutions

Migraine headache: *302*

Premenstrual
Syndrome (PMS): *307*

Prostatitis: *303*

Raynaud's syndrome: *124*

Rheumatoid arthritis: *138*

*Salmonella* poisoning: *312*

Sciatica (unspecified cause): *302*

Sinusitis (chronic): *310*

Skull fracture: *165*

## Gray Areas

Athletic performance: *53*

Exercise addiction: *287*

Excess weight: *86*

Low self-esteem: *227*

Musculoskeletal tightness: *125*

Unresolved emotional conflict: *254*

# Preface

In his book dealing with the principles of Unified Fitness, John Alton takes the ancient Chinese concept of Qi, and the role of this vital energy principle in health and disease, and translates it into the concept of reflexive exercise—a concept more palatable to our Western culture and sensibilities. However, Alton goes further. He attempts to take the poorly defined (for the Western mind) notion of Qi and frame it in the context of our current knowledge in Western medicine of the anatomy, physiology, and function of the nervous system and the immune system. He carries out his difficult task most admirably and has produced a book which is understandable to both the expert and, more importantly, to the general public.

To his great credit, Alton has also taken the Eastern concept of Qi as well as our Western medical scientific knowledge of human physiology and merged them with the emerging—and still very controversial—concept of the importance of infectious agents as the cause of many diverse chronic human diseases. Mr. Alton is to be commended for his efforts. He has produced an eminently readable and thought-provoking book.

*Thomas J. Braciale, M.D., Ph.D.*
*Director, Beirne B. Carter Center*
*for Immunology Research,*
*University of Virginia School of Medicine*

# Foreword

If you have ever seen the television drama *ER,* then you probably have an idea of what my job entails.

As a board-certified emergency physician for fourteen years, I have what I consider one of the most stressful occupations a person can imagine. On a daily basis I experience the ravages of poor lifestyles, trauma, and infectious diseases. It is not unusual in one day for me to see a shooting victim, a patient with a heart attack, another with pneumonia, a child with broken bones, and countless other patients with life-threatening problems. I never sit down in the hospital cafeteria to eat. I am on the go from the minute I step into the hospital until I leave. These realities, plus the kind of thinking built into emergency medical training, have made me a practical, logical, and goal-oriented thinker, as well as someone with a "battle frontline" mentality, with the need to see results fast.

Luckily, I recognize the need to take care of myself, and exercise has always been my main coping strategy. My need for exercise, combined with my medical background, has made me a connoisseur of every new workout fad, and a sharp-eyed critic of the science (if any exists) behind these fads. Like most emergency physicians, I'm also an "adrenaline junkie," and thus tend to move from one fad to the next, always looking for excitement and quick, decisive end results (much as in my profession). I have tried numerous physical activities, including mountain biking, marathon running, karate, weight lifting, and many others.

In a typically compulsive manner, I approached the mental aspect of fitness in the same way, reading everything from classical Western philosophy to Buddhism to New Age psychology and spirituality. Although I enjoyed each endeavor and benefited in the short run, I would usually become injured or find that I was not achieving the total, well-rounded health that I was seeking. More important, I noticed that, despite my best attempts, the stress of my occupation was affecting me. My blood pressure was creeping up, and it was commonplace for me to feel tired or irritable.

The first time John Alton and I met and discussed his approach to total fitness, his method made sense to me on many levels. It appeared to be a balanced, broad, scientifically sound approach with roots in Eastern, particularly traditional Chinese, culture. John was well read in the literature of health and fitness, and had done a lot of study on the evidence behind the techniques he advocated. I liked the fact that he incorporated many facets of fitness (i.e., stretching, cardiovascular toning, meditation) into his program. In addition, John possessed an excellent medical knowledge, which he applied towards his theories. But what was most impressive was his claim to be able to teach a student to control the circulatory and immunological systems, not only maintaining health, but also fighting off certain diseases, especially infections. As you will learn in this book, it is this special quality of his Unified Fitness program that sets it apart from other approaches to what John calls "sustainable health."

In spite of these positive impressions, emergency physicians are a suspicious and cynical lot, and I had difficulty believing the health claims John made. On the other hand, I knew that a huge amount of research in the Chinese medical literature validated the techniques he was using, and I have diligently tried to stay abreast of Western medicine's recent efforts to investigate some of these alternative methods of care. Finally, I decided that the best experimental laboratory would have to be my own body.

After training directly under John for less than five weeks, I could both feel the lower abdominal "pulse" John talks about in this book and move it up to my forehead. Since then, I have not experienced one upper respiratory infection, my high blood pressure has dropped, and my ability to deal with the stress of life-and-death decisions on a daily basis has been enhanced. I have no doubt that the Unified Fitness program, especially the part that John refers to as "reflective exercise," is responsible for all these benefits. Though at this stage it is impossible to know for sure, to me, the "pulse" phenomenon feels like a vascular, or blood-flow, event. The theories John has proposed for this "pulse" are also scientifically sound and certainly plausible. It is my great hope that this book will inspire more research to be carried out under strict conditions in medical universities so that we will come to better understand this fascinating process. In the meantime, I look forward to advancing my own "reflective skill."

A key element of John's theory involves the importance of infectious agents in many chronic, life-threatening diseases. This notion is in line with current thinking about numerous acute and chronic diseases that were once thought to have noninfectious, or sometimes unknown, causes. Take peptic ulcer disease as a case in point. For many years, it was believed that increased acid production alone caused ulcers. Recently, it was discovered that infection with the organism *Helicobacter pylori* in the stomach was also greatly responsible for ulcer formation. Groundbreaking studies on coronary artery disease (which is responsible for heart attacks) have revealed the presence of the organism *Chlamydia pneumoniae* in many blocked heart vessels at autopsy, and suggested a role for these pathogens in causing our country's greatest killing illness. John's book brings much-deserved attention to these trends in medicine, especially the work of evolutionary biologist Paul W. Ewald, who has presented compelling evidence to suggest that many of the chronic illnesses such as cancer, diabetes, and vascular disease may, in fact, have their roots in infectious agents.

These trends are important not just because of the possible link between infectious microorganisms and chronic, lethal disease, but because medical doctors are seeing an unprecedented increase in the number of bacteria (which cause the vast majority of serious infections) that are resistant to multiple antibiotics. Because of indiscriminate prescription of antibiotics by physicians and constant adaptation by bacteria, we are now seeing bacteria that are resistant to all medication. The pharmaceutical companies are unable to invent new antibiotics fast enough to keep up. The implications of an entire generation of "superbugs" are frightening.

The advantages of using the immune, circulatory, endocrine, and neurological systems to self-treat disease are obvious, but the Unified Fitness program's goal of producing all-around health and reducing risk in noninfectious disease processes (such as high blood pressure) has greater ramifications. The program accomplishes this through six exercise series, divided among three phases: physical, immunological, and mental, with a fourth phase dedicated to troubleshooting. Some of the exercises, such as those involved in the physical phase, are familiar. Others, such as those in the immunological phase, are less so, but all exercises are fully explained, illustrated, and presented in an easy-to-learn fashion. The nutritional recommendations are sensible and, we can be thankful, lacking in an emphasis on weight loss as the be-all and end-all of becoming healthy. The broad range of lifestyles, ages, and health levels of the people presented in the case studies attest to the program's accessibility and efficacy.

An interesting footnote regarding the case studies is the important role "mental fitness" seems to play in virtually every situation, from the formation of problems to the discovery of solutions. Thus, identification of mental factors would seem to be a key element in the program's ability to help people help themselves. The two exercise series devoted to the mental aspect of the program seem to be a good, nonthreatening way to cast light on troublesome emotions or mental constructs that interfere in the quest for "sustainable health."

In conclusion, the Unified Fitness program is everything an emergency physician could hope for in a self-healing routine. It's concise, scientifically plausible, effective, and efficient, as long as you stick to the prescribed schedule. This last point bears a little more emphasis, because sticking to a prescription is a mantra of modern medicine.

Even a great program like Unified Fitness will work only as long as you follow its schedule. And, like any other benefit that's worth the time and effort to earn, you have to be willing to stay at it beyond the thirty-five days it takes to work Unified Fitness into your life. Doing so is likely to help you sustain your health like nothing I've ever seen.

*Steven J. Pasternak, M. D.*
*Attending Physician*
*Department of Emergency Medicine*
*Roanoke Memorial Hospital*
*Roanoke, Virginia*

# Acknowledgments

I would like to extend much appreciation to Anne Dunn and Jane Hagaman of the Hampton Roads Publishing art department for their excellent illustrations. Thanks to Grace Pedalino for introducing me to the folks at Hampton Roads Publishing and to my editor Richard Leviton, who helped me shape the book to a form more accessible than its earlier incarnations. Thanks also to Phil Midland for all his assistance in making interactions with China go smoothly, and to Dr. Steven Pasternak for providing not only an articulate foreword, but also critical support in the early stages of the book. Dr. Phillip Kuo, whom I had the pleasure to instruct during his years in medical school, got me thinking about the immunological and biochemical mechanisms that make Phase 2 exercises so effective. I am also very thankful for Kenneth Zarski's assistance with musculoskeletal issues. Dr. Thomas Braciale, director of the Beirne B. Carter Center for Immunology Research at the University of Virginia School of Medicine; Dr. William Petri, head of the Infectious Disease Department of the University of Virginia School of Medicine; and Dr. Steve Schnatterly, professor of physics at the University of Virginia, were very helpful and encouraging during the fact-checking and editing stages of the book. Dr. Paul W. Ewald provided excellent critical advice as well as encouragement on aspects pertaining to the evolution of infectious disease.

In China, I owe a debt of thanks to Dr. Zheng Ling, secretary of the Beijing Health Promotion Society, for her generous efforts to open a dialogue with the upper echelon of traditional Chinese medicine and fitness. I am also extremely grateful to Dr. Xu Weijun, deputy director of the China National Wushu Institute, and Professor Lu Shaojun, also of the China National Wushu Institute, for sharing their time and knowledge of traditional Chinese self-healing exercise and for listening patiently to my tortured mix of Chinese and English.

Thanks also to my loyal students and friends who stood by me during very difficult times. But my deepest gratitude goes to my beloved Ania for her tireless love and support in the face of sometimes daunting circumstances.

# Introduction

Unified Fitness is a thirty-five day program that blends familiar Western exercises with more exotic Chinese ones in a single routine that makes you healthier and helps you stay that way. Along with the exercise routine, the program provides nutritional advice that combines effective Western and Chinese approaches to diet. The program also includes a series of nonphysical diagnostics to help balance and regulate the mind in daily living. Collectively, these features make Unified Fitness one of the best systems of health self-maintenance available.

Unlike less inclusive fitness programs, Unified Fitness can provide sustainable health—that is, health benefits that last and promote longevity. The program sustains your health by building vitality throughout the day, in spite of competing demands on your time and energy. It identifies major ongoing health threats, clarifies personal problems that may drain reserves, and provides specific exercises that increase your ability to manage these health issues.

The program borrows from the environmental concept of "sustainability," an ecological approach to designing products, services, and

*Unified Fitness can provide sustainable health—that is, health benefits that last and promote longevity. The program sustains your health by building vitality throughout the day, in spite of competing demands on your time and energy.*

infrastructures to last or be recycled, so that the present generation of consumers, their heirs, and the natural resources being consumed are sustained rather than depleted. Similarly, Unified Fitness allows you to see that health is a precious resource consumed by daily living. It helps you discover the body's evolved response to the daily consumption of health, and strengthens your ability to manage and sustain that response.

The Chinese exercise portion of Unified Fitness is the principal way the program sustains health. These exercises give you the amazing ability to mobilize energy and the immune system to help you cope with harmful pathogens that cause both short- and long-term health problems. Once you've learned these exercises, you can do them throughout the day, converting formerly health-draining activities such as work into health-sustaining ones. This isn't merely an opinion. Hundreds of people have experienced the power of this aspect of Unified Fitness. The real virtue of this health-sustaining power is that it makes you the primary caretaker of your own health.

The majority of people who entered the program I teach were able to learn the exercises and to begin experiencing sustainable health in thirty-five days. This time frame applies only for those willing to stick to the twice-a-day schedule built into the program. Deviating even a little from the program's schedule can slow and even block results. Thus, the thirty-five days serves as a minimum time prescription for success.

The Unified Fitness program interweaves, or unifies, three crucial aspects of fitness—the body, the immune system, and the mind—into a single exercise and dietary regimen. Fifty-one case studies (fifty-two, if you include an anecdote involving the author) provide substantial, sometimes startling, support for the claim that Unified Fitness is the simplest and best means of achieving sustainable health, even in the face of chronic illness. Asthma, allergies, premenstrual syndrome, backache, fibromyalgia, chronic fatigue syndrome, and bladder infection, which are all on the rise, are some of the health problems Unified Fitness has helped redress. The program has also helped reverse or contribute to the treatment of much greater health threats such as gastroenteritis, arthritis, cancer, and heart disease.

Unified Fitness consists of six exercise series and dietary guidelines that together increase stamina, strength, flexibility, resilience, relaxation, manipulation of blood flow, and the ability to tame infectious disease. The last two of these six exercise series help map out the main ways the mind exerts itself in life, sharpening your judgment to get the most from exercise and diet, and loosening the grip of crippling emotions or wasteful thinking so that you can cultivate a more wholesome outlook.

The six exercise series and dietary approach of Unified Fitness are presented in three phases, based on the three crucial aspects of fitness: the physical, immunological, and mental. A fourth phase sums up and troubleshoots the program. These four phases also organize the book.

# Phase 1: Physical Fitness

This phase consists of Exercise Series 1, a streamlined stretching and cardiovascular routine that emphasizes movement, flexibility, and endurance—all aspects of fitness training that medical research has identified as important signposts of health and a reduced risk of deadly disease. The first seven days of Unified Fitness help you acclimate yourself to Exercise Series 1, as well as implement dietary recommendations that fulfill both contemporary Western and traditional Chinese medical standards of good nutrition.

In addition to Exercise Series 1, Phase 1 includes an optional advanced stretching and strengthening routine with twenty exercises to enhance overall flexibility and abdominal, lower back, and upper body strength. As physical fitness increases, this advanced routine can take the place of the simpler and briefer stretches that are folded into the three-part series. Phase 1 also provides a short list of exercises for building muscle and speed, qualities that play more of a role in competitive sports than in sustainable health. These exercises, along with brief summaries of their benefits and drawbacks, may be added to Phase 1 to enhance athletic performance or physical appearance, but they are tangential to the core aim of Phase 1, which is to begin and maintain a simple cardiovascular and stretching program.

To underscore the benefits of the Unified Fitness approach to physical fitness, seven case studies are interspersed among the descriptions of the exercises in Phase 1. On the whole, these cases demonstrate how the Phase 1 exercise series and the nutritional guidelines helped individuals achieve healthier levels of flexibility, strength, endurance, and body weight. In each case, improvements fostered higher self-esteem and personal satisfaction, though the individuals varied tremendously in terms of age, sex, and physical-emotional condition.

## Phase 2: Immunological Fitness

This phase comprises Exercise Series 2, 3, and 4, which take up the lion's share of the program. Exercise Series 2, 3, and 4 help make your immune system stronger and smarter, an extremely important advantage in light of recent medical findings that suggest common infectious diseases may be linked to the four big killers: heart disease, stroke, cancer, and diabetes. These three exercise series consist of simple movement and meditation routines that help you get in touch with, and begin working with, the immune system. The three-part series is introduced one step at a time, building to a single routine that eventually leads to your ability to access your immune system on demand and use it on behalf of your health.

Also included in Phase 2 is an optional exercise that works to counter the effects of short- and long-term illness. The exercise is derived from an ancient Chinese practice that, throughout the 1980s, experienced widespread popularity in China as an "automatic" or trance-like routine. Though highly unorthodox, the exercise is presented as something purely physical (though the mind is always at work), resembling a form of Chinese martial art that acts as a specialized cardiovascular exercise.

Like Phase 1, Phase 2 presents case studies along with descriptions of the exercises. These are the majority of the cases cited in the book and corroborate the importance and efficacy of Phase 2 in sustaining health. Though individual demographics vary considerably in these case studies, most of the people involved suffered from some chronic health problem often caused by an infectious agent and usually exacerbated by mental factors.

The illnesses in these case studies range from heart disease and cancer to mysterious autoimmune diseases to the common cold. In some cases, with relatively little effort, the individuals made surprising progress; others, especially those with long-standing chronic health problems, had to invest more time and endure a greater number of set-backs. I included this range of responses to the program to demonstrate the one seeming constant: the degree to which each person stuck with the program largely determined the degree of his or her success.

## Phase 3: Mental Fitness

This phase introduces Exercise Series 5 and 6, which in a short time help you gain unique insight into your own psychological makeup and the cultural and historical forces that have contributed to it. Just as Phase 2 cites common immunological problems we all must face, so does Phase 3 identify similar emotional difficulties woven into the social fabric of our lives, especially depression and addiction to drugs and alcohol. Though Phases 1 and 2 of Unified Fitness offer consider-able deterrence to these destructive social and psychological tides, Exercise Series 5 and 6 clarify deep-seated notions about "health" and other compelling drives that naturally compete with efforts to live longer and with greater fulfillment.

With such insights, you can more efficiently structure the day-to-day life of your mind, which, like the body, has a number of minimum requirements that must be met to remain fit. You may also learn to see strengths in apparent limitations, particularly in the area of spirituality, which may have long been a source of fear, shame, or embarrassment.

Phase 3 also includes an optional meditation exercise designed to help you gain immediate relief from stress and anxiety. The exercise can be substituted for a similar meditation routine that is part of Phase 2, or it can be practiced by itself to combat an immediate problem.

This section contains five case studies and aspects of my own health story, which provide evidence that confronting and reconciling troubling emotions are necessary for sustainable health. Though the importance of mental fitness is hinted at in all the case studies, these final examples underscore the power of the mind to either assist or block sustainable health.

# Phase 4: Troubleshooting Unified Fitness

This phase concludes the book, with two chapters detailing problems that can develop in Phases 1 and 2, and a final chapter tallying up the program's benefits. Potential difficulties in Phase 1 are related to current trends in physical fitness, and two more case studies demonstrate how these trends, motivated by either competitive sports or hyped-up notions of having "the perfect body," can create confusion about the meaning of health. In each case, Unified Fitness helped the individuals transform what were essentially elaborate forms of punishment into long-term rewards.

Problems stemming from Phase 2 are a bit more complex because so little is understood about the mechanism of the effect of these unique exercises on the immune system and the microorganisms that inhabit our bodies from cradle to grave. After outlining an array of symptoms that can occur during Phase 2 practice, particularly if a chronic illness is involved, this chapter presents sixteen case studies that demonstrate the tremendous healing range of Phase 2 exercise.

The final chapter of the book summarizes the program schedule and recounts the main features of the six exercise series and three optional exercises. It also underscores the theoretical mechanisms by which Unified Fitness works, with an emphasis on its potential influence on the evolution of infectious disease. Also, the chapter lists the large number of illnesses Unified Fitness effectively improved or eliminated in all but one of the fifty-one case studies.

I have taken great care in crafting the instructions and collaborating on the illustrations to help you learn Unified Fitness solely from this book. Having said that, I should also point out that the video presentation of the program, made to assist the goals of the book, will greatly enhance your understanding of the flow and sequence of the exercises, especially those in Phase 2. The last page of the book contains information on how to purchase the video presentation.

## Program Summary of Unified Fitness

The first week of Unified Fitness focuses on Phase 1, which consists of Exercise Series 1 (stretches and cardiovascular exercise) and a nutritional regimen. Exercise Series 1 and the dietary guidelines are the most "mainstream" aspects of the program, and their tenets are fully embraced by the medical and fitness communities. Research over the past thirty years has shown that proper cardiovascular exercise and appropriate eating habits lower your risk for—and may even help prevent—heart disease, stroke, cancer, and diabetes (Type II). The general public is also very much aware of the role of cardiovascular exercise and diet in shaping health. But many are not so aware that cardiovascular exercise also tightens muscles and damages the skeleton and its connective tissue. These inherent drawbacks make safe, appropriate stretches before and after exercise essential.

The remaining weeks of the program concentrate largely on Phase 2, Exercise Series 2, 3, and 4, which bring immunological fitness into the mix. Immunological fitness consists of three simple directives: breathe with the abdomen, move slowly, and be still. In more specific terms, attaining immunological fitness amounts to combining subtle movement with abdominal breathing and paying special attention to the sense of touch, a unique traditional Chinese fitness regimen that heightens the role of the mind in exercise. Meditation also helps involve the deep, non-thinking aspect of the mind, which controls the systems that maintain and guard our lives against injury and disease.

Though Exercise Series 2, 3, and 4 have fairly well-known Chinese names, I have relabeled them collectively as "reflective exercise." The title works well on a number of levels. For one, it gets across the notion of how the mind invariably ponders or reflects on experience of all kinds, including exercise. But, more important, the term *reflective* conveys how the exercises work. The exerciser directs the sense of touch to the surrounding air, which in turn becomes a mirror, reflecting back signals emanating from within the body. Over time, the exerciser can follow these reflected signals to their sources, effectively learning to sense and eventually control internal processes.

Exercise Series 1–4 go a long way to contributing to mental fitness, which requires a kind of durable happiness. But sometimes the mind is far too powerful to be hemmed in by exercise or meditation. Thus, Phase 3 of Unified Fitness introduces Exercise Series 5 as a means of uncovering and restructuring boundaries and relationships that affect the pursuit of sustainable health. Exercise 6 offers another mental exercise that helps illuminate deeply felt assumptions about spirituality, an area of the mind that the medical community has come to recognize as having a significant impact on health and the ability to recover from illness.

Armed with this knowledge, you can better judge assumptions, attitudes, and even behaviors that you might otherwise take for granted or deem irrelevant. Thoroughly adapting to this new self-knowledge may take longer than thirty-five days. Aside from sticking to task and schedule, this adaptation is the most important factor in achieving sustainable fitness.

Phase 4 troubleshoots Phases 1 and 2 (which automatically spill over into Phase 3). It helps you avoid the pitfalls of focusing too narrowly on physical fitness, which can lead to injury and psychological distortion. Phase 4 also prepares you for occasions when your immune system alters the course of an infection—long or short term—and produces unexpected or seemingly incongruous symptoms. A summary of Unified Fitness benefits, the range of illnesses it has helped reverse, and the theoretical explanations of how Unified Fitness works, leaves you with a concise sense of purpose that can help you maintain the will to make Unified Fitness a central part of your life.

The thirty-five day schedule of Unified Fitness helps you develop a single self-care routine that can lead to sustainable health, as the case studies demonstrate—but only if you make the lessons of the program a part of your daily life well beyond the thirty-five days. This is especially true for Phase 2, or reflective exercise, which should be practiced twice a day, once together with Phase 1 exercise and a second time by itself.

Eventually, the skill developed through reflective exercise becomes accessible on demand, allowing you to feel inside your body and muster immune response to the site of an infection the moment you detect it. If you want such a skill, you must be willing to invest the time and effort required to hone and strengthen it. There are no push-button, pill-popping means to acquire this skill.

The thirty-five days of Unified Fitness follow this schedule:

*The thirty-five day schedule of Unified Fitness helps you develop a single, self-care routine that can lead to sustainable health, as the case studies demonstrate—but only if you make the lessons of the program a part of your daily life well beyond the thirty-five days.*

## Days 1–7. Learning Phase 1: Getting Physically Fit

**Learn Exercise Series 1 and implement dietary regimen.**
Exercise Series 1 includes:

A. Self-Mobilization (2–4 minutes)
B. Lower Body Stretches (5–7 minutes)
C. Cardiovascular Exercise (10–30 minutes)
D. Repeat Series 2—Lower Body Stretches (5–7 minutes).

*Optimal time: 48 minutes; minimum time: 34 minutes.*

If Advanced Stretching and Strengthening is substituted for B and D, the time increases to 15–20 minutes for those portions of Phase 1, increasing the maximum time to 88 minutes and the minimum time to 64 minutes.

During Days 1–7 the focus should be on learning and following the routine. People who never or rarely exercise should be especially careful not to overdo Exercise 1C, Cardiovascular Exercise, which consists of either brisk walking, moderate jogging, or swimming. The Unified Fitness recommendation is to alternate weight-bearing cardiovascular exercise (walking or running) with swimming, every other day.

If Exercise 1C makes your feet, legs, hips, or lower back sore, do only the bare minimum (ten minutes) at a pace that causes you the least discomfort. The stretches, though perhaps equally uncomfortable, should be performed consistently. In all probability, it will take more than thirty-five days for your flexibility or endurance to increase significantly, especially if you have a history of inactivity or have never done such exercises before, but the benefits start to accrue the moment you begin the Unified Fitness program.

## Day 8. Learning Phase 2: Opening the Door to Immunological Fitness

### Learn Exercise Series 2:

A. Abdominal Breathing
B. Six Subtle Movements.

*Time: approximately 25 minutes.*

Abdominal Breathing can be learned in a little more than five minutes, but then it has to be integrated into the Six Subtle Movements, which take approximately twenty minutes. Once learned, Exercise Series 2 takes about four minutes to complete.

## Day 9. Phase 2 Continued: The Door Opens Wider

### Learn Exercise Series 3:

A. Standing Reflective Meditation
B. Sensing the Middle Center
C. Closing Sculpt
D. Seated Reflective Meditation.

*Optimal time: 35 minutes; minimum time: 19 minutes.*

Standing Reflective Meditation and Sensing the Middle Center follow Exercise Series 2, are purely experiential, and clearly demonstrate the appropriateness of the term "reflective." During these portions of Exercise Series 3—which take approximately ten minutes—the hands sense subtle bodily emanations, such as heat, magnetism, vibrations, and static electricity, absorbed and reflected by the surrounding air. After the Sensing the Middle Center portion of the routine, the hands perform an action referred to as the "Closing Sculpt," which helps encourage the unification of the tactile nerve center in the brain with deeper brain stem nerve centers.

At this stage, Seated Reflective Meditation, Exercise 3D, begins, and can last anywhere from five to twenty minutes. Exercise Series 2 and 3 should be practiced twice daily, without exception.

# Days 10–15. Unifying Phases 1 and 2

Integrate Exercises Series 1 with Exercise Series 2–3. Let the numerical sequence set the order of the exercises.

*Optimal time: 1 1/2 hours; minimum time: 34 minutes.*

The Second Phase 2 practice has the same maximum and minimum limits as described in Day 9 (35 and 19 minutes respectively).

# Days 16–30. Deepening Phase 2: Going Through the Door

## Learn Exercise Series 4:

A. Gentle Chaosercise of the Low Center (Days 16–22)
B. Gentle Chaosercise of the Three Centers (Days 23–29)
C. 16-Step Acupressure Massage (Day 30).

*Unified Fitness (Phases 1 and 2 combined) optimal time: 1 1/2 hours; minimum time: 38 minutes.*

*Second daily practice (Phase 2 or reflective exercise only) optimal time: 41 minutes; minimum time: 26 minutes.*

The term *chaosercise* illustrates the means by which Exercise Series 4 works: an experiential routine wherein, over time, apparently random energetic signals the body projects into the surrounding air begin to form consistent, detectable patterns. The entire exercise consists of sensing and engaging these patterns.

Exercise Series 4 implements its two components in two stages. In stage one, Exercise 4A, Gentle Chaosercise of the Low Center, replaces Exercise 3B, Sensing the Middle Center, and unfolds over the course of a week; during which time, only patterns around the Low Center (pelvic region) are engaged. The routine takes approximately eight to ten minutes.

The second stage kicks in a week later, and introduces a method of sensing patterns around both the Middle and High Centers (chest and head, respectively). This method then combines with Gentle Chaosercise for the Low Center to make a single routine, lasting approximately eight to ten minutes.

Seated Reflective Meditation follows with the same minimum and optimal time limits (five and twenty minutes, respectively).

At this point, Exercise 4C, a 16-Step Acupressure Massage routine, which takes approximately four minutes to complete, should follow Seated Reflective Meditation (3D).

## Days 31–32. Phase 2 Continued: Taming Germs

*Optimal time: 46 minutes; minimum time: 29 minutes.*

Optional Exercise 4D, Rigorous Chaosercise, can take the place of Phase 1 in the event that short- or long-term illness precludes Cardiovascular Exercise (Exercise 1C). Rigorous Chaosercise should be included in Phase 2, following the Six Subtle Movements (Exercise 2B).

In a nutshell, Rigorous Chaosercise involves shaking and gyrating the body and using the hands to strike up and down the front and back of the torso. This should be done for eight to ten minutes, followed by two minutes of cool-down, wherein the arms sway gently from side to side. Once the heart rate calms, the hands sweep the air around the head, and down the centerline—an action referred to as "sculpting"—for approximately two minutes.

At this point, Exercise 4B (Gentle Chaosercise of the Low, Middle, and High Centers) comes into play for approximately two minutes, followed by the Exercises 3C (Closing Sculpt), 3D (Seated Reflective Meditation), and Exercise 4C (16-Step Acupressure Massage).

## Days 33–34. Phase 3: Prone Relaxation Meditation, Mapping the Mind, Using the Map, Discovering the Spirit

*Optimal time: 20 minutes; minimum time: 5 minutes.*

Optional Exercise 4E, Prone Relaxation Meditation, involves meditating in a prone position in order to reduce stress and anxiety while using Relaxation Abdominal Breathing, a pattern that is the opposite of Reverse Abdominal Breathing (2A). Exercise 4E can take the place of Exercise 3D, Seated Reflective Meditation, or it can be used to combat sleeplessness as a separate exercise.

## Begin Exercise Series 5

A. Mapping the Mind
B. Using the Map.

### *Time: approximately 25 minutes.*

Exercise 5A, Mapping the Mind, is a brief self-examination that allows you to understand your mental/emotional priorities in much the way nutritional guidelines help delineate the body's dietary needs. The emotional guidelines provide a framework for daily and long-term living. Exercise 5B, Using the Map, helps you create a daily schedule that supports and sustains mental stability and happiness.

## Begin Exercise 6: Discovering the Spirit

### *Time: approximately 20 minutes.*

This series presents a brief inventory of questions that help uncover basic assumptions about spirituality and primal history. By helping you discover these assumptions, Exercise 6 guides you to better understand your inherent spirituality, based on early learning and childhood experience. Like Exercise Series 5, the information brought forth by Exercise 6 is ongoing and potentially limitless.

# Day 35. Phase 4: Troubleshooting Unified Fitness

This phase of the program addresses fallacious notions of physical fitness and off-putting difficulties arising from reflective exercise.

# *The 35–Day Program at a Glance*

## Days 1–7. Learning Phase 1: Getting Physically Fit

Exercise Series 1:    1A Self-Mobilization

1B Lower Body Stretches

1C Cardiovascular Exercise

1D Advanced Stretching and Strengthening

Dietary regimen.

*Optimal time: 48 minutes; minimum time: 34 minutes.*

## Day 8. Learning Phase 2: Opening the Door to Immunological Fitness

Exercise Series 2:    2A Abdominal Breathing

2B Six Subtle Movements

*Time: approximately 25 minutes.*

## Day 9. Phase 2 Continued: The Door Opens Wider

Exercise Series 3:    3A Standing Reflective Meditation

3B Sensing the Middle Center

3C Closing Sculpt

3D Seated Reflective Meditation

*Optimal time: 35 minutes; minimum time: 19 minutes.*

## Days 10–15. Unifying Phases 1 and 2

Combine Exercise Series 1 with Exercise Series 2–3.

*Optimal time: 1 hour and a half; minimum time: 34 minutes.*

Second Phase 2 Exercise

*Optimal time: 35 minutes; minimum time: 19 minutes.*

## Days 16–30. Deepening Phase 2: Going Through the Door

Exercise Series 4:  4A Gentle Chaosercise of the Low Center (Days 16–22)

4B Gentle Chaosercise of the Three Centers (Days 23–29)

4C 16-Step Acupressure Massage (Day 30)

*Unified Fitness (Phases 1 and 2 combined) optimal time: 1 hour and a half; minimum time: 38 minutes.*

*Second daily practice (Phase 2 or reflective exercise only) optimal time: 41 minutes; minimum time: 26 minutes.*

## Days 31–32. Phase 2 Continued: Taming Germs

Exercise 4D (Rigorous Chaosercise), inserted in Phase 2, following Exercise 2B, Six Subtle Movements.

*Optimal time: 46 minutes; minimum time: 29 minutes.*

## Days 33–35. Phases 3 and 4: Prone Relaxation Meditation, Mapping and Using the Mind, Discovering the Spirit, Troubleshooting Unified Fitness

Optional Exercise 4E Prone Relaxation Meditation

*Optimal time: 20 minutes; minimum time: 5 minutes.*

Exercise Series 5:  5A Mapping the Mind

5B Using the Map

*Time: approximately 25 minutes.*

Exercise 6: Discovering the Spirit

*Time: approximately 20 minutes.*

Phase 4: Troubleshooting Unified Fitness

*Time: approximately 20 minutes.*

# Case Studies in Support of Unified Fitness

I am not a scientist and don't have the wherewithal to sponsor sophisticated scientific research, but I have taught Unified Fitness to more than five hundred individuals, most of whom now enjoy greater sustainable health. By way of proof of the program's efficacy, I offer the fifty-one case studies, presented throughout the book. These case studies demonstrate a range of health problems, from the common cold to heart disease, from gastrointestinal disorders to premenstrual syndrome, from exercise addiction to drug and alcohol abuse. In all cases, the individuals were able to improve their conditions using Unified Fitness. Some of them achieved full cures. Though proud of their accomplishments, I have preserved each person's anonymity by changing names and key identifying details.

I have also included pertinent autobiographical detail to demonstrate how the methods of Unified Fitness evolved and made a difference in my life. Over years of public speaking, I have found that personal anecdotes build effective bridges to others, especially those struggling with despair, even if the stories cast an unflattering light on the speaker. My sense is that expert advice always seems more credible when the expert drops the pose of superiority and admits to having feet of clay.

The success of the individuals cited within, along with my own compelling experience, provided the fire to write this book. I am solidly thankful for the love and support my students have given me through the years. Without them, I might never have had the courage to dig as deeply into the life and death questions raised and answered here.

# Origins of the Program

Unified Fitness is the summary wisdom of the more than thirty years I've put into questing for fitness and understanding its ramifications. Such a statement undoubtedly prompts the question "So who are you?" Here's my answer.

I am not a sports champion. I am a writer and a teacher of exercises that yield health and longevity. My devotion to these exercises, however, stems from my early exposure to competitive sports. I dropped sports in the early 1970s while I was in high school, owing largely to my size (I was only five feet, four inches tall) and to the anti-conventional mentality of the counterculture that swept into fashion around then, which made participation in organized sports "uncool."

In college, sometime near the end of my twentieth year, I rediscovered the benefits of exercise and started a thirteen-year binge of physical development. During that time, I revisited much of my training as a young athlete, learned the hard way how to distinguish between health and athleticism, and eventually achieved a respectable level of physical fitness, which I came to understand as a kind of balance between cardiovascular stamina and strength. To test my development, I constantly timed my runs and swims, entered an occasional race or contest, and earned a couple of black belts in karate, where my strength and stamina could be measured in more direct ways.

At thirty-three, my life took a dramatic turn—East. I lived in China for two years. As exotic and fun as this may sound, my reason for going to China was anything but. Two years earlier, I had injured my wrist in a bicycling accident.

Instead of having the wrist properly looked at, I assumed it was sprained and wore a brace on and off for a year. When I finally went to an orthopedist, he informed me that the navicular scaphoid—an easily overlooked bone at the base of the thumb—was broken into several pieces that weren't likely to knit back together without surgery. Even then, he could only guarantee me a fifty-fifty chance of recovery.

Desperate to try anything, I turned to my martial arts training, from which I had seen and read enough to make me believe there was something special about traditional Chinese medicine and healing techniques. I took a job teaching English at Beijing University, where I became the personal student of the coach of the Beijing University martial arts team. He was also a master of the traditional self-healing practice called Qigong ("Breath work"), and with his help I not only healed my wrist, but also unlocked the ability to regulate my immune system, an aspect of fitness that conventional medical wisdom in the West considers virtually out of reach.

Cradling this new knowledge as if it were a precious infant, I returned to the U.S., continued practicing what I had learned, and eventually began teaching. News of what I could do spread fast, and before I knew it, there were enough interested people for me to form a school which I called the Three Emperors, after my teacher's tradition in China. The Three Emperors grew to serve more than a hundred full- and part-time students in central Virginia. In the eleven years I have operated the school, more than a thousand students have passed through the system I developed.

*The six exercise series of Unified Fitness are an optimal blend of Western and Chinese self-care methods that can be learned in thirty-five days. However, you should make the program part of your life. Doing so allows you to sustain health in a way that resembles current efforts to sustain natural resources.*

After seven years of watching people heal themselves and change their lives in ways that probably would not have been otherwise possible, I wrote *Living Qigong: The Chinese Way to Good Health and Long Life* (Shambhala Publications, 1997). This book focused largely on my experiences in China and the healing methods my teacher passed on to me. The book broadened my credibility as a teacher of Chinese martial and self-healing exercises, but I wasn't satisfied with that label, which insists on ancient Chinese medical theory for both validity and justification. The incredible physiological experiences my students and I enjoyed deserved serious treatment from the Western medical viewpoint as well.

It took a couple more years, but I finally got the necessary support from an unlikely but familiar source: China. My book had gotten into the hands of prominent Chinese doctors who practiced both traditional and Western medicine. At their invitation, I flew to Beijing again and met with a number of leading traditional healers who felt I might be capable of arguing their case in Western medical terms. During a year of collaborative visits, exchanges, and e-mails, I changed my school's name to Health Masters International Studio to signal my intention to blend traditional Chinese and Western medical approaches to fitness. After another two years of assembling all the input, the result is what you see before you now: an original work whose concepts and practices have been approved at the highest official level by mainland China's traditional health community.

The six exercise series of Unified Fitness are an optimal blend of Western and Chinese self-care methods that can be learned in thirty-five days. However, you should make the program part of your life. Doing so allows you to sustain health in a way that resembles current efforts to sustain natural resources. Instead of squandering precious sustenance, enlightened businesses and governments employ careful management and long-range strategies that encourage the rate of growth to exceed the rate of depletion.

Similarly, Unified Fitness begins with the assumption that health is a personal resource that powers every effort. Blind or careless self-management represents a waste that is often irretrievable. Enlightened self-care through Unified Fitness will not only sustain health, but give you amazing control over it. Imagine stopping an upper respiratory infection at will or overcoming a seemingly hopeless chronic health problem. Unified Fitness makes this, and more, possible.

The nature of the exercises in Phase 2 (Immunological Fitness) chiefly determines the thirty-five-day schedule for achieving the goals of Unified Fitness. Phase 2 exercises activate subtle bodily processes that must be sustained at least twice daily for a minimum of three to four consecutive weeks. While this schedule has delivered results with very few failures for fifteen years, it cannot guarantee success. Small schedule deviations, unexpected stress, or hidden emotional problems can thwart progress. Still, the Unified Fitness methods practiced and learned in thirty-five days provide the tools with which to succeed. I offer one case study here to make my point.

# A Successful Unified Fitness Cure: Norman Routs Heart Disease

Norman, forty-two, walked into my studio with the express purpose of learning reflective exercise. A tall, muscular man with a square jaw and a Gary Cooper manner of quiet strength, Norman calmly informed me at the end of the first session that he suffered from heart disease, with which he was diagnosed at age thirty-six. Prior to that, Norman had been a physical dynamo: marine, black belt in Tae Kwon Do, competitive cyclist. Now he could hardly do light yard work without getting out of breath. His doctors had told him he had a ninety-eight percent blocked coronary artery, which they attributed to inherited factors (his father had suffered from heart disease).

After almost six years of taking cholesterol-altering drugs and having virtually no improvement, Norman was game to try anything. His background in Korean martial arts gave him an understanding and respect for traditional Chinese fitness, and made him an exceptional student. He followed the program to the letter, practicing far beyond the minimal requirements I laid out.

During the fourth week, while resting one night in his recliner, he suddenly felt a pulse come to life in his lower abdomen and travel with his breath up to the middle of his chest, where the sensation lingered. His chest seemed to expand from within in a warm fullness that traveled up into his face, and his eyes welled with tears. (This abdominal pulse is central to Unified Fitness, and I discuss it in detail in Phase 2.)

The next day, Norman and his wife worked together in the yard. Though ordinarily she could outwork him by hours, this time she had to sit down and rest while Norman continued working. After two hours, he hopped on his bike and rode for several miles, something he hadn't been able to do in more than six years. Norman contacted me with the astounding news, and I advised him to visit his doctor.

A few days later, Norman had his blood lipids tested and was further astounded (along with his doctors) to learn that all of his readings had dropped from abnormal into the normal range for the first time since he had been diagnosed with heart disease. The doctors asked what Norman had been doing. When he told them, they shook their heads in disbelief. They said it was possible the medication he had been on for the past six years was finally working. Norman didn't tell them that he had stopped taking the medicine.

Thoroughly persuaded that he was onto a cure, Norman asked me to take him further into Unified Fitness, which involved prolonged meditation and an array of unorthodox exercises. Though the exercise and meditation made a powerful physical impression, Norman's psychological reactions were even more pronounced. During his second session, he experienced such emotional release that later he said he felt as though he had expressed "tons" of anger and wept a "million" tears all at the same time. He also discovered sensations in the liver and kidneys that seemed connected to the former sense of constriction in his chest, all of which he has subsequently been able to dissipate.

With the passing of those symptoms, Norman noticed increased stamina and a sense of wellness. The leap in fitness that Norman gained exceeded anything he had ever gone through, and he became quite understandably devoted to Unified Fitness.

Unified Fitness restored Norman's health in thirty-five days. In the same amount of time, it can enhance your physical fitness with flexibility and cardiovascular exercise. Even more importantly, it can introduce you to the incredible power of your immune system, abdominal pulse, and mind. It will make you feel better and more secure about your health.

The health problems Unified Fitness improved or cured in the people described in this book cover a wide spectrum. Life-threatening diseases, such as cancer and coronary artery disease, as well as debilitating chronic conditions, such as arthritis, fibromyalgia, and chronic fatigue syndrome, respond to the program's self-healing methods. Fresh and chronic physical injuries in joints and bones improve. Harmful addictions and troubling emotions give way to a sense of better health and control. Such broad efficacy suggests that the number of health threats Unified Fitness can treat or reverse is potentially limitless. All you have to do to gain these benefits is invest thirty-five days of your life, and the Unified Fitness program will do the rest.

# Physical Fitness Exercises

# Chapter 1

## Days 1–7: Getting Physically Fit

### Exercise Series 1, A, B, and C: Flexibility and Endurance

Your first week of Unified Fitness begins with cardiovascular exercise and flexibility training, which medical and fitness research has shown to have a clear, positive impact on health. To make intelligent choices about these keys to physical fitness, you need a little background.

Exercise that most easily and efficiently works the cardiovascular system uses either the lower body through exercises that approximate running or both the upper and lower body, such as when swimming or using so-called "cross-trainer" machinery, such as a skiing track which works the whole body. These prolonged sets of movements cause the heart (cardio) to pump blood throughout the circulatory (vascular) system. Along with proper dietary support, cardiovascular exercise helps lower your risk for the four big killer diseases: heart disease, stroke, cancer, and Type II (adult-onset) diabetes. It may even help prevent these diseases.

But cardiovascular exercise requires efficient and thorough use of the musculoskeletal system, namely, the muscles, ligaments, tendons, and bones—especially those of the lower body. To keep this essential engine of bodily motion in top form, an effective stretching routine is a must.

Stretching increases circulation and range of motion so that the musculoskeletal system can perform freely and efficiently during cardiovascular exercise. Proper stretching also guards against injury, and it tones and fortifies all the elements of the musculoskeletal system, including the bones. Stretching again after exercise ensures that the muscles, ligaments, tendons, and bones recover and maintain resilience and flexibility.

The following stretching regimen yields maximum results in a minimal time. It's easy to learn and maintain, as well. Beginning and ending your workout with this routine will give you more mobility and flexibility, and can help stave off the punishing effects of cardiovascular exercise on your musculoskeletal system.

# Exercise 1A: Self-Mobilization

Before plunging into a full-bore stretching routine, you should prime the musculoskeletal system with the following self-mobilizations, or brief movements into tight positions that are held for approximately three seconds. Each self-mobilization should be repeated twice, unless otherwise indicated.

# Neck Self-Mobilization

### Backward and Forward Neck Mobilization

1. Gently lean your head back and hold, then lean your head forward and hold. Repeat the mobilization.

### Sideways Neck Mobilization

2. With your head lowered, turn your head left and hold, then turn it right and hold. Repeat the mobilization.

5

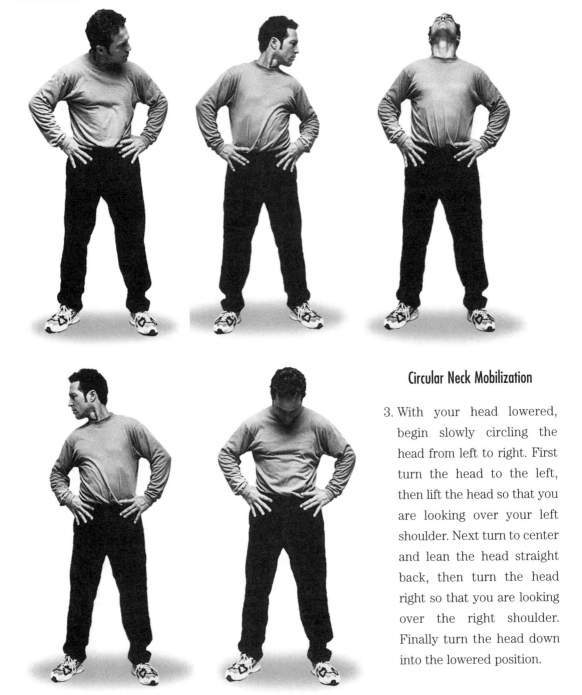

### Circular Neck Mobilization

3. With your head lowered, begin slowly circling the head from left to right. First turn the head to the left, then lift the head so that you are looking over your left shoulder. Next turn to center and lean the head straight back, then turn the head right so that you are looking over the right shoulder. Finally turn the head down into the lowered position.

Repeat the circle one more time from left to right, then reverse the circle from right to left two times.

## Forward and Backward Shoulder Rotations with Hands Touching Shoulders

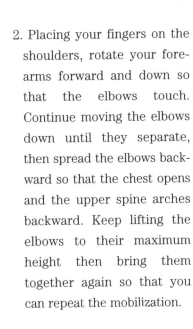

2. Placing your fingers on the shoulders, rotate your fore-arms forward and down so that the elbows touch. Continue moving the elbows down until they separate, then spread the elbows backward so that the chest opens and the upper spine arches backward. Keep lifting the elbows to their maximum height then bring them together again so that you can repeat the mobilization.

Do this mobilization a total of four times then reverse the sequence four times. Do this mobilization only once in each direction.

## Tuck and Extend Neck Mobilization

4. Without bending the neck, tilt your head forward so that your chin tucks into your neck, and hold. Then extend your chin forward, stretching the neck away from the shoulders, and hold.

Then repeat the mobilization.

# Shoulders Self-Mobilization

## Backward and Forward Shoulder Rotations

1. Lift your shoulders and rotate them backward four times, then lift and rotate your shoulders forward four times. Do this mobilization only once.

## Forward and Backward Shoulder Extensions

3. Making loose fists with your hands, hold your arms in front of you at chest height. The arms are straight, but the muscles should be loose and the elbow and wrist joints unlocked. Then push the left shoulder forward, which extends the left arm a few inches farther than the right arm. Describe a small forward circle in the air. At the bottom of this circle, retract the left shoulder and bring the entire left arm back. At the same time, extend the right shoulder, causing the right arm to move ahead of the left. While moving forward, describe, with the right fist, a forward circle similar to that of the left.

In this way, extend each arm a total of eight times, then reverse the pattern, also a total of eight times. Do this mobilization only once in each direction.

# Low Back, Hip, and Leg Self-Mobilizations

## Hand-to-Side Sweep for Low Back, Hip, and Leg Self-Mobilization

1. Standing with feet a comfortable shoulder-width apart, lay the back of your left hand just above your tailbone, then lift the right hand from the right side, reach overhead, and brush down the left side of the body. Bend at the waist, and continue the brushing movement until the right hand reaches the left ankle. Then turn to the center and rise up slowly.

2. Place the back of the right hand along the lower spine, above the left hand, which is still resting on the tailbone.

3. Drop the left arm to your side, then rise and sweep overhead, brushing down the right side of the body, bending at the waist. When the right hand reaches the left ankle, return the head and torso to the

center and rise up slowly. Place the back of the left hand on the spine above the right hand, which drops to your side, then rises to sweep overhead, stroking down the left side to the left ankle, as you bend at the waist.

4. Repeat with each arm three more times. Each time, place the returning hand on the spine just above the other hand.

5. Return the head and torso to center, stand slowly, then finish by placing the left hand in the palm of the right, which should be high on the back, roughly between the shoulder blades. Push up as far as possible with both arms and hold for three seconds, then relax your arms at your sides.

Elbow-to-Foot Mobilization for Low Back, Hip, and Leg

6. Standing with feet a comfortable shoulder-width apart, fold your arms at chest level. Turn left and sink your weight to the right leg, carefully bending your right knee. At the same time, fully extend your left leg, locking the knee and lifting the toes of the left foot so that only the heel touches the floor.

7. Then, with your arms still folded, raise your right elbow overhead and bend the whole body to the left, with the right elbow aimed down toward the left toes.

8. Hold this position, stretching your right side as well as the back of the extended left leg. Then rise up to your original shoulder-width position, unfold your arms, then refold the arms at chest level and repeat the mobilization to the right. Sink your weight to the left leg, carefully bending your left knee. At the same time, fully extend your right leg, with the right knee locked and the right toes lifted so that only the heel touches the floor.

9. Then, with your arms still folded, raise your left elbow overhead and bend the whole body to the right, with your left elbow aimed down toward the right toes. Hold this position, stretching your left side and the back of the extended right leg. Return to your original upright position, unfold, then refold the arms at chest level and repeat the mobilization to each side one more time.

## Exercise 1B: Lower Body Stretches

After completing the above self-mobilization routine, follow the stretching program outlined below, which works the area of the musculoskeletal system involved in land-based cardiovascular exercise, especially the lower back, pelvis, and legs.

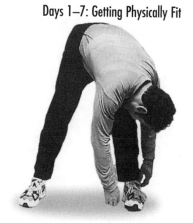

## Gentle Bend

This gentle stretch begins with setting the legs one shoulder-width apart, straight, without being locked. Then, gently lean forward so that you hang the torso between your legs. Hold for twenty seconds in the center. Without lifting the head, pivot right and hold for another twenty seconds, then again without lifting the head, pivot left and hold another twenty seconds. Return to center, then rise up slowly, feeling the blood drain from the head back into the chest.

This musculoskeletal exercise gently stretches the back, gluteal, and hamstring muscles. It also flexes without excessively stressing the lumbosacral region and works with only the natural weight of what that region was designed to bear.

## Calf Stretch

With your right leg extended and locked behind you, bend and put the majority of your weight on the left leg. At the same time, lay your forearms against a wall or stationary object and lean forward, keeping the right foot flat on the ground so that you feel a pulling sensation in the right calf muscle. Hold for twenty seconds, then switch legs and repeat the process for twenty more seconds.

# Elevated Leg Stretch

Elevate the right leg on a chair or some object suited to your natural flexibility, with your left support leg and hips pointed straight ahead. If you can't elevate your leg because of poor flexibility or balance problems, then perform the stretch in a seated position.

# Seated Leg Stretch

Keeping your head craned back so that the only joint involved is the sacroiliac, at the base of the spine, exhale and lean into the extended leg until you feel a tight spot. Inhale deeply, then exhale while going an inch or so into the tight spot, then inhale and return to the top of the tight spot. Do this ten times, exhaling as you go down, inhaling as you come up. After ten repetitions, hold into the tight spot for twenty seconds. Switch legs and repeat the procedure.

This easy stretch elongates the hamstrings as well as the muscles and ligaments of the gluteals and lower back. At the same time, it helps to build leg strength and balance in the support leg.

# Small Split with Braced Foot

With feet spread about two shoulder-widths apart, lock the knees. Keep your feet straight ahead, left foot braced against a wall on your left side to keep the leg alignment straight while you focus on stretching the unbraced leg. Grab the foot, ankle, or calf of the unbraced leg and hold twenty seconds. Switch legs and repeat the process. This stretch further elongates the muscles and ligaments worked in the Elevated Leg Stretch.

# Seated Hamstring Stretch

Sitting on the floor, with your left leg folded into your groin and your right leg fully extended, grab either the back of the knee, calf, ankle, or toes of the right leg and gently pull your chest down toward your right knee. Hold for twenty seconds, then switch legs and repeat the process for twenty more seconds. This stretch allows for maximum stretch of the low back, gluteal, and hamstring area.

# Quadriceps Stretch

### Option 1: Standing Quadriceps Stretch

Stand on the left leg and bend the right leg at the knee so that the foot rises up toward the right gluteal. Reach behind and grab the right foot, keeping the shin in alignment with the thigh. Pull the right foot until you feel a tug in the right quadriceps. Hold for twenty seconds, then repeat the process. In addition to the quadriceps, this stretch elongates the shin and ankle muscles and ligaments.

### Option 2: Prone Quadriceps Stretch

While lying on your left side, bring your right foot toward your right gluteal and grab the foot with your right hand. Pull on the right foot until you feel a tug in the right quadriceps and hold for twenty seconds. This stretch works the same muscles and ligaments as the Standing Quadriceps Stretch, but doesn't force you to balance on one leg while performing the stretch.

## Jackknife Stretch

Sitting on the floor, bent knees pressed into the chest, grab the ankles and fully extend the legs, trying to keep the chest on the knees. Hold twenty seconds. The Jackknife Stretch fully elongates the lower back, gluteals, hamstrings, and calves.

## Crossover Stretch

Sitting on the floor, cross the right leg over the left, then place the left arm against the right knee area and turn behind to the right as far as you can. Hold twenty seconds, then switch legs and repeat the process in the other direction, also for twenty seconds. The Crossover Stretch pulls the quadriceps and gluteals, and increases range of motion in the pelvis, waist, and lower back.

After completing the above routine, you can begin exercising the cardiovascular system. Once you've finished cardiovascular exercise, the above stretches should be repeated.

# *Abner Limbers Up*

A tall, lanky man with a thick head of white hair, Abner was one of the most unusual mid-sixty-year-olds I had ever worked with. In his younger days, he was an officer in military intelligence, but after retiring, he became the follower of a Western guru who had formed a nearby ashram that followed an East Indian mystical tradition.

Abner's lifestyle choices struck me as incongruous, until he confided that he was interested in doing brain wave research on the method of meditation practiced at the ashram. However, life on the ashram apparently involved much more than meditation. Abner confessed that the ashram's guru insisted that everyone jog naked in winter, which was taking a toll on Abner's health. In particular, his joints ached, and his back was weak and stiff. He was hoping I could teach him some exercises that would mitigate the effects of the guru's program.

The first thing I did was recommend he stop jogging naked in winter. Abner smiled sheepishly and dropped his head, a silent acquiescence to the not-so-subtle suggestion that he had been foolhardy. Then I put him on a regimen of stretching and lower body strengthening, followed by a session of reflective exercise, careful to make certain he started modestly and didn't push himself, to counteract habits leftover from his days in the military. Three days a week, he drove to my school from the ashram for training, but he kept up a daily practice on his own as well.

Within three weeks, Abner reported a considerable increase in his flexibility, range of motion, and general sense of well-being. In particular, his back and lower body felt better than they had in years. Though he never went back to jogging naked in winter, Abner did go on gentle runs fully clothed, but always began and ended with the stretching routine. This, he followed with reflective exercise, into which he mixed his guru's methods.

In a less than a month, Abner's joints and back ceased to be a problem, as long as he stretched and practiced reflective exercise. With his health stabilized, he was able to devote more of his attention to setting up his brain wave experiments, which continue to this day.

# Days 1–7 Continued

## Exercise 1C:
## Cardiovascular Exercise and Endurance

After stretching, begin the cardiovascular step of Unified Fitness. The program offers a variety of options, but focuses on two basic exercises—moderate jogging or brisk walking and swimming—because they are the simplest and most effective ways to get the benefits of cardiovascular exercise. For optimum results, Exercise 1C should alternate between land-based exercise and swimming. The following background information on these cardiovascular exercises enables you to get the most out of this routine or to find an exercise that suits your needs and benefits you the most.

Though health and longevity should be the aim of building the cardiovascular system, increased endurance is a sure sign of progress. Increased endurance—the ability to move longer and harder—means that the cardiovascular system is becoming more efficient in delivering fresh, oxygenated blood to the skeletal muscle fibers, of which there are three kinds: red, white, and intermediate.

Red muscle fibers are rich in myoglobin (a protein with properties similar to hemoglobin) and contract in response to slow, repetitive motion, thus earning the name "slow-twitch" muscle fibers. They tend to concentrate in places that perform a lot of slow, repetitive motion, such as the legs; or that continuously help stabilize the body, such as the ribs. White muscle fibers contain less myoglobin, are larger in size than red fibers, and are called "quick-twitch" muscle fibers because they contract in response to rapid, short-lived motion, such as that used in weight lifting and sprinting exercises. Intermediate muscle fibers have characteristics of both the red and white kinds (Krause 1981).

Endurance exercise consisting of relatively slow, continuous motion, such as modest jogging or brisk walking, undoubtedly works all three kinds of muscle fiber, but the white and red fibers come into play at different points in the process. White muscle fibers help set the body into motion and force the heart to pump blood to muscles in the legs,

19

arms, and trunk. Red muscle fibers keep the body in prolonged motion, so that the cardiovascular system circulates blood at a rapid pace over a period of time. As a result, the heart and muscle fibers develop resilience and suppleness.

A good length of time for beginners to exercise the cardiovascular system is approximately twenty minutes, though people who rarely exercise should aim for a shorter time, perhaps only ten minutes or less. After achieving a twenty-minute threshold, the next step is to sustain it. As the routine becomes easier, you can increase the time of movement to thirty minutes.

## Running or Walking: The Easiest and Most Natural Cardiovascular Exercise

Modest running or walking seems to deliver the best results in terms of sustainable health. Running at a fast pace can harm the musculoskeletal system, even with proper musculoskeletal care, and the effects of fast-paced running get worse with age.

The best thing about modest running or brisk walking is they require so little in the way of preparation. So long as you're able to move without pain, you're good to go. There are, however, a few preliminaries to consider.

### Footwear

Aside from taking the time to stretch before and after running or walking, choosing the right footwear is the next important consideration. In this matter, the endurance trainer shouldn't play cheap. A good pair of running shoes—which can cost as much as several hundred dollars—is essential in preventing foot, shin, and even knee injury. To achieve adequate protection, however, a sixty-five to eighty dollar pair of shoes should suffice, but use them only for exercise. Any additional use will shorten the life span of the footwear, which, if worn every other day may last from six months to a year, depending on terrain and how strenuous your regimen is.

Make sure your shoes have solid arch support. Most quality running shoes have extra arch support built in or include arch cushions that you can place in the shoes. Also make certain that your shoes fit well. If the fit appears to be poor, first make certain that the problem isn't your socks, which should be tight and utterly conforming to the foot, with no bunches or creases. Barring a sock problem, you should also keep in mind that new running shoes often take a little breaking in, which can result in a few blisters. After using the shoes two or three times, however, they should start conforming to your feet and causing little or no discomfort. If your feet continue to be bothered, return the shoes and get a new pair or your money back.

## Running or Walking Surface

Another important consideration is the surface you run or walk on. Asphalt and concrete are especially punishing to the lower parts of the legs, even with good shoes. For this reason, stretching before and after running or walking is not only helpful, it's mandatory. Even so, run or walk on soft surfaces if you can, such as the ground or running-track surfaces, which are designed to cushion the impact of footfalls.

To lessen the burden running or walking puts on your lower body, use the maximum shock-absorption capacity of your feet. To do this, simply make surface contact with the heel of the extended leg. As your weight transfers to the extended leg, ride the entire sole of the foot, from heel to ball, which causes the foot to act roughly like the rim of a wheel, reducing the impact of the weight shift on the structure of the leg and lower back.

## Progress

As for gauging your progress, monitoring your heart rate is a popular choice, advocated by physicians and fitness professionals. An inexpensive way to measure heart rate is with the stopwatch function of a digital timepiece. A good digital watch with a variety of features can be bought for less than twenty dollars. Far more expensive is a heart monitor, which you wear around your chest; these retail for forty to eighty dollars. For some people, the convenience and accuracy they provide compensate for the extra cost.

If using a watch, at the completion of your workout, for twenty seconds count the number of beats in your wrist or neck pulse, then multiply that figure by three (which equals one minute, or sixty seconds). To see what your measurement implies, compare it to the number you get by subtracting your age from 220; then multiply that figure by seventy percent (0.7) if you consider yourself fit or by sixty percent (0.6) if you consider yourself unfit. A fit forty-year-old man should have a heart rate per minute that comes close to 220 minus forty, multiplied by seventy percent [(220–40) x 0.7], which equals 126.

In using this or any other formula, realize that such calculations serve only as signposts and do not by themselves define states of health. For people at risk of heart problems, all formulas that don't involve your physician in the work of assessing their significance should be tossed out the window.

The simplest approach to determining progress is to observe how long it takes for you to cover a set distance. As you cover the same ground over less and less time, you know you're making headway. At that point, you might want to test your endurance by increasing either your time or distance.

Though in some cases gauging progress with timepieces or heart monitors makes sense—as in cases of competitive athletes or people with heart disease—my advice is not to get caught up in measuring your performance. Signs of improvement can bolster self-esteem, but you want to avoid the trap of equating personal worth with exercise performance. For most people, the goal of cardiovascular exercise should be to improve health and reduce the risk of deadly disease, and nothing more. The main things to focus on are keeping a consistent routine and paying attention to how you feel. Barring the initial nuisance of soreness that all beginners experience, exercise should make you feel better.

## Weather

Another point to bear in mind is the weather. Running in cold, wet weather isn't a good idea. Walking poses less of a hazard, unless you have a weakened condition due to disease or musculoskeletal infirmity. If you're in good health and dress appropriately, ensuring that the head and extremities are warm and insulated, walking in damp cold may be fine. In other, more tolerable forms of cold weather, wear a cap or hood to keep heat from escaping the head, which radiates a tremendous amount of thermal energy. In addition to a long-sleeved T-shirt, a sweatshirt and a light synthetic jacket protect the torso from wind and chill. Wear gloves, sweat pants over long underwear or tights, and thick socks to protect your extremities.

Tolerably warm weather dictates an opposite strategy. The body should be allowed to ventilate, so wear loose, light clothing.

Indoor running tracks with controlled temperatures provide an option when the weather gets either too cold or hot. The surfaces of most indoor running facilities are designed to be easy on the feet, but like their outdoor counterparts, indoor tracks can be boring. If you're like me, however, the repetition of going around in circles isn't that big of a turnoff. As long as I'm in steady motion and observing all the rules for avoiding injury, I'm getting done what needs to be done. Just make sure when you finish your workout and return to the outside weather you've managed to avoid, that you are appropriately dressed.

## The Mind

One final consideration in running or walking, which is also a concern with device-based methods of cardiovascular exercise (discussed later), is what to do with your mind during the exercise period. Some people use headsets to listen to their favorite music; others like to watch television. My advice is to leave your ears and eyes unfettered. Instead, pay attention to your body and breathing. Stay alert to how you're using your muscles. If you unnecessarily tighten your shoulders, focus on relaxing them. Coordinate your exhalations with the push of your legs, and notice whether or not you're matching that push off with the downswing of the arm opposite the push leg. If you are—which is natural for most runners—challenge yourself by swinging forward the same-side arm of the leg that pushes and trails behind.

Movement and the body's response are inherently rhythmic, and therefore poetic, in the sense that poetry is made up of lines of rhythmic language. Let your mind play with the rhythm created by your movement. Either in your mind or in a whisper, count, use affirmative slogans, or recite verses or songs that have meaning for you, but let your body and the motion determine the meter, not the verse or song. In this way, you can make what is essentially a physical exercise into more of a mind-body experience.

When I ran in college, usually before dawn, I used this method to fully engage my studies. I canted Latin poetry that depicted the beauty of the rising sun in time with my breath. From my perspective along the grassy shoulder of the highway, the rise and fall of the road became a manifestation of the curved lines my math teacher drew on the blackboard. The predawn darkness allowed my imagination greater freedom to join the experience of moving and breathing. As a result, my workouts often seemed magical and were edifying. When I stopped imposing my will and let my mind do what it wanted, unforeseen connections between ideas and bursts of problem-solving insight presented themselves.

There is nothing new in what I experienced. Writers from thousands of years ago recommended getting out in nature and allowing the mind to interact with it. Not surprisingly, many physicians now see this method of exercise as the right medicine for most people. So try not to limit your mind's involvement in exercise. You might find that you're able to hear things in that pop tune you like that you never heard before, or better still, you may be inspired to think about something far more interesting and helpful.

## Swimming: Exercising in Water

Considered the cardiovascular equal of running or walking, swimming involves the red, slow-twitch muscles of the upper body as well as the legs. Swimming is like running or walking in at least two more ways: Moderation produces best results, and some paraphernalia are essential, such as swimwear, towels, and leak-proof goggles (the equivalent of good shoes, proper clothing, and non-punishing surfaces in running or walking), while others, such as performance-measuring devices, aren't.

Here the similarities end. Unlike running or walking or other forms of endurance training, swimming doesn't make the musculoskeletal system experience continuous impact against the ground, so it is easy on the joints and tendons. It is also not as natural as running or walking and must be learned.

There are a variety of strokes, and each works the muscles in a slightly different way. Here's a brief catalog of the swim strokes you can use to develop your endurance:

### Freestyle

This stroke is performed lying face-down in the water, using the arms to pull the body through the water, assisted by the continuous kicking of the legs. The swimmer turns the head to the side on the inhale, then turns the face back into the water on the exhale—a technique called "rhythmic breathing," which allows continuous motion and maximum cardiovascular workout.

*So try not to limit your mind's involvement in exercise. You might find that you're able to hear things in that pop tune you like that you never heard before, or better still, you may be inspired to think about something far more interesting and helpful.*

### Butterfly

This is the most demanding and skill-intensive stroke. Like the freestyle, the face is directed into the water. But in terms of kicking, the whole body, not just the legs, performs an undulating whip action known as the dolphin kick. At the same time, the arms reach forward and push down, lifting the swimmer out of the water. The swimmer inhales, only to point the arms, dive underwater, and exhale, where both the arms and dolphin kick lift and propel the swimmer forward again. Of all the strokes, the butterfly forces the body to work the hardest and on the most levels.

### Breaststroke

This stroke is also performed face down, and the head is lifted out of the water on the inhale and submerged on the exhale. As the arms pull the swimmer forward—known as the "pull" portion of the stroke—the legs separate, then press quickly together. This shoots the swimmer forward, arms pointed straight ahead in a position known as the "glide." Performing these movements continuously maximizes the cardiovascular effect.

### Backstroke

This stroke doesn't force the swimmer's face into the water; instead, the swimmer lies on the back and continually reaches with the arms, out of the water, above the head, to pull the body through the water in the manner of the freestyle. Similarly, the legs steadily kick to help the arms create forward motion.

### Elementary Backstroke

This stroke also places the swimmer on the back, so breathing isn't impeded by having the face immersed in water. Unlike the backstroke, the arms don't leave the water, moving instead out from the sides to pull the body through the water. Coordinated with these arm movements, the legs separate and come together in a manner similar to the breaststroke kick. Elementary backstroke is taught primarily as a way to swim without overtaxing the system, but if performed over a long period of time, it can condition the cardiovascular system.

### Sidestroke

This stroke puts the swimmer on the side, using the arms to pull the body forward while the legs perform a scissors-like action referred to as the "scissors kick," which greatly enhances forward motion. The head remains above water. Though primarily used as a lifesaving technique, the sidestroke generates constant motion for cardiovascular benefits.

All swim strokes work all the major muscles of the upper body, especially the arms (triceps), back, chest, and abdomen. The kicking action of the strokes works the pelvic muscles (gluteals and hip flexors) and the legs (quadriceps). Like running, swimming involves a number of issues that require awareness and care.

### Weather

In fresh or salt water, swimming is something best suited to warm outdoor weather (my personal experience with outdoor winter swimming doesn't jibe with the claims of those who extol its benefits), but even in warm weather, swimmers have to protect their skin from sunburn and their ears from infection. While a simple step like resisting the allure of sunbathing and using plenty of sunscreen can help guard the skin, keeping the ears free of infection is a bit trickier.

## Ear Maintenance

"Swimmer's ear" refers to the chronic condition swimmers sometimes develop, which is an allergy-like reaction often triggered by swimming. The condition probably begins when a viral or bacterial infection scars and roughens the area on or around the eardrum so that it becomes a breeding ground for future irritations, such as water filling the ear canal. This may trigger an immune response that leads to inflammation or fluid collecting in the ear. Once you develop the condition, it is difficult to get rid of, even with medication.

To avoid swimmer's ear, some swimmers wear earplugs, which, though inexpensive, can be uncomfortable and a nuisance because they are small and easy to lose. My solution is to squirt an eyedropper full of rubbing alcohol into each ear immediately after I get out of the water. After letting the alcohol sit in the ear canal for about twenty seconds (I do this by cocking my head so that the ear filled with the alcohol points up), twist the end of your towel and put it in the opening of the alcohol-filled ear, then tilting your head down, gently swab out the ear with the towel. This procedure sterilizes the ear canal, flushes out any water trapped inside, and kills microorganisms.

## Warm Inside, Cold Outside

Indoor swimming pools make weather a nonissue for swimmers, though the problem of swimmer's ear is just as serious. Moreover, the controlled temperature of the indoor facility can instill false confidence in the swimmer during winter. Many times I have watched accomplished swimmers march wet-headed into freezing outdoor temperatures, and invariably I have seen them a short time later nursing a cold or sinus condition. Make sure you dry your head thoroughly and are dressed for the outdoors when you leave an indoor pool in winter.

### Chemicals

Pools, both indoor and out, pose another problem with the chemicals used to treat their water. Most modern facilities have switched from chlorine to a chemical called bromine to purify their water, banking on assurances from the manufacturers that bromine is safer. The reason for the switch is that chlorine is a much harsher chemical and has been linked to the development of certain forms of cancer. Bromine is also supposed to be easier on the skin and hair, which take quite a beating from the water with frequent exposure. That's not to say that bromine isn't without side effects. Many swimmers have corroborated my experience that bromine can cause odd allergic responses in the skin and nasal sinuses. To counter this potential problem, shower immediately after your swim, making sure that you rinse your hair and skin thoroughly. This gets the chemical off quickly before it can penetrate your skin.

### Goggles

One piece of advice concerning goggles: Make sure they fit the contour of your eye sockets. Leaky goggles not only distract from your ability to keep up continuous movement, but they introduce pool chemicals and microorganisms into the eyes, an area of the body extremely vulnerable to infection. Goggles will fog unless you first swab them with spit then rinse out the inside with a little water before putting them on.

## An Exercise Caution from a Veteran

Running and swimming have been my personal choices for cardiovascular exercise for the past twenty-five years because they deliver the best results with the least amount of trouble. Once you've acquired the basics—with swimming the investment is considerably higher than for running—you're good to go. With running, all you need is the right gear for the right weather, and the same is true for swimming.

But I would be remiss if I didn't underscore the importance of learning to avoid potential problems with running and swimming.

When I first began making cardiovascular exercise a part of my life, I went through a naïve, euphoric phase, convinced that only good results would ensue from my exertions. In running, I was careless about footwear, surfaces, and foot position. As a result, I developed shin splints, a painful condition in which the tendon of the shin begins to separate from the shin bone, making it almost impossible to walk, much less run. The idea of stretching before and after exercise, and the risks of excessive training and of not adapting to weather conditions, were bits of wisdom I won at a cost.

It was the same regarding the pitfalls of swimming. I had turned to swimming to help rehabilitate damage done by my excessive running and strength training. Though swimming helped me initially, I soon discovered it had rules that needed to be respected. As with running, I was slow on the uptake, but this need not be the case for you. Don't learn the hard way.

## Other Cardiovascular Options

For those who either can't perform or don't like modest running, brisk walking, or swimming, fitness centers and health clubs provide further options. These options, like swimming, are limited because they either require special spaces or are device-dependent, so they put the exerciser in the position of either paying a fee to join a club or purchasing an expensive device that has to be maintained.

A current popular favorite is the treadmill, which allows the endurance trainer to derive all the benefits of moving for twenty minutes or longer without having to go outside. In using a treadmill, all of the rules regarding pre- and post-movement stretches and proper footwear still apply.

The same stretching and footwear rules affect cycling, stationary or mobile, now a popular form of endurance training because it wears and tears the legs far less than running, especially the ankles and knees. But exercising with stationary and mobile equipment should be given a bit of thought in advance, especially if you're going to purchase a device. A stationary cycle is more convenient and makes weather irrelevant, but cycling outdoors provides fresh air and aesthetic benefits that stationary indoor cycling cannot. With outdoor cycling there is also the added need for protective gear against wrecks and the elements. Wearing a helmet, appropriate clothing, and pads for the knees and elbows address this potential problem.

### Cross-Trainer Machines: Skiing Tracks or Stair Climbers

For those who want a full-body workout, but who also don't like the water and its hassles, there are cross-trainer machines. NordicTrack and StairMaster have become almost synonymous with the category; these devices not only simulate running and walking, but recapitulate the upper body actions performed in swimming, snow skiing, rock climbing, or canoeing. They combine the best of all these exercises: The lower body bears the body's weight, while the leg and hip muscles continually work. At the same time, the upper body is put into strain and motion.

### Aerobic Dance

Once the reigning cardiovascular workout at most fitness centers, aerobic dance has recently lost some popularity. As with running, research has shown high-impact aerobics can be harmful in the long term, especially if stretching and cooling down techniques aren't added to the routine. Because the arms and upper body are put into play, aerobic dance can produce results similar to that of NordicTrack or StairMaster exercise without locking the exerciser into an isolated position on a treadmill or stair machine. Moreover, the exerciser can hold small weights in the hands and build muscle and cardiovascular fitness all at once. Proper footwear is also an issue, though perhaps less so than for running because aerobic dance is usually performed on a wooden floor, which is kinder to the feet than the hard ground.

### Eastern and Western Martial Arts

Though primarily a white, quick-twitch muscle exercise, both Western and Eastern martial arts can be performed as endurance routines. Western martial arts, or boxing, use swift, coordinated explosions of leg and upper body muscles, and can be converted to cardiovascular exercise when applied to a heavy punching bag or a speed bag. Wear gloves to protect the hands from injury. In the case of the heavy bag, strike it continuously for five to ten minutes, and in so doing, you will develop strength, speed, and endurance. A speed bag requires greater skill and should be struck over a longer period of time. Boxers can bypass both of these apparatuses and simply practice moving and striking in the air, or shadowboxing, over five to ten minute intervals.

Eastern martial arts have developed shadowboxing to a fine art, using choreographed movement routines that require explosive punching and kicking movements that work the whole musculoskeletal system far more elaborately than Western boxing. As a result, it requires a time investment for learning the skills.

Having studied a variety of East Asian martial traditions, I can say that the Chinese systems, especially those practiced in Mainland China for sport, are the most physically demanding and sophisticated, with movements similar to those of floor gymnastics. Korean martial arts such as Tae Kwon Do provide the next level of physical challenge, followed by Japanese and Okinawan traditions, which tend to stress power and martial efficiency over speed, endurance, and flexibility.

## Jump Rope

Used extensively as a way to augment martial arts skill, jumping rope involves a good bit of practice to maintain a challenging pace, but once acquired, it can build the cardiovascular system on a level equal to, if not exceeding, that of running. In addition, it strengthens calf and ankle muscles to accentuate your ability to spring quickly. Begin by jumping rope for at least one-minute intervals in five sets, resting briefly between each set. Eventually build to jumping for five minutes continuously. Longer durations can be achieved using a similar set structure, though you should reduce the number of sets as you increase the length of your intervals.

## Other Endurance-Enhancing Activities

These include tennis, basketball, racquetball, squash, rock climbing, white-water canoeing, ice-skating, cross-country skiing, and water aerobics (a good idea especially for seniors and for those who have difficulty with weight-bearing exercises).

## Summary of Guidelines and Benefits of Endurance Training

For the optimal effect on the cardiovascular system, endurance exercises should last from about twenty to thirty minutes, and should be performed a minimum of three or four times a week. In the beginning, however, especially in the case of people unaccustomed to exercise, stop once you reach a mild level of discomfort. Stretching should begin and end all exercises.

In addition to building the cardiovascular system, all endurance exercises, except swimming, increase bone density in the lower torso. Endurance exercise also improves skin condition by promoting sweat. This is true even of swimming in relatively cool water. Once you get out of the pool, your skin will perspire. Endurance exercises that involve the upper body increase the musculature of that region, but swimming provides the most thorough upper body workout, especially for red, slow-twitch muscles.

## Summary of Endurance Training Drawbacks

In general, land endurance training punishes the entire musculoskeletal system, especially the legs and lower back. For this reason, augment land endurance exercises with complete stretching routines both before and after exercising. As I mentioned previously, swimming represents a kind of antidote to the harmful effects of land sports. But swimming can cause tightness in the upper body muscles and in the lower body as well if kicking is performed rigorously. Swimming also forces the exerciser into contact with chemicals used to treat pools, which may have a long-term deleterious effect on health.

Almost all endurance exercise is a form of repetitive motion, which means the body keeps working the same musculoskeletal components in the same directions over and over, leading to a breakdown in those components or a limitation in their directional capacity. For example, chronic swimmers tend to develop shoulder problems, while chronic runners are plagued with knee and ankle trouble.

## Tony Tones Up

A former commando in the U.S. military, Tony was a great slab of a man with the biggest forearms and hands I had ever seen on someone of his height (five feet, ten inches). He came to me when he was in his early thirties, about six or seven years after sustaining a massive head injury from an explosion during combat. The incident had almost killed him, leaving him paralyzed for two years. By sheer determination, Tony had used swimming to rehabilitate himself to the point where he could walk, but he still suffered from neurological problems such as seizures, numbness, and limited mobility which made it difficult for him to find work commensurate with his skills. He was also about thirty pounds overweight, which hurt his self-esteem.

I started Tony out with flexibility exercises and reflective exercise, and these had remarkable effects on all of his problems. His balance and mobility were the first to improve, then feeling began to return to areas his doctors had assured him would remain numb.

By comparison, his weight was little affected, so when he seemed strong enough, I suggested that he combine swimming with his reflective exercise routine. Tony was happy to oblige, but he wasn't so happy when I asked him to stick to a low-fat diet. However, the progress he had made so far persuaded him to go along with the program.

In about two weeks, Tony dropped twenty pounds, and his confidence soared along with his health. Unfortunately, he went back to his hard-core physical fitness habits and began to exhibit an unhealthy aggressiveness that reflective exercise seemed to only reinforce. He got into brawls, and though he was never the instigator, it was clear he had gone out of his way to seek rather than avoid conflict. The worst incident occurred when he ventured into one of the most violent areas of a major city. In an alley, he was assaulted by three men, one of them holding a baseball bat, with which he struck Tony in the back. Tony took the blow then knocked all three men unconscious. In fact, the men were hurt so badly that they later tried to sue Tony for use of excessive force.

The blow to Tony's back threw a monkey wrench into his progress. Unable to maintain his routine for a few weeks, he regained some weight, which sent him into a depression. I encouraged him to self-treat with the reflective exercises I had taught him, and he responded well to my assurance that he could get back to where he was before the assault. Tony not only recovered, but pushed himself into an even more accomplished level of fitness, which again provoked overconfidence and destructive impulses that led to more injuries, a return of lost pounds, and low self-esteem.

*In general, land endurance training punishes the entire musculoskeletal system, especially the legs and lower back. For this reason, augment land endurance exercises with complete stretching routines both before and after exercising.*

It took about a year, but Tony increasingly freed himself from the hold of his commando machismo and developed a more health-oriented set of fitness reflexes. Though less heavy than when he began training with me, he became comfortable carrying the few extra pounds that would never have been acceptable in his twenties. He started working as a bodyguard for local celebrities, and for several years taught others some of the martial arts I had taught him, along with some highly effective commando techniques he had learned in the military.

## Jeff Hits His Stride

While shopping in a local mall one Christmas season, a voice called me from behind with a formal "Excuse me, sir." When I turned, there stood a thirteen-year-old boy with wide, expectant eyes.

"Aren't you the guy who teaches kung fu?" he wanted to know, and after I acknowledged that I did, the young man bowed, shook my hand, and introduced himself as Jeff. He said he wanted to train at my school, then abruptly walked away.

At this time, most of my students tended to be middle-aged and older, so I doubted I would see Jeff again, but he showed up a few days later, raring to go. About a month later, Jeff brought along his best friend, Carl, who would eventually become my top student.

Over the course of a year, Jeff and Carl learned as much from me as they could, especially hard-style Chinese martial arts, and an intense but constructive rivalry broke out between them. Both became highly flexible very quickly, able to drop to the floor in full splits without effort, and both quickly developed the coordination, speed, and strength needed to master the basic forms. Quickly, Jeff's awkward, adolescent body developed a distinct musculature. Carl, who was already in good shape, simply got better.

Though Carl was a tough act to match, already an accomplished athlete who played for his school's football and basketball teams, Jeff, who had never used his body with such commitment, nipped constantly at Carl's heels. It wasn't long before he and Carl were trying stunts such as back flips that were outside the curriculum of my program. Eventually, they both got injured and became crestfallen.

Because Carl seemed used to such setbacks, I focused on Jeff, who had twice as much aggressive energy as did Carl. This energy, along with the enthusiasm Jeff had shown in throwing kicks and punches during kickboxing, suggested his best interests would not be served in martial arts. Instead, I recommended that he channel his energy into noncombat sports, such as track and field and gymnastics, for which he had both the talent and interest to excel, and in which he had less chance to hurt someone else.

Jeff took my suggestion and literally ran with it. He joined the track team and in a short time went from being among the slowest to one of team's best long-distance sprinters. He also attended a summer gymnastics camp, where he learned acrobatics. Upon completing the camp, Jeff visited my school and offered to demonstrate an "aerial," a difficult maneuver that was part of the school curriculum; essentially it is a cartwheel done without using the hands. To everyone's amazement, Jeff popped off three aerials in a row, a feat that was far beyond even what Carl could do.

At this point, Jeff seemed satisfied, as though the acquisition of extraordinary flexibility, speed, and gymnastic skill had scratched a terrible itch that had been bothering him for some time. Soon, Jeff turned his attention to mastering the piano and developing his study skills. He succeeded on both counts, gaining a scholarship to a prestigious music college where he settled in with confidence, thanks in large part to his three-year devotion to physical fitness exercises.

# Chapter 2

## Optional Exercise 1D:
## Advanced Stretching and Strengthening

Though the stretches outlined in the previous chapter are fine for countering the harmful effects of cardiovascular exercise on the musculoskeletal system, the following routine imparts greater flexibility and strength to the overall musculoskeletal system, especially the lower back and pelvis. The exercises are a time-tested mixture of yoga, East Asian martial arts, and Western exercises and stretches. I have been using and teaching them for more than twenty-five years with great success.

If you want to achieve greater flexibility and range of motion, eventually replace the previous routine (from chapter 1) with this advanced regimen, which adds approximately fifteen to twenty minutes to your exercise time. All the competitive or high-performance athletes I've taught use the advanced routine to tone and maintain their musculoskeletal systems. In the long run, though, anyone who spends the extra time will find that the effort is worth it.

Though some degree of discomfort can be expected, skip any exercise that causes sharp or continuous pain. People with musculoskeletal problems, especially conditions of the knee, hip, or lower back, should

consult their physician or physical therapist before even trying these exercises. Warm up with the Gentle Bend, and do all stretches gently at first, according to your own capability. Don't force yourself to stretch too far and don't bob too vigorously. Do all stretches on both sides and begin on the right; each should last for twenty seconds, unless otherwise indicated.

The routine includes abdominal and lower- and upper-body strengthening exercises because of the importance of these muscles in keeping the back stable and resilient. Do the strengthening work every other day, until the muscles become strong enough to tolerate the exercises more frequently.

## Advanced Elevated Leg Stretch

Observing all the guidelines of the previous version of this stretch, elevate the stretch-leg to a challenging height, with hips and support leg facing straight ahead. Grab the toe, ankle, or calf of the elevated leg with the same-side hand. Place the back of the support-leg hand on the forehead to keep the head back so that the only joint involved is the sacroiliac. Exhale and lean into the elevated leg until you feel a tight spot. Inhale deeply, then exhale while going an inch or so into the tight spot, then inhale and return to the top of the tight spot. Do this ten times, exhaling as you go down, inhaling as you

come up. Hold into the tight spot for twenty seconds. Switch legs and repeat the procedure.

## Small Split with Braced Foot

With feet spread about two shoulder-widths apart, lock the knees with your feet straight ahead, left foot braced against the wall. Grab the foot, ankle, or calf of the unbraced leg and hold twenty seconds. Switch legs and repeat the process.

## Tiger Stretch or Full Squat

The Tiger Stretch is more advanced than the Full Squat, and can be done directly from the Small Split stretch. Keeping both feet flat on the floor, adjust the unbraced leg until your shoulder is even with the knee, then bend the knee of the unbraced leg. The braced leg should be fully extended. Keep both braced and unbraced feet flat on the floor. Hold twenty seconds, then repeat the process on the other side.

To do the Full Squat, simply squat to the floor and keep both feet flat on the ground.

# Full Split

With hands on the floor, spread the legs to the sides as far as can be tolerated without pain. Hold only ten seconds.

# Full Right Split

The sideways splits have both advanced and modified versions. The advanced version should only be performed by people with no noticeable musculoskeletal limitations. Otherwise, the stretch won't work the proper muscle groups. The modified version helps focus on the psoas and iliac muscles.

### Advanced

Turn the whole body to the right, fully extending the right leg and adjusting the right foot so that it sits on its heel, the left foot lying on its top (instep). Lean back as far as possible and hold for twenty seconds.

## Modified

Turn the whole body to the right in the same manner as the advanced stretch, but instead of fully extending the right leg, bend the knee with the right foot resting on its sole. Lean back as far as possible and hold for twenty seconds.

# Full Left Split

### Advanced

Turn the whole body to the left, fully extending the left leg and adjusting the left foot so that it sits on its heel, the right foot lying on its top (instep). Lean back as far as possible and hold for twenty seconds.

### Modified

Turn the whole body to the left in the same manner as the advanced stretch, but instead of fully extending the right leg, bend the knee with the right foot resting on its sole. Lean back as far as possible and hold for twenty seconds.

## Wider Full Split

From the finishing position of the advanced Full Left Split, turn your torso to the right until you return to the center to a Wider Full Split position. This time hold for twenty seconds.

## Sitting Full Split

With the legs spread as far as can be tolerated without pain, sit on the floor and keep the legs spread apart.

Then do the following three stretches:

## Sitting Full Split to Right

    With the back erect, straighten the left arm overhead and lean to the right, reaching toward the right foot, ankle, or calf with the right and left hands. Hold for twenty seconds.

## Sitting Full Split to Left

    With the back erect, straighten the right arm overhead and lean to the left, reaching toward the left foot, ankle, or calf with the left and right hands. Hold for twenty seconds.

### Sitting Full Split to Middle

Straighten the back and keep the head up by placing the backs of the hands on your forehead. Then bend at the waist, leaning the torso forward into the center space between your legs. Hold for twenty seconds.

## Butterfly Stretch

From a sitting position, bring the legs together so that the soles of your feet are pressed against one another. Grab the ankles and pull up with the hands while pressing down with the elbows into the knees. Hold for twenty seconds.

## Jackknife Stretch

Sitting on the floor, bend the knees so that they press into the chest. Then grab the ankles and fully extend the legs, trying to keep the chest on the knees. Hold twenty seconds.

# Crossover Stretch

Sitting on the floor, cross the right leg over the left, then place the left arm against the right knee area and turn behind to the right as far as you can. Hold twenty seconds, then switch legs and repeat the process in the other direction, also for twenty seconds.

# Quadriceps Stretch

### Option 1: Standing Quadriceps Stretch

Stand on the left leg and bend the right leg at the knee so that the foot rises up toward the right gluteal. Reach behind and grab the right foot, keeping the shin in alignment with the thigh. Pull the right foot until you feel a tug in the right quadriceps. Hold for twenty seconds, then switch legs and repeat the process.

## Option 2: Prone Quadriceps Stretch

While lying on your stomach, raise both feet toward the gluteals and grab each foot with your hands. Pull on the feet until you feel a tug in the quadriceps of each leg. Hold for twenty seconds. This stretch works the same muscles and ligaments as the Standing Quadriceps Stretch, but works the upper back muscles and stretches the shoulders at the same time.

## Exercise 1D, Continued:
## Lower and Upper Body Strengthening

## Leg Raises

Lying flat on your back, inhale and raise the legs in locked position (if tension is excessive in the lower back, pelvis, or legs, bend the knees slightly). Exhale as the legs pass overhead and the toes touch the floor behind. The hands can press down at the sides to help keep the back flat on the floor, or they may grip any floor-level structure to take pressure off the back. Adjust this according to your own ability. Repeat a maximum of thirty times. Afterwards, roll over and stretch the stomach muscles.

If you have a neck, upper back, or lower back problem, you should either skip this exercise or do it gently, without extending the legs fully overhead.

### Leg Raises with Bent Knees

## Sit-ups

With feet anchored under a sofa or bed, or held by another person, start from an upright position with the knees well bent, hands placed in an unclasped position behind the head. Inhale and arch backward, looking up at the ceiling, arms spread behind your head like wings. Don't let the back touch the floor. Exhale and keep the back straight as you come forward, crossing the right elbow to the left knee, switching sides on the next repetition. Repeat a maximum of thirty times. Roll over and stretch the stomach muscles.

This exercise is also potentially harmful for those with neck, upper back, or lower back injuries. In the event of such a problem, do the exercise gently, with very few, if any, repetitions.

# Lower Back Push-ups

### Beginner Lower Back Push-ups

Face a wall and stand two or more feet away from it. Place the fingertips close together on the wall above the head. Come forward, sagging and touching the abdomen into the wall and riding up on the balls of the feet. Locking the muscles, push off from the wall. As your proficiency increases, stand farther from the wall, although the farther back you stand, the less able you will be to touch the wall with your abdomen, thus putting more pressure on your shoulders.

### Advanced

A more advanced position is lying flat on the floor in push-up style, hands placed on floor above the head.

### Most Advanced

The most advanced position involves fully extending the arms and pressing up with the fingertips. Maximum repetitions: twenty.

# Triceps and Shoulder Push-ups

Lying face-down on the floor, chin touching, place your hands on the floor so that the arms fit tightly against the sides of the torso. If the hands are rotated slightly outward, the arms will automatically assume such a fit. Without letting the abdomen touch, lock the stomach muscles and press up until the arms are fully extended, then lower the body until the chin touches the floor. Afterward, repeat the process for as many repetitions as you can (but no more than thirty) without performing sloppily.

## Modified Version

If you have trouble with push-ups, perform the process using the knees instead of the feet to support the lower half of the body. Maximum repetitions: thirty.

49

# Back Bend

With your back to the wall, stand a comfortable distance from it and spread the feet apart about a shoulder-width-and-a-half. Fold the hands together and extend them backward, arching the head, neck, and back along with the hands. Touch the wall, then return to the original position. Maximum repetitions: ten.

## Full Back Bend

If you can bend all the way backward without any support, then do only one. Hold the full back bend for ten seconds.

# Alternating Arm Swings

Lift the right arm to the right, inhale, then exhale and turn the waist to the left while simultaneously swinging the arm to the left. Use the waist to bring the arm all the way around until the hips are square and the arm returns to the right hip. Repeat the process with the left. Alternate back and forth until you have done ten arm swings on both sides.

# Arm Swings in Unison

Using the hips and waist as in the previous exercise, swing both arms to the left in circular motion until they are over your head, inhaling on the way up. Then continue the circular swing back to the starting position, exhaling on the way down. Do ten, then do ten to the right.

# Alternating Arm Circles

On the inhale, bring the right arm forward and raise the left arm behind, hips and palms turned to the left. Bring the arms together overhead, hips turned straight. Exhale and drop the left arm in front, the right behind, hips turned to the right. Drop the arms at the sides, hips turned straight. Repeat ten times. Then reverse the process, also ten times.

# Rear Arm Swings with Small Split

Exhale and spin to the left, turning all the way around, striking the left shoulder with the right hand, legs locked at the knees and spread apart about two shoulder widths. Inhale quickly, then exhale and spin to the right, mirroring the previous actions. Do ten on each side.

## *Jack Makes a Comeback*

I met Jack when he was twenty-seven. Standing six feet, two inches, with shoulders so broad he looked as though he had to angle his way through most doorways, Jack was once the number-one player on a well-respected university tennis team. From the time he was a kid, all the way through his college career, Jack was expected to emerge as one of the top professional players in the game, but by the time he came to me he had long fallen away from his lofty goal.

Jack had spent his four years at the university partying in the manner to which most college athletes are accustomed. When he graduated, he landed a job as tennis pro at one of the premiere country clubs in the U.S., where the debauchery continued. He fell in love with a woman, and the two of them tore each other's hearts to pieces. At that point, his decline began in earnest.

First his health took a dive, starting with nagging little injuries, then a constant barrage of minor infections. He took vitamins, he brewed herbs, but the results were negligible. He quit the country club and spent two years questing to get back his lost vitality, searching all the hotbeds of alternative medicine, from San Francisco to Boulder to New York City, where he went through yoga and Qigong retreats held by famous masters. Still Jack felt little or no improvement, though he had seen enough to make him believe in East Asian approaches to health.

The first thing I taught Jack was subtle movement and meditation techniques that unleashed his ability to fight infectious disease and helped him recover his stamina. From the movement routines, he learned how to augment his serves and volleys in unusual ways that allowed him to dominate his opponents. By the time tennis season rolled around, he was unstoppable. For two years he dominated men's tennis in the area and went on to become the Virginia men's clay court champion of 1995.

In spite of his success on the court, Jack decided to go back to school and get an MBA, which he earned with a 3.5 grade-point average, something he never would have thought possible during his undergraduate years. According to Jack, he used the meditation I had taught him to increase the flow of blood to his brain.

Once Jack graduated, he took up tennis teaching and competition, and during the winter he worked as a ski instructor, which led him into injury. Almost as good at skiing as he was at tennis, Jack got into what started as a friendly rivalry with another instructor. In trying to outlast his rival, Jack ignored a weak sensation in his knee until he tore the cartilage.

Jack was reluctant to undergo surgery, yet I assured him that he could rehabilitate his knee afterwards using reflective exercise. Jack had the surgery, did the exercises, and within three months was back on top of his game. Shortly after, he married, took a job as the general manager of a country club in northern Virginia, and went on to become the number one tennis player in his age bracket for the Mid-Atlantic States.

# Mack Keeps Running

Mack was a track and field coach at a state university. Prior to that, he had distinguished himself at the 1968 Olympics as a bronze medalist in distance running.

By the time Mack began his training with me, he was in his early forties, tremendously fit in the aerobic sense, but in such immense musculoskeletal pain that he had to have daily full-body massages to counter the effects of the grueling runs he put himself through every day.

Before we began, I warned Mack that he would have to scale back his running so that he could spend more time on reflective exercise. An extremely disciplined and principled man, Mack agreed, and kept his promise. However, because the routine restored him physically, he was back to his addiction of daily running in no time, exceeding his previous performance times, he proudly told me.

Again I warned Mack that he would slow his progress if he didn't curtail his runs, but the program we had agreed upon was at an end, and I could only encourage Mack to stay in touch and let me know how things were going. From his massage therapist, who was also my student, I learned that Mack continued using reflective exercise to enhance his performance and recover from his runs.

Eventually, Mack took another coaching job at another university and I lost touch with him. Though I disagree with the way that Mack chose to apply what I taught him, which I believe to have been inspired by his flawed understanding of physical fitness (a fallacy addressed in Phase 4), instead of a deep grasp of the meaning of fitness, I respect his decision. In a sense, Mack had so devoted himself to this flawed principle, both professionally and personally, that he effectively rejected all other choices. Mack may have begun running for compulsive or pathological reasons, but at a certain point he transformed those reasons by the sheer exertion of his will to the pure love of movement—at any price.

# Kendra Gets Her Flexibility Back

Kendra and I were introduced when I taught a course in Chinese martial arts through the local university where she was studying law on a military scholarship. Kendra had distinguished herself by graduating from West Point, one of only a few women in her class. But even more impressive was her determination to seek out physical challenge after undergoing surgery for a ruptured disc a few years earlier. Kendra had also gotten reconstructive surgery on one of her knees. This, combined with stiffness and poor range of motion, almost made her ineligible for the martial arts class. Nonetheless, I decided to accept Kendra into the class and to use her drive to succeed to help her reduce her musculoskeletal difficulties.

Kendra was a stocky, powerfully built woman who loved to box. In fact, she had taken the class hoping to mix it up, but the martial arts movements required flexibility, speed, and strength, in that order, which made her full engagement of the stretching routine a necessity. Once Kendra understood the procedure on how to advance, she applied herself with maximum effort, careful to follow my coaching on walking the fine line between moderation and exertion.

In less than two months, Kendra had the knee, thigh, hip, and lower back flexibility and strength to do the movements correctly, and her general comfort zone of motion had significantly expanded. She was more limber and stronger in extended positions than she had been since having to get back surgery.

Until Kendra graduated from law school—approximately two years later—she continued to train at my school, learning reflective exercise as well as hard-style Chinese martial arts. When she left to assume a post overseas, her back and legs were far better off than before either of her surgeries, and she had a number of exercises, including the flexibility and lower-body strengthening routine she could count on to keep them that way.

# Strength Training

There is a place in most everyone's lives for a degree of athleticism. For one thing, our culture so completely adores images of muscular, sculpted bodies that it will reward any progress toward such ideals with attention and admiration, which in turn bolster pride and self-esteem. The same goes for demonstrable improvements in performance. In this way, the relatively simple notions of exercise and physical fitness can become powerful allies in the development of mental fitness.

To assist in this potentially helpful aspect of athletic fitness, I offer the following section on strength and speed development, along with contraindications. Enhancing physical strength involves increasing the size of muscles in the neck, arms, shoulders, chest, back, abdomen, pelvis, and legs. The muscles that respond most readily to this sort of training are the white, quick-twitch, used for short-term bursts of exertion.

More recently, strength-training advocacy has gotten a boost from reports that adding new muscle tissue helps the body burn fat. The program responsible for this renewed focus on muscle building as the key to fitness is called "SuperSlow," a method pioneered by the creators of the Nautilus weight machines. According to SuperSlow, the commonly held belief that rapid, multiple repetitions most efficiently build muscle and strength is wrong. The SuperSlow approach involves fewer, slower repetitions, which fatigues the muscles fairly quickly. This reduces the time spent lifting weights, while building more muscle and strength. The SuperSlow optimum target time for each phase of lifting weights (lifting and releasing) is ten seconds. The same principle can apply to calisthenics, such as pull-ups, push-ups, and sit-ups. Each phase of the exercise—pulling, pushing, or sitting up and releasing—can be extended to last ten seconds, thus exhausting the muscles being worked more quickly and theoretically making them stronger and thicker, and thus capable of metabolizing fat more quickly and efficiently.

Whatever the benefits of the SuperSlow program, extreme concentration on strength appears to have little value in terms of longevity and well-being. But modest strength training is important for maintaining the integrity of the musculoskeletal system so that ordinary chores, such as yard work or moving furniture, don't end up creating chronic health problems. In addition to building muscle, strength training increases bone density and fortifies tendons.

### Weightlifting

This is perhaps the quickest and most efficient exercise for building muscles. The following routine works most of the major muscle groups and, together with the abdominal exercises described in chapter 2, can be used as a guideline for developing overall muscular strength. Each weightlifting exercise should be done in repetitions of ten, and the entire routine should be performed three times. These routines are based on weight machines, not free weights, which pose difficulties in terms of balance and control. Nautilus machines don't apply either, since they are designed to work multiple sets of muscles. Moreover, the routine can be adapted to the SuperSlow model (fewer repetitions performed very slowly) if you are interested in building muscle and strength fast.

Bench Press: for chest, back, shoulders, and arms (triceps)

Seated Overhead Presses, facing or with back to the weights: for shoulders, back, and arms (triceps)

Curls: for arms (biceps, forearms, wrists, and hands)

Reverse Curls: for arms (forearms, wrists, and hands)

Kneeling Pull-downs: for back (latissimus dorsa), neck, and arms (forearms, wrists, and hands)

Leg Raises (see earlier this chapter for illustration and description): for abdomen, pelvis (hip flexors and gluteals), lower back, and legs (quadriceps)

Sit-ups (see earlier this chapter for illustration and description): for abdomen, pelvis (gluteals and hip flexors), lower back, and legs (quadriceps)

Seated Leg Presses: for pelvis (gluteals) and legs (quadriceps, calves, and ankles)

Seated Leg Curls: for pelvis (hip flexors) and legs (quadriceps, shins, and ankles)

Face-down Leg Curls: for pelvis (gluteals) and legs (hamstrings and calves)

## Calisthenics

Calisthenics are a convenient way to build muscle without expensive apparatuses, relying instead on schoolyard chinning bars and on the exerciser's body weight and capacity for movement. Because of this, the number of repetitions of a calisthenic exercise will depend on the strength of the exerciser, thus limiting calisthenic ability to build strength quickly for the beginner. For those with a reasonable threshold of strength, however, the benefits of calisthenics can exceed those of weightlifting because calisthenics can involve greater range and variety of motion than does weightlifting. Also, because calisthenics work using only the body, the kind of muscular strength it helps develop is better suited for the demands of ordinary life. As with weightlifting, calisthenics can be performed with the SuperSlow method—lengthening the time it takes to do a single repetition.

Push-ups (see earlier this chapter for illustration and description): for chest, back, shoulders, arms (triceps, forearms, wrists), and abdomen

Pull-ups: for neck, back, shoulders, arms (triceps, forearms, wrists, and hands), and abdomen

Chin-ups: for neck, chest, shoulders, arms (biceps, forearms, wrists, and hands), and abdomen

Body Presses (Dips): for neck, back, shoulders, chest, arms (triceps, forearms, wrists, and hands), and abdomen

Leg Raises (see earlier this chapter for illustration and description): for abdomen, pelvis (hip flexors and gluteals), lower back, and legs (quadriceps)

Sit-ups (see earlier this chapter for illustration and description): for abdomen, pelvis (gluteals and hip flexors), lower back, and legs (quadriceps)

Calf Extensions: for calves and ankles

### Resistance or Isometric Training

Isometric training is similar to calisthenics in that it doesn't rely on overspecialized apparatuses, but it is different in that it is static rather than dynamic. In resistance, or isometric, training, a muscle or group of muscles is pitted against a static object such as a wall or even against an opposing set of muscles. The muscles are flexed and held for a period of ten seconds or longer, during which time good, erect posture should be maintained. The routine is repeated three times.

Clasp hands behind neck and pull the head forward, resisting the pull of the hands and arms with the neck muscles. For back of neck, back, and arms (shoulders, triceps, forearms, and wrists).

Press palms into forehead, using the neck muscles to resist the push of the palms. For front of neck and arms (shoulders, biceps, forearms, and wrists).

Press right palm into the right side of the head, using the right-side neck muscles to resist the press of the right palm. Press left palm into the left side of the head, using left-side neck muscles to resist the press of the left palm. For sides of neck and arms (shoulders, biceps, forearms, and wrists).

Holding arms horizontally at chest level, press palms into each other with equal force, causing the chest muscles to tighten. For chest, back, and arms (forearms and wrists).

With elbows bent at ninety-degree angles, hold the left palm upward, lay the right palm down onto the left palm, and lock fingers. Push up with the left palm and down with the right palm. Then with elbows bent ninety degrees, hold the right palm upward, lay the left palm down onto the right palm, and lock fingers. Push up with the right palm and down with the left palm. For chest, back, shoulder, biceps, triceps, forearms, and wrists.

With arms held horizontally at chest level, hook the fingers together in a locked position, then pull in opposing directions without breaking the fingers from their locked position. For neck, back, shoulders, and arms (triceps, forearms, wrists, and hands).

Lean your back against a wall and lower arms to your sides so that the palms rest against the wall. Then press the palms into the wall and use the legs to push, keeping your body pressed against the wall. For neck, shoulders, and arms (triceps, forearms, and wrists), and legs (quadriceps, calves, and ankles).

Lie on your back and fully extend your legs so that the tops of the feet sit underneath a bed or couch. Then lift the legs from the hip so that the tops of the feet press into the bed or couch. For abdomen, back, pelvis, and legs (quadriceps).

Lying on your back or sitting in a chair, cross the legs at the ankles. Then pull the legs in opposing directions. Recross the legs so that the leg that was on top is now on bottom and repeat the exercise. For pelvis (hip flexors) and legs (quadriceps, hamstrings, calves, shins, and ankles).

Sitting in a chair, grab the side edges of the seat on both sides. Then pull down equally hard with each hand and tense the abdomen. For neck, shoulders, back, arms (biceps, triceps, forearms, wrists, and hands), and abdomen.

## Moving Resistance Training

This involves the same principle as static resistance training, but it has some range of movement. The primary device is a thick elastic or rubber band, similar to the inner tube of a bicycle tire, which provides resistance and range of motion. This technique is employed by physical therapists to help impaired or injured patients regain strength in damaged or compromised muscle groups. The exercises parallel those in the previous section, but with some modification due to the use of the elastic band. In each case, do a maximum of ten repetitions.

Place the band behind the back of your head and push the head back with your neck muscles until you reach maximum extension, then relax the neck and let the band return the head forward. For back of neck, back, and arms (triceps, forearms, wrists, and hands).

Place the band across your forehead and use your neck muscles to press the head forward until you have maximum extension, then relax the neck and let the band return the head backward. For front of neck and arms (biceps, forearms, wrists, and hands).

Holding the band in each hand, position the left hand behind the back of your head and the right hand overhead. Holding tightly to the band, keep the left hand in position as you pull up with the right hand and reach maximum extension. Then, while resisting the downward pull of the band, slowly lower the right hand until the band is no longer taut. Switch hands and repeat on the other side. For back, shoulders, and arms (triceps, forearms, wrists, and hands).

With one end of the band held down by the foot, grab the loose end of band with your right hand and pull your gripped fingers up toward your chin, then let the band return the right hand to its starting position. Switch hands and repeat on the other side. For chest, shoulder, and arms (biceps, forearms, wrists, and hands).

Holding the band at chest level, with each hand close to the band's center, pull the band apart then let the band slowly bring the hands back together. For neck, back, chest, shoulders, and arms (triceps, forearms, wrists, and hands).

Repeat the above actions with the band held behind the back of your head. For neck, shoulders, back, chest, and arms (forearms, wrists, and hands).

Sit on the floor, lay the band over the top of your right foot, and grip the ends of the band with both hands. Then, still holding the ends of the band, lie either face-down or on your left side and bend your right knee, letting the band bring your right heel to your right gluteal muscle. Extend your right knee until the leg straightens, then slowly let the band bring your right foot back to the right gluteal muscle. Switch legs and repeat on the other side. For neck, back, shoulders, arms (forearms, wrists, and hands), and legs (quadriceps, shins, and ankles).

While seated in a chair or sitting on the floor, hold both ends of the band with each hand and hook your right foot into the band as though it were a stirrup. Then flex the right ankle so that the toes push against the band, then let the band slowly bring the foot back into starting position. Switch legs and repeat on the other side. For shoulders, arms (biceps, forearms, wrists, and hands), and legs (calves, shins, and ankles).

### Other Strength Enhancing Activities

You might like to try rock climbing, white-water canoeing, or gymnastics.

## Drawbacks to Strength Training

The immediate drawback of strength training is a loss of flexibility and range of motion. This, in turn, can lead to a loss of agility or fine movement control. As muscle size and strength increase, more attention should be paid to flexibility exercises. If an exerciser puts too much emphasis on strength, eventually the musculoskeletal system will break down, thus limiting the cardiovascular system's ability to maintain itself through movement.

## Speed Training

Though speed is a quality that is typically unrelated to sustainable health, at earlier times in human history it was necessary for survival. Those who weren't quick enough to get away from a lunging predator lived a shorter life compared to those with speed. In my childhood, speed enabled me not only to successfully outmaneuver bullies, but also to outrun biting dogs or nests of furious yellow jackets. In Beijing, I could dash to catch a departing bus, thus saving me an hour of waiting in a polluted, overcrowded street. When my two sons were toddlers, being speedy allowed me to stay on top of their constant potential for havoc.

Speed essentially involves marshalling strength and endurance for a burst of short-lived effort. It is largely a white, quick-twitch muscular quality.

### Wind Sprints

These are used by most team sports to develop speed, and by distance athletes to develop the capacity to exert more effort at the end of an endurance event. The sprinter runs a short distance—a maximum of eight hundred meters and a minimum of the length of a basketball court—rests for a brief interval, then repeats the process. Because of the traumatizing effect of this kind of running, repetitions should not exceed ten. Because wind sprints are relatively short bursts of physical action, the red, slow-twitch muscles aren't brought into play as much as the white, quick-twitch muscles in the legs and pelvis. Thus, wind sprints tend to build quick-twitch muscle in the lower body. They also build quick-twitch muscle in the upper body, because the arms pump and flex in coordination with the action of the legs.

## Sprint Swimming

This is the aquatic equivalent of wind sprints. The swimmer uses a particular stroke to cover one to several lengths of a pool as quickly as possible. After resting a brief period, the swimmer covers the interval distance again. As with wind sprints, sprint swimming puts a lot of strain on the muscles, especially those of the upper body and so repetitions should not exceed ten. Sprint swimming primarily develops quick-twitch muscles in the back, shoulders, and arms.

## Body Weights

Like the jump rope, these are devices used by team sports participants to enhance speed. To increase lower-body speed, wear ankle weights during training or while walking around. Weights on the wrists have a parallel effect on the arm and shoulder muscles. Weight belts worn around the waist, or weighted packs worn on the back help increase trunk, pelvic, and leg quick-twitch strength.

## Jumping

This is performed with one or both legs. This non-apparatus exercise builds the quick-twitch muscles of the entire lower body and enables the exerciser to leap faster and higher than would be possible without the exercise. For one leg jumping, place the jumping leg on a chair or platform. Then spring up into the air using both legs, but push harder with the elevated leg. During the descent, switch legs, landing the previously elevated leg on the floor, and place the previously grounded leg in the elevated position. In using both feet, crouch as low as the knees will permit, then spring into the air, returning to the crouch position upon landing. Do no more than ten repetitions for each form of jumping.

## Other Speed-Enhancing Activities

Applicable here are all team sports, such as football, basketball, and soccer, plus individual sports such as track and field, tennis, racquetball or handball, squash, swimming, speed ice-skating, or downhill skiing.

# Benefits and Drawbacks of Speed Training

Like endurance training, speed training builds cardiovascular potential, increases bone density, and improves the skin by encouraging sweat (with swimming, the sweat comes after you get out of the pool).

But as with endurance exercise, speed training, especially the land-based sort, punishes the musculoskeletal system, resulting in tight muscles, sore joints, and traumatized bones, particularly in the spine. These drawbacks of speed training make stretching even more important than in endurance training. As noted earlier, speed is primarily a quality required in competitive sports, all of which take a tremendous toll on one's physical and mental fitness. Therefore, as exercisers age, the use of speed-enhancing routines should diminish if not cease altogether.

# Chapter 3

## Days 1–7 Continued:
## Eating Right and Well—Unified Fitness Nutrition

As soon as you begin Unified Fitness, you must provide enough of the right kind of fuel needed to help you sustain a regular exercise program. Before you begin unfolding your napkin, two contemporary assumptions linking nutrition to fitness need to be addressed. Comparing these dietary assumptions with the nutritional principles of traditional Chinese medicine creates the basis for Unified Fitness nutrition. This approach to diet supplements the Unified Fitness goal of sustainable health.

## Weight Loss and Nutrition

In the field of contemporary nutrition, weight control has become synonymous with physical fitness. This assumption began over twenty years ago, when research started showing a link between obesity and a variety of diseases such as heart disease, stroke, diabetes (Type II), and certain cancers. This research led to the condemnation of dietary fat as the cause of many health problems and to the evolution of the height-weight standards currently used to measure obesity. The key dietary authorities whose books and programs proceed from such weight control assumptions are Drs. Barry Sears, Dean Ornish, and Robert Atkins. Ornish and Atkins are medical doctors, and Sears holds a doctorate in biochemistry. While each advocates weight loss through his nutritional program, they strongly disagree on what sorts of foods produce the loss.

Traditional Chinese nutrition would consider weight control irrelevant, except in a case of clear-cut obesity (approximately thirty to fifty pounds overweight). But its dietary recommendations come closest to those advocated by Dr. Sears in his book *The Zone*. The Sears program's basic prescription for each meal is 20 to 30 percent fat, 40 to 50 percent complex carbohydrates such as fruits and vegetables, 30 to 40 percent lean protein, and eight, eight-ounce glasses of water. These percentages match those in a traditional Chinese meal, but the metaphorical terms *yin* (a metaphor for "darkness") and *yang* (a metaphor for "light") take the place of "fat," "carbohydrate," and "protein."

> *Traditional Chinese nutrition would consider weight control irrelevant, except in a case of clear-cut obesity (approximately thirty to fifty pounds overweight). But its dietary recommendations come closest to those advocated by Dr. Sears in his book* The Zone.

Yin and yang constitute the ends of a spectrum for classifying food and drink. Yin foods and drinks recapitulate the properties of darkness, such as cold, wetness, and slow breakdown and absorption. Fatty meats, dairy products, nuts, and seeds fall at the yin end of the spectrum. Yang foods and drinks manifest the qualities of light, such as heat, dryness, and quick breakdown and absorption. Refined sugars, starches, and lean meats are at the yang end. Most fruits and vegetables are on the yin side, though more toward the center. Water and soothing teas are yin beverages, whereas alcohol and stimulating teas are yang.

The balance between fats, carbohydrates, and protein in the Sears meal prescription approximates the yin/yang balance of traditional Chinese nutrition largely because of Sears' insistence on the kinds of carbohydrates that should be consumed. Sears argues that grains and cereals are highly glycemic carbohydrates. This means they turn rapidly into glucose in the digestive tract, much as sugar does, causing the body to overproduce insulin.

Thus, grains and cereals get digested fairly quickly, satisfy less, and create insulin problems. Fruits and vegetables, on the other hand, are less glycemic. They take more time to break down, satisfy hunger more effectively, and don't wreak havoc with insulin production. This argument is consistent with traditional Chinese nutrition, which uses extremely yang (highly glycemic) side dishes like rice or noodles in much the same way as breads function in a traditional American meal. The lion's share of calories comes from meat and vegetables, which bring the meal toward the middle of the yin/yang spectrum.

Sears and the traditional Chinese differ on the issue of water. According to the Chinese view, drinking eight, eight-ounce glasses of water in a day would overtax the kidneys, which are believed to play a vital role in overall health, and introduce yin excess into the diet. Though specific recommendations on water intake vary with individual conditions, no more than six teacups a day is the general recommended limit.

My recommendation for water consumption is to use a spectrum similar to that of yin/yang, with Sears' sixty-four ounces at one end and the Chinese six teacups at the other. If you have been especially active (thus perspiring heavily) or if you regularly indulge in dehydrating habits, such as drinking caffeine and alcohol, your water consumption should be near the Sears' recommendation. If you are not so active, or if you don't have any dehydrating habits, then you're probably safer at the Chinese end of the spectrum.

While the Sears diet touts weight loss as a primary benefit, it seems less strongly rooted in the pathological association between obesity and disease than the Ornish and Atkins programs. Dr. Ornish's meal plan is high-carbohydrate, low-fat, and low-protein. It evolved from his research, which suggested that his plan along with an exercise program, can reverse coronary artery disease. Dr. Atkins promotes a diet high in protein but low in fat and carbohydrates. It has helped millions rapidly lose lots of weight, a desirable outcome for someone diagnosed as clinically obese.

In some cases involving obesity and related pathologies, traditional Chinese nutrition would find some common ground with the

Ornish and Atkins programs. Conventional medicine uses tests to measure blood pressure, blood lipids, and blood sugar to determine obesity-related pathologies, but to classify someone as obese, which suggests an increased risk for obesity-related disease, only muscle-fat measurements, body type assessment ("apple" or "pear"), and height-weight ratios are necessary.

Traditional Chinese medicine might arrive at similar conclusions through the language of yin/yang. For example, a traditional Chinese doctor would classify a short, round, pale, fat person as too yin, a pathological condition similar to obesity. Other qualities might determine whether to prescribe an Ornish vegetarian diet, rich in yang-type carbohydrates such as pasta, or an Atkins meal plan high in yang protein sources but low in yin carbohydrates and fats.

The traditional Chinese doctor would examine the obese patients through indirect means, such as examining the tongue and a variety of wrist pulses, and assess muscle tone and bone strength. If the patient has good muscle tone and strong bones, with signs of excess yang on the tongue and in the wrist pulse, the Ornish diet, with its predominately yin emphasis on vegetables, might prove the best nutritional regimen to balance the patient's condition. If the muscles and bones appear weak and the tongue and wrist pulse show signs of yang deficiency or yin excess, the Atkins diet, with its preference for high yang protein, might make a better course of treatment.

Thus yin/yang analysis of variations within obesity classification schemes casts obesity and its attendant health problems in a more complex light than does the conventional medical logic on which the Ornish and Atkins programs are premised. For example, conventional medicine might classify a barrel-chested, red-faced person as a case of apple-shaped obesity and prescribe either the Ornish or Atkins diet. Traditional Chinese medicine views such a person as excessively yang, a term also associated with thinness. The highly glycemic carbohydrate sources of the Ornish diet give it a yang component that would make it inappropriate. Though the Atkins' high protein formula is less yang than Ornish's, it is still more so than that of Sears, which would likely satisfy the traditional Chinese recommendation in this case. Sears advocates fruits and vegetables as primary carbohydrate sources, which, on the whole, traditional Chinese medicine considers yin foods.

Interestingly, evidence collected by Glenn Gaessar, nutritional expert and author of *Big Fat Lies,* shows that apple-shaped people are at risk for a variety of health problems, including coronary artery disease, certain cancers, and diabetes. If diabetes is an issue, then the highly glycemic Ornish diet might prove counterproductive. Similarly, Atkins' high-protein approach, especially if the protein sources are animal, might not be the best thing for someone with coronary artery disease, due to the high cholesterol content of animal protein. Thus, for an apple-shaped obese person, the Sears-like traditional Chinese diet is probably the safest bet.

In general, traditional Chinese nutrition finds more affinity with the Sears dietary program than with those of Ornish and Atkins, whose approaches would probably be prescribed only in certain cases of "yin" obesity. But, in general, traditional Chinese nutrition isn't as concerned with weight control as Sears, Ornish, and Atkins. The reason for this may be that obesity is very much an American problem, with which traditional Chinese medical nutrition never had to contend. Recent statistics confirm that the United States is the fattest nation on Earth, but a number of factors suggest that a rush to judgment about the relationship between weight and disease may be unwise. For one, the height-weight ratio method for determining obesity is specious, and Glenn Gaessar's *Big Fat Lies* does a good job of debunking this method. Another factor may have to do with the role that infectious disease plays in the epidemiological evidence used to indict obesity as a health threat. It may be that germs are the primary cause of the health problems currently attributed to weight, a thesis taken up in greater detail in later chapters.

## Nutritional Medicine

Another pervasive nutritional assumption is that natural foods are healthier than processed foods. Two lines of reasoning underpin this assumption. First, processed foods are more likely to be tainted with health-damaging additives and pesticides that have been linked to cancer or other life-threatening conditions. Second, natural foods have chemical properties that can act as preventive and curative medicine.

Medical scientists have scrutinized these claims, and found evidence both for and against the natural foods argument. As a result of this scrutiny, the Food and Drug Administration has restricted the health claims of natural food products. At the same time, there have been enough findings on the good health effects of natural foods and the bad effects of additives and pesticides in processed food to strengthen the association between natural foods and improved health. An influential authority to emerge on behalf of natural foods is Dr. Andrew Weil, also a successful advocate of natural healing approaches.

Traditional Chinese medicine supports the natural foods assumption on a number of fronts. Traditional Chinese medicine considers nutrition the second most important form of medicine (below mind-body exercise, but above massage, acupuncture, and herbology). It prefers whole grains, such as rice and noodles made from wheat, to processed grains. It advocates eating fresh meats, fruits, and vegetables in season. It flavors and colors meals with ingredients which add immune-boosting antioxidants, substances which help prevent the breakdown of tissues. These include red and green chili peppers, garlic, green leafy vegetables, mushrooms, water chestnuts, bamboo shoots, radishes, and sweet, sour, salty, or pungent sauces. The constant drinking of teas, especially green tea, provides an even richer source of antioxidants.

Another dietary staple, often served at breakfast, is chicken soup with rice, black beans, and minced vegetables, seasoned with garlic and onions. Chicken soup by itself contains the amino acid cysteine, which is similar to a chemical used to treat cold symptoms. Ingredients such as black beans, garlic, and onions enhance the antioxidant potency.

Aside from being good for you, a traditional Chinese meal should be pleasurable, stimulating a variety of tastes, smells, and sights— hence the emphasis on colors and flavor. Chinese tradition also places a high value on crafting dishes that are not only pleasant to taste but finely wrought. *Dim sum*, a smorgasbord of small, finely crafted dumplings and pastries, demonstrates this aesthetic attention to shape and size. Fashioning dishes and carving decorative radishes into animal, floral, or a variety of symmetrical designs are also typical ways to enhance the pleasure of a meal.

Such aesthetic considerations have been lacking in most natural foods approaches, but Dr. Andrew Weil's recent book on diet, *Eating Well for Optimal Health,* has brought the issue of meal pleasure to the fore-front. Dr. Weil's point is that eating healthy isn't enough. Foods should also stimulate complex sensory reactions, thus adding a psychological benefit to good nutrition. Thus, Dr. Weil brings the natural foods approach into greater alignment with that of traditional Chinese medicine.

Without being an expert in traditional Chinese cooking, you can con-coct a natural foods diet that parallels the Chinese use of medicinal foods and preparation strategies. Including ordinary fruits and vegetables such as grapes, bananas, oranges, broccoli, carrots, onions, garlic, and red, green, and yellow bell peppers ensures high antioxidant content. Treats or desserts containing dark chocolate or yogurt have helpful properties. Dark chocolate has antioxidant flavonoids similar to those found in Chinese teas, and yogurt is rich in acidophilus (helpful bacteria), which can aid digestion. In addition to including these healthy ingredients, use them to create meals that are aromatically and visually stimulating.

Other traditional Chinese notions about the health effects of food and drink also merit serious consideration. Some of these may seem peculiar, even to a natural foods advocate. For example, traditional Chinese medicine disparages ice-cold fluids, a favorite of many Americans, even in cold weather. Next time you down an ice-cold drink, pay attention to your hands. If they grow cold, then you've expe-rienced a breakdown in peripheral circulation, which means the blood has less space in which to flow, and means the pressure is rising. You feel the same thing when you take a cold shower. Because of bodily reactions such as these, the Chinese perspective generally regards cold (a yin phenomenon) as pernicious, especially to the heart, which is associated with heat (a yang phenomenon).

On the other hand, extremely hot foods and drinks are equally suspect in the Chinese view. This suspicion has also been corroborated by research. Overcooked foods tend to lose nutritional value, and charred or burned foods have been linked to cancer, as has the consumption of liquid served at near-boiling temperature. For this reason, traditional Chinese cooks use a lot of oil to keep the surface of foods from getting burned. They brew tea by bringing the water to a full boil, then they pour the water into a pot where it cools for several minutes before the tea leaves are added. This keeps the medicinal substances in the tea from being destroyed by the heat.

Following these traditional Chinese rules can make your meals healthier and more interesting. Though not a panacea, a meal plan that combines these rules with modern natural foods practices and the principle of balancing fats, carbohydrates, and protein offers good support for the Unified Fitness exercise program. The following suggested daily menu exemplifies such a meal plan. Though you can benefit by following it to the letter, it is intended as a guideline. The next section on nutrition provides information that may give you some ideas on how to vary the suggested menu.

# Unified Fitness Suggested Menu

## Breakfast

### Warm and Hot Weather

Fresh, seasonal, non-citrus fruit (bananas, cantaloupe, peaches, strawberries, blueberries); one egg; whole grain bread or bagels (cheese is okay for active people); nuts (peanuts, almonds, sunflower seeds); yogurt; Chinese teas (especially green or black tea); juices.

### Cool and Cold Weather

Rice porridge (oatmeal, Cream of Wheat, or grits as substitute); lean meat or meat substitute (tofu, tempeh); one egg; whole grain bread or bagels (cheese is okay for active people); Chinese teas (especially green tea); oranges (avoid substituting sour citrus fruits such as grapefruit).

## Lunch

### Option 1 (Year-round)

Rice-noodle soup (wheat noodles if rice noodles unavailable); lean meat and some vegetables (broccoli, carrots, cabbage) cooked into the soup; tempura vegetables (broccoli, carrots, zucchini); Chinese teas (variety); water (okay to sweeten with pure juices for non-glucose-challenged people). Dessert: pumpkin or sweet potato pie, frozen yogurt in warm or hot weather, berries in season.

## Option 2 (alternate days)

1. Organic turkey breast sandwich (whole wheat bread); cheese optional for active people; soy-based mayonnaise substitute or oil and vinegar as garnish; tomato slices; sprouts or green leaf lettuce; baked corn chips (lightly salted); Chinese teas (variety); water (okay to sweeten with pure juices for non-glucose-challenged people). Dessert: 0.75–1.5 grams of pure chocolate, eaten with Chinese tea.

2. Albacore tuna in spring water, mixed with soy-based mayonnaise substitute, on whole wheat bread; cheese optional for active people; tomato slices; sprouts or green leaf lettuce; baked corn chips (lightly salted); Chinese teas (variety); water (okay to sweeten with pure juices for non-glucose-challenged people). Dessert: 0.75–1.5 grams of pure chocolate, eaten with Chinese tea.

In warm or hot weather, salads are fine additions that can take the place of portions or whole items from the above, but salads should rarely constitute whole meals.

# Dinner

## Meat Entrée

Light salad (fruit or leaf); lean meat entrée (fish, chicken, or lean organic beef); green, red, orange vegetables (broccoli, spinach, Chinese cabbage, carrots, tomatoes, red bell pepper, yellow squash); whole grain rice (long- or short-grain basmati); whole wheat rolls; Chinese teas (noncaffeinated); water (juice-sweetened for non-glucose-challenged people). Dessert: carrot cake, frozen yogurt in hot weather, berries in season.

### Vegetarian Entrée

Stir-fry vegetables: green, red, orange vegetables (broccoli, spinach, Chinese cabbage, carrots, tomatoes, red bell pepper, yellow squash); one cup of cooked lentils, seasoned with soy or amino acid sauce; whole grain rice (long- or short-grain basmati); a crunchy garnish such as sesame sticks; Chinese teas (noncaffeinated); water (juice-sweetened for non-glucose-challenged). Dessert: carrot cake, frozen yogurt in hot weather, berries in season.

## Exercise and Nutrition

The following discussion offers insight into the basic mechanics of nutrition, the impact of exercise on metabolism, and a detailed roster of nutrients and foods. This information enables you to vary the suggested menu by creating your own culinary masterpieces that satisfy the Unified Fitness nutritional standards of balance and health promotion.

Physical exercise strongly influences metabolism: the process by which the body uses food energy to maintain and build itself. The first step in metabolism occurs when food or drink enters the mouth. Solid food must be chewed and mixed with saliva, which prepares it for further breakdown in the stomach. Liquids go straight to the stomach, where the first crucial steps in nutrient extraction occur. Acids in the stomach immediately begin decomposing the food or drink into smaller compounds that can be absorbed by blood vessels lining the stomach.

After the stomach, breakdown continues in the small intestine, which absorbs more nutrients and passes them into the blood. In response to mere taste as well as the absorption function of the stomach and small intestine, the pancreas secretes insulin, a hormone that regulates blood sugar levels. These levels increase as digestion converts food and drink into glucose. The final nutrient extraction occurs in the large intestine, from which solid and liquid waste passes out of the body.

All the while, nutrient-rich blood travels from the digestive organs to the liver, where a complex variety of metabolic functions occur, such as the conversion of sugars into fats. In the end, the metabolic process reduces food and drink to tiny packets of energy that can then be transported by the circulatory system to places in the body where energy is needed.

Exercise depletes these energy reserves, especially in the muscles. Therefore, diet should include lots of lean protein to help build and replace muscle tissue, plenty of carbohydrates for sustaining the muscles and nerves, and an adequate amount of fat to provide the body with a store of energy to draw upon once the carbohydrates have done their job. Exercisers must also obtain from their meals the minerals necessary for bone development, and they should drink plenty of water to replenish losses brought on by profuse sweating, which also depletes the body of electrolytes. Electrolytes are chemicals in the blood that carry electrical charges. Sweating leeches some of these chemicals—especially sodium and chlorine—from the blood and slows down some of its functions. Thus, minerals such as sodium and chlorine (in the form of salt) must be restored through the diet.

The body metabolizes these various food substances at different rates, and to help make sense of this aspect of the process the term *calorie* comes in handy. Essentially a unit of measurement that denotes the amount of energy used to metabolize a quantity of food, calories help nutritionists differentiate between the various metabolic properties of proteins, carbohydrates, and fats. For example, one gram of fat contains nine calories, whereas one gram of protein or carbohydrates has only four calories. Thus, it takes more metabolic energy to burn one gram of fat than one gram of either protein or carbohydrate.

> *Exercise depletes these energy reserves, especially in the muscles. Therefore, diet should include lots of lean protein to help build and replace muscle tissue, plenty of carbohydrates for sustaining the muscles and nerves, and an adequate amount of fat to provide the body with a store of energy to draw upon once the carbohydrates have done their job.*

Calorie-counting became an annoying spawn of the nutrition craze that erupted in the 1970s, but recent research has steered the medical and fitness communities away from devoting so much time and interest to calories. The caloric spread mentioned at the beginning of this chapter provides a good rule of thumb for healthy eating (30 to 40 percent of calories from protein, 40 to 50 percent from carbohydrates, and 20 to 30 percent from fat), with a much lower fat percentage in the case of obesity or other health-compromising conditions.

Protein is important in an exerciser's diet because it builds muscle that exercise tends to break down. Good sources of protein include:

Poultry

Beef

Pork

Fish

Eggs

Cheese

Yogurt

Legumes (such as lentils or soy beans), mixed with rice

Soy products, such as bean curd (tofu) and soy milk

Corn

Nuts and seeds

Forty to fifty percent of calories should come in the form of carbohydrates, mostly of the complex variety, as opposed to the simple—refined sugar being the least favored. Carbohydrates are essentially sugars that serve as the main energy source for all the cells of the body, especially the muscles and the nerves that control them. Prime sources of complex carbohydrates include:

Vegetables

Grains (breads, pasta, rice)

Fruits

Fats are another piece of the nutritional puzzle. Though currently the scourge of food experts throughout the West, fat is not held in such deep contempt in the East (in China being called "fat" can be a compliment). Americans certainly eat too much fat, but a certain amount of fat in the diet and on the body is necessary. For example, young women's bodies need fat in order to perform the basic endocrine function of menstruation. Women who exercise excessively, or who suffer from full-blown eating disorders, tend to menstruate irregularly or not at all. Problems from too little body fat aren't strictly limited to women. Men can also damage their health by trying to become too lean. This problem is addressed at length in the final section of the book.

Fats must therefore be factored into the nutritional equation, just like carbohydrates. And, as with carbohydrates, fats come in varieties, some of which are more helpful than others. In general, animal fats tend to be more harmful than vegetable fats, so if protein sources are largely animal, then the fat intake is likely to be high as well. In general, animal fats are referred to as saturated while the term "unsaturated" applies to most vegetable sources. There are exceptions, however. Coconut oil, a non-animal source of fat, is highly saturated. A good source of fat comes from vegetable cooking oil, such as olive or canola oil.

In addition to balancing the diet with protein, complex carbohydrates, and vegetable fats, the exerciser's menu must include foods and drinks rich in calcium, the mineral responsible for making strong bones. This is especially important for exercisers who engage in bone-punishing endurance training. Runners, for example, should make sure their diet offers as much as 1000–2000 mg of calcium daily. Sources of calcium include:

Milk

Cheese

Yogurt

Sardines

Soy beans

Salmon

Peanuts

Sunflower seeds

Dark green, leafy vegetables

Water makes up seventy-five percent of the body, so sweat-inducing activities necessitate fluid replacement, and for that purpose, there is no substitute for water. Fruit juices and soft drinks can't do the job and may cause complications because they have such high sugar content. Caffeinated drinks, such as coffee and tea, can cause further fluid loss because they promote urination. It's difficult to assess how much water should be drunk, since so much depends on body type and amount of exercise, but six eight-ounce glasses of water a day is a good rule of thumb for an active person.

Though balancing protein, carbohydrates, and fats, along with consuming calcium-rich food and keeping the water intake high are important, they are by no means the end of our nutritional concern. Exercise, especially when performed rigorously, depletes the body's stores of vitamins and minerals that are necessary for fitness. The following vitamin and mineral lists and suggested food sources can help exercisers keep track of what needs to be replaced as a result of their training.

Vitamin A: Fish-liver oils, broccoli, dark green, leafy vegetables, cantaloupe, sweet potatoes, apricots, carrots, pumpkins, squash, cheese, butter

Vitamin $B_1$ (thiamin): pork, liver, brewer's yeast, bran, wheat germ, whole grains, enriched bread, cereals, pasta

Vitamin $B_2$ (riboflavin): organ meats (liver, heart, and kidneys), poultry, milk, eggs, brewer's yeast, wheat germ, whole grains, enriched bread, cereal and pasta, almonds, legumes, and dark green, leafy vegetables

Vitamin $B_3$ (niacin): tuna, liver, lean meat, poultry, fish, whole grains, enriched wheat products, nuts

Vitamin $B_5$ (pantothenic acid): all plant- and animal-based foods, especially organ meats, poultry, egg yolks, whole grains, nuts, brewer's yeast, and dark green, leafy vegetables

Vitamin $B_6$ (pyridoxine, pyridoxal, and pyridoxamine): whole grains, liver, beef, avocado, cantaloupe, bananas, nuts, and dark green, leafy vegetables

Vitamin $B_{12}$ (cyanocobalamin): only in animal-based foods, such as tuna, salmon, organ meats, beef, pork, eggs, milk, cheese

Folicin (folic acid): brewer's yeast; organ meats, legumes, broccoli, carrots, asparagus, and dark green, leafy vegetables

Vitamin C (ascorbic acid): fresh fruits and vegetables, especially citrus fruits, leafy green vegetables, tomatoes, strawberries, melon, green peppers, broccoli, Brussels sprouts, cabbage, potatoes

Vitamin D (chalecalciferol): fish-liver oil, milk, dairy products

Vitamin E (tocopherol): cold-pressed vegetable oils, wheat germ, whole grains, liver, raw seeds, margarine

Vitamin K: kelp, brussel sprouts, cabbage, cauliflower, peas, liver, fish-liver oil, and dark green, leafy vegetables

Vitamins fall into two broad categories: water-soluble and fat-soluble. Vitamins A, D, E, and K are fat-soluble, and so require fat in order to be metabolized. The B vitamins and vitamin C are water-soluble and are easily passed from the body by excess urination. Thus, drinking too many caffeinated drinks can cause a loss of B and C vitamins, and not having enough fat deposits makes it difficult for your body to process fat-soluble vitamins.

In addition to vitamins, minerals are important aspects of nutrition. Calcium has already been singled out. The following roster is a list of essential minerals and food sources. Combined with the previous lists, it can help exercisers fulfill nutritional requirements imposed by their particular regimens.

Copper: legumes, whole wheat, prunes, beef liver, shrimp and most seafood, leafy green vegetables, almonds

Iodine: all seafood, kelp, sea salt, iodized salt

Iron: liver and other organ meats, oysters, lean meat, leafy green vegetables, whole grains, dried fruits, molasses, eggs, oatmeal, nuts

Magnesium: raw leafy green vegetables, almonds, cashews, soybeans, whole grains, milk, figs, corn, apples

Manganese: whole grains, nuts, seeds, eggs, leafy green vegetables, fruits

Phosphorus: lean meats, poultry, fish, eggs, whole grains, seeds, nuts

Potassium: citrus fruits (especially oranges), bananas, potatoes, leafy green vegetables, whole grains, pumpkin seeds, sunflower seeds

Selenium: brewer's yeast, organ meats, eggs, dairy products, fish and shellfish, whole grains, onions

Zinc: liver, lean meat, eggs, whole grains, brewer's yeast, wheat bran, wheat germ, raw seeds

As long as exercisers eat within the broad range of foods outlined above, they should be getting the vitamins and minerals they need. Though supplements can provide many of these nutrients, exercisers should consider the complex biochemical processes involved in metabolism of food. Our bodies have evolved a means of extracting these essential nutrients from our food and drink, so perhaps an over-reliance on supplements could lead to physiological lethargy in that means of extraction.

An opposing view comes from a vocal contingent of nutrition experts who have argued that virtually all foods have lost their nutritional value because of farming and land development practices over the past century. According to this view, conventional farms produce foods lacking essential minerals, and therefore constitute empty calories. Most who express this view advocate taking supplements that are chelated, that is, chemically designed for better absorption.

I am suspicious of this argument for two reasons. First, while there may be some evidence of mineral depletion in conventional farm products, I have seen no convincing proof that natural foods grown with organic methods lack sufficient mineral or vitamin stores. Second, companies selling chelated vitamins and minerals often exaggerate the "depleted foods" threat, encouraging people to overlook the possibility that buying fresh, natural produce reduces, if not eliminates, the need for chelated vitamins and minerals.

The easiest way to confirm or reject theories about nutrition is to pay attention to how you feel after following a dietary regimen for a couple of weeks. If you feel more energetic, then you're most likely on the right track. If you feel weak or lethargic, modify your food intake until you feel better.

# Fiber

Often referred to as roughage or cellulose, fiber is a complex carbohydrate that the pancreas, liver, and digestive organs cannot break down. It stimulates peristalsis, the propulsive action of the digestive tract that moves food through the body. Fiber also cleans the intestinal lining. There are two kinds of fiber—soft and rough—and each has a more pronounced effect on different aspects of digestion. Soft fiber tends to act more on the small intestine, and has been shown to reduce the manufacture of harmful cholesterol in the liver. Rough fiber affects the large intestine. Fruits, such as apples and pears, and grains such as oats contain soft fiber. Whole wheat breads and cereals and vegetables, such as cabbage and broccoli, are good sources of rough fiber.

Aside from these benefits, the fitness effects of fibrous foods have come under suspicion. While past studies have shown that increased fiber intake reduces the risk of cancers of the lower digestive track, more recent findings show no such relationship. Even so, the fiber in fresh vegetables, whole grains, and fruits clearly aids digestive regularity and provides other nutritional advantages that enhance Unified Fitness.

## Cholesterol

The body produces cholesterol naturally. It is the chemical basis for hormone production, which is essential for growth and healing.

There are good and bad kinds of cholesterol. The bad kind is referred to as LDL (low-density lipoprotein) cholesterol; the good kind is called HDL (high-density lipoprotein) cholesterol. When under stress, the body produces LDL cholesterol in the liver, which causes tissues to break down. LDL cholesterol has been implicated in the development of the plaque that obstructs blood flow in coronary artery disease. HDL cholesterol helps maintain and repair the body's various systems and tissues, and appears to play an important role in preventing coronary artery disease.

In addition to what our bodies manufacture, food and drink provide another source of cholesterol. Foods high in saturated fat tend to be high in cholesterol, but eating low-fat food doesn't necessarily ensure low cholesterol. Shellfish, for example, are low in fat but high in cholesterol.

To help keep cholesterol levels in check, you should partake moderately of foods and drinks that are high in cholesterol or that encourage the body to manufacture LDL cholesterol. Therefore, eating lots of fatty meats, which are high in cholesterol, and drinking too much alcohol, which encourages the liver to manufacture LDL cholesterol, will undermine Unified Fitness.

## Short List of Unified Fitness Nutritional Guidelines

The following guidelines provide a logic for preparing healthy meals, and an overlay of contemporary Western and traditional Chinese principles of good nutrition.

- If you are less than thirty pounds of your height/weight standard, prepare meals that have the following caloric breakdown: 30 to 40 percent protein, 40 to 50 percent low-glycemic carbohydrates (mostly fruits and vegetables), 20 to 30 percent fat (unsaturated).

- If you are thirty pounds or more over your height/weight standard, reduce the percentages of fat and protein and increase the percentage of low-glycemic carbohydrates.

- As a rule, use grains (bread, pasta, rice) as side dishes, not as main courses.

- Eat vegetables and fruits rich in antioxidants, vitamins, and minerals.

- Include fiber in meals and keep cholesterol low (mostly saturated fat sources).

- Eat soups and porridges.

- Drink warm fluids, especially green tea.

- Match your fluid intake to the degree of your exertions. Maximum: eight, eight-ounce glasses of water; minimum: six teacups of water (tea counts as half a glass or teacup)

- Cook with canola or olive oil; season with garlic and antioxidant spices (red or green chili pepper, curry, or cumin).

In conclusion, the Unified Fitness nutrition program combines traditional Chinese principles with modern approaches to natural foods and calorie distribution. Unless you are clearly obese (thirty to fifty pounds over the weight prescribed by standard height/weight ratios), weight control should be the least of your concerns. Even if weight is a problem for you, Phase 1 exercises, supported by the Unified Fitness Suggested Menu, will help you achieve and maintain a healthy weight. More important, your dietary regimen will provide good nutrition and be pleasing to eat. It will infuse your body with disease-fighting antioxidants, essential vitamins, and minerals. It will restore energy reserves depleted by stress and your exercise routine.

There is little more you should expect from nutrition. Diet alone cannot protect against health threats, as exemplified by the harmful LDL cholesterol the liver creates due to stress. Phase 1 exercises aren't enough either. You need the other phases of Unified Fitness to help to achieve and sustain fitness.

## Peggy Decreases Arthritis Pain and Loses Weight with Diet and Exercise

I had serious doubts that I could do much for Peggy when she showed up at a reflective class at the local senior center. In addition to being almost one hundred pounds overweight, Peggy suffered from crippling osteoarthritis of the spine and severe diabetes, which had ravaged the circulation in her feet. She could barely stand for thirty seconds before the pain overwhelmed her, and any damage to her feet brought up the fear of limb amputation. In her middle sixties, Peggy had suffered from this condition for twenty years, ever since the premature death of her husband, a trauma that had helped spur Peggy's decline.

Peggy's face practically shouted desperation. She had tried seemingly every medical intervention possible, and the doctors she had worked with were only barely sympathetic. She had no place left to turn except to someone like me. After explaining that absolute devotion to the routine was the only way she would ever see results, I accepted Peggy into the class, where she worked diligently for a month. During that time, she went from being able to stay on her feet no more than thirty seconds to almost twenty minutes.

Encouraged by her progress and ability to stick with the routine, I took her on as a private student, and she made even more progress. At the same time, I brought in other healthcare practitioners, students of mine I knew and trusted, to help out with Peggy's pain and weight problem. For pain, she saw an acupuncturist regularly; his traditional Chinese medical assessment was that she was "yang deficient," which produces an appearance of "excess yin," such as an apple-shaped body and red face. The acupuncturist managed not only to complement the pain reduction Peggy was already getting from her exercise routine, but was also able to improve the circulation in her feet.

For her weight problem, Peggy worked with a board-certified family practice doctor who also specialized in nutritional therapy. The doctor placed her on an extreme no-fat diet. For cardiovascular exercise, she rode a stationary bike for twenty to thirty minutes every day, followed by a session of reflective exercise.

Under this regimen, Peggy lost almost fifty pounds in about three months. The pain that once kept her a prisoner of the nearest armchair and a supplicant in the offices of insensitive or indifferent healthcare practitioners didn't go completely away, but she was happier and freer to move for longer periods than she had been in almost twenty years.

After about nine months, Peggy, the doctor, the acupuncturist, and I agreed that she should reintroduce protein and fats into her diet, especially chicken soup. The increase in protein and fat in her diet has not affected her weight loss, which has leveled off. She continues treatment with the acupuncturist and uses reflective exercise to treat herself every day. She calls me on a regular basis to report on her progress and setbacks, but each time Peggy affirms that she hasn't felt so good in twenty years.

> Under this regimen, Peggy lost almost fifty pounds in about three months. The pain that once kept her a prisoner of the nearest armchair and a supplicant in the offices of insensitive or indifferent healthcare practitioners didn't go completely away, but she was happier and freer to move for longer periods than she had been in almost twenty years.

## Jenny Conquers Her Fear of Fat

Jenny was still in high school the first time she dropped by to investigate the buzz made by a group of her friends who had been training with me for a couple of months. She was small, pale, and thin, with a look of unflagging confidence on her young face that dared anyone to try and impress her. She trained for a couple of weeks, then vanished, apparently unimpressed, drawn to the more exciting world of teen society.

About three years later, Jenny reappeared with at least two years of college under her belt. She looked basically the same, only the confidence had been replaced by a tired, vacant expression. Asking for privacy, she discussed what had been going on with her, in particular a number of health problems, especially a constant upper respiratory infection and insomnia. While she talked, I studied her wan, pallid face and dark circles under her eyes. Though well-muscled—part of what she was telling me had to do with her exploits in rock climbing—she couldn't have weighed more than just over one hundred pounds. Before she finished talking, I reached the conclusion that I was listening to a young woman with an eating disorder.

In addition to her physical appearance, there were other indications, such as a driving perfectionism, which I later learned came from her family, all of whom were distinguished intellectuals who had managed to escape from communist-bloc Eastern Europe in the early 1980s. It didn't take a genius to guess that adjusting to life in U.S. was difficult for Jenny and her family. In spite of almost fifteen years of residency, her family still did not speak English in their home, and a sense of distrust toward their new moorings warred with their desire to settle down and relax. In the hotbed of these conflicts, with roots that ran back at least to the trauma of the Second World War, Jenny had fallen into the American teenage-girl trap of using her weight to control an overwhelming sense of emotional chaos.

I accepted Jenny as a student, but I knew she was going to be tough. Getting anyone to admit to having an eating disorder is like pulling teeth. I understood this situation both first and second hand, through my own compulsions with physical fitness and through encounters with young anorexics and bulimics among the hundreds of students I taught every year as a college instructor. Once it is admitted to, the eating disorder fights back, as though it has a life of its own.

Jenny followed my expectations to the letter. She found inventive ways to question and sabotage the reflective exercises I taught her, taking a step backward for every step forward. Still, she managed to progress, and was able to reduce the chronic sinus infections she suffered from, and that kept her from giving up.

Her problems with insomnia and general malaise continued. In my opinion, they were the result of chemical imbalances caused by her addiction to slow self-starvation. She also menstruated irregularly, another predictable consequence of not having adequate fat stores. Though failing to menstruate seemed more like a blessing than a curse, the problem with insomnia got to the point where she couldn't stand it anymore. When she complained to me that the exercises I had taught her were doing nothing for her sleeplessness, I confronted her about her eating disorder more bluntly than I probably should have.

Jenny instantly went into denial, claiming that she ate "huge amounts" of food all the time. When I asked her to list everything she ate in a day, she came up ludicrously short of the calories her body needed. Strictly a vegetarian, Jenny usually ate only two daily meals, one of which consisted of plain oatmeal. This was all the fuel she was giving herself, in spite of the fact that she was trying to keep up an athlete-level exercise schedule.

At this point, I intervened with dietary suggestions and made her compliance a necessary condition for further training. The diet was basically "*Zone*-friendly," with about thirty percent of calories coming from fats such as olive oil, cheese, and nuts. Meat was another fixed item on her menu, which caused an uproar at first, but the increase in waking energy and nighttime relaxation she experienced was so pleasant that she grudgingly accepted chicken and fish as necessary "evils."

It took almost two years from the time that Jenny first began her training, but finally she gained the fifteen pounds her body needed to function better. With the weight gain, her insomnia all but vanished, her menstrual cycle evened out, and the persistence of her sinus infections faded to something she could manage with reflective exercise. None of this would have been possible had Jenny not improved her diet.

# Boyd Beefs Up

Similar in temperament to Jenny, Boyd was a fourteen-year-old boy who wanted to become a martial arts standout, but was tied to the notion of pure vegetarianism, a diet which didn't deliver the strength and endurance he needed to accomplish his goal. Compared to most kids his age, Boyd's physical fitness struck me as above average, but he wanted to do extraordinary things, such as the flips and high acrobatic kicks he had seen his classmates Carl and Jeff attempt and eventually perfect. With his tall, lanky frame (he was about six feet), fueled largely by grains and vegetables, he found it difficult to keep up.

When I questioned Boyd about his diet, he launched into a philosophical defense of vegetarianism that was basically Buddhist: we should not eat living things because living things are us. At the time, Boyd was sporting spiked, dyed-blond hair; prior to that, his hair was purple; before that, it was red—fairly typical behavior for a bright, unconventional kid. I suspected that vegetarianism was rather like his hair color: He was simply trying it on.

For the moment, it felt right to him and certainly agreed with many of the apparently politically correct codes of behavior reflected back through popular culture (for example, the Dalai Lama, a Buddhist vegetarian, appeared at a 1999 rap concert). But now Boyd was at a crossroads where an essentially social matter was getting in the way of a physical fitness goal. When I suggested this theory as a way to frame the problem, Boyd shrugged indifferently as though saying he disagreed that there was a problem to begin with.

A few months later, Boyd had let his hair return to its natural dark blond. He also had more color in his face and was suddenly able to do physical movements that were formerly beyond him. When I asked him how he had broken out of his rut, Boyd smiled sheepishly and admitted to eating a little meat, which, he confessed, had made an almost instant difference.

Not wanting to make too big of a scene for fear of encouraging him to go in an opposing direction, I complimented Boyd and let the matter drop. The tactic seemed to work, because in the days that followed, Boyd's renewed vigor persisted.

Though Boyd still ate mostly vegetarian and tried to rely on vegetable sources of protein, he made the move to more of a Zone or traditional Chinese diet on his own. Though he never achieved the high acrobatic level of his classmates Carl and Jeff, he came close and probably would have overtaken them if he hadn't been drawn to other interests, such as acting and academics.

Still, Boyd became one of my best students, absorbing and internalizing the lessons of Unified Fitness in ways I could never consciously convey. In my view, Boyd had a knack for recognizing the advantage of balancing out the demands and desires that impinged on his life. It's a knack I would have wished for at his age.

# Immunological Fitness

# Chapter 4

## *Day 8: Opening the Door to Immunological Fitness*

### Exercise Series 2, A and B:
### Abdominal Breathing and Subtle Movement

Once you have Exercise Series 1 (stretching and cardiovascular exercise) and nutrition on your agenda, you're ready to begin Phase 2. This is the most crucial step to sustainable health, because it entails immunological fitness. This means learning reflective exercise, a mind-oriented routine that consists of the following:

• Abdominal breathing
• Subtle movement
• Using subtle movement and meditation to sense the body's relationship to the surrounding air
• Using meditation to sense a physiological pathway that allows the transfer of immune-enriched blood from the gut to the nasal sinuses and other regions of the body.

It may seem impossible, but the first three elements of reflective exercise can be learned in two days, after which you may add them to your stretching and cardiovascular exercise routine. Following your final stretch with reflective exercise is the key to immunological fitness.

If you're still doubting the importance of immunological fitness, reconsider the case of Norman, who had all the elements of physical fitness in place and at a high level. He was struck down in his prime by what has remained the biggest killer in the U.S. since the statistics on public health were first compiled. Norman's doctors used every drug and technical form of intervention they had, except open-heart surgery, which poses such a risk that doctors are usually willing to do it only when the patient is in danger of immediate death. Once Norman invested thirty-five days in developing immunological fitness through reflective exercise, the symptoms of his heart disease vanished in terms of blood pressure and lipid measurements and in his ability to exert himself.

Norman's recovery baffled his doctors, but it can be explained with an unorthodox, but medically plausible, theory. For many years, medical doctors have observed that heart disease shows traces of inflammation, a medical term used to describe the body's immune response to infection. More recently, a related branch of science called evolutionary biology has presented compelling logic and evidence that many lethal, chronic health problems—including heart disease, stroke, cancer, and diabetes—are actually later, more virulent stages of common infections, especially upper respiratory disease, that plague human beings from infancy to old age, and whose treatment accounts for the largest percentage of primary care efforts.

These findings have big implications, not the least of which is that living a long, healthy life may be a matter of managing the progression and permutations of infectious diseases. Reflective exercise may be a highly effective, inexpensive way to do this.

I can say this with conviction because Norman's reaction to reflective exercise isn't unique. Over the many years prior to his case, I had seen a large number of miraculous turnarounds. In each case, I was certain a medically acceptable explanation lay just beyond our discernment. The source of my certainty began fourteen years ago, when I had my first exposure to the immunological power of reflective exercise.

On a dark, cold November night in Beijing, I sat on the floor of my room at Beijing University, dutifully practicing a meditation and breathing exercise my Chinese teacher insisted I perform twice daily. It seemed like a ludicrous waste of time, because I had been practicing a similar meditation and breathing exercise for at least two years and had experienced nothing unusual. There had been no stunning lights or spiritual revelations, the big things you read about in Eastern meditation lore. Even worse, my head was stuffed with cold symptoms, and an eerie wind was blowing in from Mongolia, banging the loose-fitting window like an angry spirit trying to get in. Rumor had it that my building was a former headquarters for the Gang of Four, the nickname for the political leaders who joined forces with Mao's widow in the late 1970s to rule China by terror. There was also talk that my room was the site of a young woman's suicide, which made things even spookier.

*Suddenly, out of nowhere, a pulse thumped a few times in my lower abdomen, then shot straight up into my head, and all at once I had the sense of knowing the exact spot where the cold was located. In that instant, the pulse struck the locus of the cold like a laser. My sinuses opened, and the cold symptoms dissipated in seconds.*

Suddenly, out of nowhere, a pulse thumped a few times in my lower abdomen, then shot straight up into my head, and all at once I had the sense of knowing the exact spot where the cold was located. In that instant, the pulse struck the locus of the cold like a laser, though the sensation seemed vascular and organic, not energetic or otherworldly. My sinuses opened, and the cold symptoms dissipated in seconds.

From that point on, I never questioned the value of my practice and worked to become strong and confident enough to teach others. After fourteen years, I estimate I have taught more than five hundred people to attain a lower abdominal pulse that rises and ameliorates upper respiratory and more serious problems, a collective success that virtually cries out for serious investigation.

To my knowledge, no research has been conducted to verify this phenomenon. To be sure, the mechanisms will be difficult to observe, but this doesn't mean the superficialities can't be measured. In fact, Tom, one of my students who was also a medical researcher, once monitored it in me.

Using a kind of pulse monitor that was supposed to measure internal blood flow in lab animals, Tom hooked four surface sensors up and down my centerline—one below the navel, one at the center of the chest, one at the throat, and one in the middle of my forehead. Then, I began sending the pulsing sensation up and down the vertical line. The sensor readings showed regular, symmetrical spikes in the first three locations, obviously caused by the domineering acoustics of the heart and aorta, but the forehead reading was flat, until about the tenth spike of the chest readings. At that point the forehead sensor registered an odd, fairly tall, two-humped wave, then fell flat. The two-humped wave appeared with regularity, matched to an equal measure of the other spiky regions and to my inhalations. Tom was impressed, and I reported the results to several physicians who conceded that such a reading in the forehead with the monitor we used was not something they would have expected.

Though our little informal test was by no means rigorous science, it suggests that the pulsing phenomenon can be superficially measured. At this point, I have only anecdotal evidence and personal testimonies as to the existence of this pulsing sensation that can be moved by breath up and down a frontal path of the body, enlivening and healing ailing sinuses and more.

Two questions about this mysterious pulse immediately present themselves: Where does the pulse come from and how does it facilitate healing? To answer both questions, you need basic medical knowledge of the nervous system, human anatomy, the physical dynamic between human beings and the surrounding air, and recent discoveries in the biochemistry of the immune system. But those answers can wait. First you need to get started learning reflective exercise, and the place to begin is to reacquaint yourself with something most people take for granted: breathing.

## Optional Exercise 2A: Relaxation Abdominal Breathing

Most Eastern fitness traditions such as yoga and Taiji (T'ai Chi) start people with relaxation breathing in order to help them stretch and reduce tension in the muscles of the lower abdomen. This is a place on the body that typically receives little attention, especially in the West. Of all the various forms of abdominal breathing, relaxation breathing is the easiest and is therefore less likely to raise anxiety levels for beginners and for those who may have difficulty with breathing exercises.

Relaxation breathing is a fairly deep kind, though the lungs shouldn't be filled to the bursting point, and is done through the nose. As air is pulled in through the nostrils, the muscles of the lower abdomen expand, causing the thoracic and navel region to swell like a balloon. On the exhalation, the abdominal muscles relax, returning the belly to a normal state. The inhale and exhale should take between three to five seconds each.

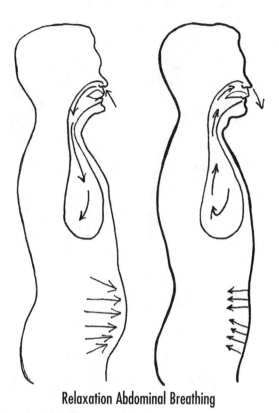

**Relaxation Abdominal Breathing**

A beginner who has difficulty with abdominal breathing should practice relaxation breathing at least twice a day, in cycles of fifty complete breaths (one breath equals one inhale and one exhale). After a minimum of two weeks of this form of abdominal breathing, the novice may begin practicing the next breathing technique.

Though relaxation breathing is useful for people who have trouble with abdominal breathing, most people I've worked with can and should go straight to the next, slightly more difficult method, known as Reverse Abdominal Breathing.

## Exercise 2A: Reverse Abdominal Breathing

As the name implies, this form of abdominal breathing reverses the pattern of relaxation breathing, but there are a number of fine distinctions that deserve comment. First, Reverse Abdominal Breathing engages only the lower abdomen, the superpubic region just below the

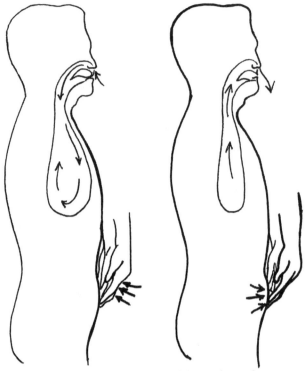

**Tongue Position and Reverse Abdominal Breathing**

navel. Contract these muscles lightly on the inhalation, then relax them on the exhalation; all breathing occurs through the nose. Second, the lungs expand and contract simultaneously with the expansion and contraction of the lower abdominal muscles. This makes the breathing light, taking up only about half of the lung capacity. Third, the tongue is curled or lifted so that the tip rests comfortably on the upper palate.

Once the tongue is in position, sit or stand while placing the hands over the lower abdomen just below the navel. Then on the inhale, press the hands inward while you contract the lower abdominal muscles. On the exhale, relax both the hands and the muscles so that the lower abdomen protrudes into the hands. Don't force the lower abdomen out. Let it relax into expansion. Do this exercise for fifty complete breaths once daily. As you get used to the exercise, you can stop using the hands. Practice whenever possible, such as while stalled in traffic, sitting at a desk, or watching television.

## Exercise 2B: Six Subtle Movements

The true power of reflective exercise cannot be achieved without subtle movement, the basis for the Chinese fitness exercises known as Taiji (T'ai Chi) or Taijiquan (T'ai Chi Ch'uan) and Qigong (Ch'i Kung) which I have taught and studied for more than fifteen years. The problem with Taiji and even the simpler Qigong is that they are learning-intensive, time-consuming practices that carry the added burden of not being able to explain their benefits to a non-Chinese audience.

For these reasons, I developed the Six Subtle Movements. This simple routine, in condensed form, delivers the essence of the far-more-involved Taiji, thus saving the novice the worry of having to learn hundreds of complex movements and postures whose function extends into, and is therefore clouded by, the issue of self-defense. Likewise, Qigong, generally regarded as a breathing and meditation exercise, also involves subtle movement, with so many thousands of overlapping varieties that trying to learn them all would be impossible. Some Qigong routines take almost two hours to complete, tasking the practitioner with meticulous details such as standing on one leg while raising the other and rotating the foot eighty-one times in each direction, repeating the process on the other leg, all the while holding the hands overhead, palms pressed together as though preparing to dive headlong into the sky. In contrast, the Six Subtle Movements can be learned in less than half an hour and mastered by almost anyone in less than a week's time.

Each of the following six movements has a number of rules, designed to help the practitioner perform them effectively. Each move has two phases regarding breath: the inhale and exhale phases, each lasting approximately three seconds. Inhales occur either at the beginning of a movement or during a transition from one movement to the next. Inhales happen when the hands contract toward the body, exhales when the hands expand away.

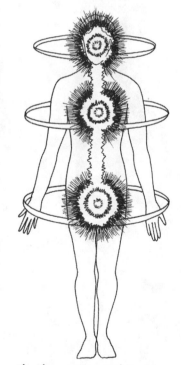

In addition, five other factors characterize the movements. First, each movement is performed three times. Second, all are performed to the left and right, motion beginning on the left. Third, the movements involve the hands, the lower body, and the shifting of weight from one leg to the other, all occurring at the same time. Fourth, all motion originates from the hips. Fifth, hands, arms, and all upper body muscles remain relaxed throughout the routine.

Each of the six movements makes a series of circular or elliptical patterns in the air surrounding the head, chest, and hips, defined as the High, Middle, and Low Centers, respectively. Throughout the Six Subtle Movements, the hands sweep

**The Three Centers and Patterns Created by the Six Movements**

through the airspace of each of the three centers, creating opposing circular patterns on each side of each center. Seeing the patterns the hands trace in the air helps the practitioner understand the simple way the movements engage and shape personal space. These three centers have great immunological significance, but I'll forego explanations for the moment in favor of introducing the exercise.

## Opening:
### Begin, Raise Arms, Drop Arms and Sink, Draw in Hands

Prior to moving, the feet should be shoulder-width apart, facing straight ahead, the legs straight without being rigid. Though some natural movement of the feet will occur due to weight shifts and hip rotation, this foot position is maintained throughout the six movements.

The Six Subtle Movements begin the same way as do the most popular forms of Taiji. Starting with arms relaxed at your sides, raise the arms upward to about shoulder level and inhale slowly, using Reverse Breathing. Keep the arms straight without tension, the hands relaxed and bent at the wrist joints. All at once, drop the arms, slightly bend the knees, and begin a slow exhale. As the arms descend, bend the elbows and flex the hands at the wrist joints, as though stroking an invisible wall.

Continue to drop the hands until they are in front of the pelvis, then draw them toward the navel. Inhale slowly while doing this. The legs shouldn't be bent enough to create too much stress, but later, as aptitude increases, bend the knees further in order to build the quadriceps.

### First Movement: Low-Forward Circle Left and Right
#### Low-Forward Circle Left: Begin Circle, Shift Back, Return to Origin

#### Low-Forward Circle Right: Begin Circle, Shift Back, Return to Origin

As mentioned before, the movement starts on the left. With a slow exhale, the motion originates from the pelvis, where the hands have been placed from the opening movement. On the exhale, slowly turn the hips left and shift the body's weight over the left leg. At the same time, have the hands mirror the lower body movement, describing a low circular pattern that ranges out from the left side of the Low Center. Then, as the hands line up with the left hip, draw them inward, inhaling and shifting the weight back onto the right leg, without turning the hips. Then turn the hips back to their original position, and bring the hands to their original placement in front of the pelvis.

Repeat this action two more times, then in identical fashion perform three forward circles to the right.

### Second Movement: Low-Rear Circle Left and Right
#### Low-Rear Circle Left: Turn Behind, Farthest Extension, Return to Origin

## Low-Rear Circle Right: Turn Behind, Farthest Extension, Return to Origin

After exhaling and completing the last forward circle to the right, inhale softly and turn the waist so that the body returns to its original, forward-facing position and the weight is equally distributed on both feet. Return your hands to your pelvis. Then, continuing to inhale, turn left so that the whole body, including the hands, faces behind your left shoulder. At the same time, shift the weight onto your right leg.

Exhale and shift the weight to the left leg, then turn your waist back toward the front, at the same time tracing a low circle on your left side with the hands, opposing the frontal circle outlined by the first movement. As the waist and hands return to their original, forward-facing position, redistribute your weight evenly, then take a long, slow inhale and shift the weight back to the right leg to begin the process again.

Repeat this rear circular movement two more times, then perform three identical rear circles to the right, matching your breathing to the movements, just as you did on the left side.

As mentioned earlier, the first two movements define opposing circles in personal space. The first movement traces two circles that radiate out from the front of the Low Center. In counterpoint to the circles of the first, the second movement's circles run from the rear of the Low Center to the front (see page 101).

### Third Movement: Middle-Forward Circle Left and Right. Transition from Low-Rear Circle Right

After completing the second movement on the right, inhale and return to the central, forward-facing position and raise your hands to chest level, turning the palms so that they face outward.

### Middle-Forward Circle Left: Begin Circle, Shift Back, Return to Origin

As in the first movement, slowly turn the hips left, shifting the body's weight so that it sits primarily over the left leg. Let the hands follow the lower body, describing a circular pattern that ranges out from the left side of the chest, or Middle Center. Then, as the hands achieve a perpendicular position to their beginning position, turn the palms inward, drawing them toward your chest as you inhale. Shift the weight back onto the right leg, then turn your hips back to their original forward position, returning the hands to their original spot in front of the chest. Again, turn the palms to face outward.

Repeat this action two more times, then in identical fashion perform three middle-forward circles to the right.

## Middle-Forward Circle Right: Begin Circle, Shift Back, Return to Origin

## Fourth Movement: Middle-Rear Circle Left and Right

### Middle-Rear Circle Left: Turn Behind, Farthest Extension, Return to Origin

After exhaling and completing the last middle-forward circle to the right, inhale softly and turn so that the body and hands face their original forward position and the weight is equally distributed on both feet. Then, without pause, continuing to inhale, turn left so that the whole body, including the hands, faces the rear in a manner identical to the second movement, palms facing outward, weight shifted onto the right leg. Next, exhale and shift the weight onto the left leg, at the same time tracing a left-rear circle with the hands similar to the low rear circle of the second movement, except that the palms face outward until the inhale. Then they are turned inward and pulled toward the chest. All subsequent breath and weight-distribution issues are the same as in the second movement.

**Middle-Rear Circle Right: Turn Behind, Farthest Extension, Return to Origin**

Repeat this mid-level, rear circular movement two more times, then perform three identical rear circles, with the same breathing pattern, to the right.

As with the first two movements, the third and fourth movements define opposing circles in personal space that radiate out from the chest (see page 101).

### Fifth Movement: High-Forward Circle Left and Right.
### High Forward Transition

After completing the fourth movements, inhale and bring the hands and weight around to the forward position, but move the hands and arms up to engage the head or High Center, the right palm several inches above the crown, facing downward, the left palm extended up, about shoulder height. On the exhale, have your hands describe a high circular pattern similar to the low and middle forward circles, except that the palms are on different levels, aimed in opposite directions. This causes the movements to trace a pair of ellipses in the air, one hovering above the other, like a pair of smoke rings.

## High-Forward Circle Left: Begin Circle, Shift Back, Return to Origin

As with the low and middle forward circle movements, the hands exaggerate the lower body's shift over to the left leg, and draw inward on the inhale when the weight shifts back onto the right leg. Turn the hips back to their original forward position, and put the hands back where they started. Repeat this action two more times.

## High-Forward Circle Transition

The transition to the right side is more complicated than the parallel movements at the Low and Middle Centers. After the third high-forward circle is completed to the left, inhale and shift back on the right leg, slowly turning the hips to the forward position. At the same time, the left hand moves to the overhead, palm-down position, while the right turns palm-up and drops to shoulder height.

At this point, the high-forward circles to the right mirror those of the left.

### High-Forward Circle Right: Begin Circle, Shift Back, Return to Origin

# Sixth Movement: High-Rear Circle Left and Right

## Transition

Aside from the position of the arms and hands, the transition to the sixth movement parallels the rear-circular patterns at the Low and Middle Centers. The arm positions involve returning the hands to the beginning posture of the high-forward left movement.

Returning on the inhale to a forward-facing position, weight equally distributed on both feet, move the right hand to the palm-down, overhead position while dropping the left and turning it palm-up at shoulder level.

## High-Rear Circle Left: Turn Behind, Farthest Extension, Return to Origin

Without a pause, and continuing to inhale, turn left so that the whole body, including the hands, faces to the rear in a manner identical to the other rear movements. At the same time, shift the weight onto the right leg.

Next, exhale and shift the weight to the left, at the same time trace parallel ellipses with the hands opposing those of the fifth movement on the same side, rotating the hips and hands forward until they return to their original forward position and weight is equally distributed

Repeat this high-level, rear-circular movement two more times.

### Transition to the Right

Transitioning to the right involves reversing the hands as in going from left to right in the fifth movement.

## High-Rear Circle Right: Turn Behind, Farthest Extension, Return to Origin

Once the hands are inverted, perform three identical rear circles with the same breathing pattern to the right.

As with the first two sets of movements, the fifth and sixth movements define opposing circles in personal space that radiate from the left and right sides of the head (see page 101).

## Closing

Upon completing the last of the high-rear circles to the right, lower the left hand and simultaneously turn over the right. Gently lower the hands to the sides and straighten the knees.

Repeat the routine (all six movements) a minimum of two more times, a maximum of six.

# Six Subtle Movements Versus Traditional Chinese Taiji and Qigong

Once you've completed the last of the high-rear circles, you may proceed to the next stage, Reflective Meditation (see chapter 5), or begin the six movements again, if you prefer. In the beginning, three repetitions of the whole routine yield good results (taking twelve to fourteen minutes), and more repetitions produce even better results.

*Studies reveal that both Chinese systems can lower blood pressure about the same as does cardiovascular exercise, with the added benefit of preserving the integrity of the lower body muscles, joints, tendons, and bones.*

By repeating sets of the Six Subtle Movements, you may feel the air surrounding the three Centers thicken in your hands. This sensation marks an increase in your reflective response—that is, your tactile sense of the air surrounding the three Centers. As your reflective response grows more acute, you can reduce the number of repetitions to a single set, which takes about four minutes.

By comparison, a simplified Taiji routine takes only about two minutes more to complete, but learning the intricacies of such a form takes at least several months of daily committed practice. Getting to the point where you're performing the Taiji smoothly and feeling your body's reflections in the air takes much longer.

In spite of these time and learning barriers, however, research on traditional Taiji and Qigong has shown that practitioners invest their time well when they perform these exercises. Studies reveal that both Chinese systems can lower blood pressure about the same as does cardiovascular exercise, with the added benefit of preserving the integrity of the lower body muscles, joints, tendons, and bones.

The most widely accepted research has shown that Taiji can reduce the risk of falls in the elderly better than any other exercise. Moreover, Taiji and Qigong fit the body's physics. Both exercises are weight-bearing activities, which have been shown to strengthen and build bones, the loss of which, in the form of osteoporosis, is a big problem as we age. In contrast, the arms move freely through space, the only burden being the weight of the arms themselves. The resulting increase in peripheral circulation builds cardiovascular health without tearing down the rest of the body, which is one of the risks of orthodox cardiovascular exercise.

Though important, this research has a narrow, mechanical focus that overlooks the profound immunological issues alluded to at the beginning of the book and this chapter. Making matters worse, traditional Chinese medicine and fitness models insist on explanations and proof grounded in pre-scientific metaphors, which Western medicine has difficulty understanding and respecting. These traditional Chinese accounts revolve around the notion that the lower trunk, pelvis, and legs contain the body's most precious healing potential or "Qi," often translated as "vital energy." In Chinese acupuncture and massage, for example, the therapist works from an understanding that long-term health can only be gained by accentuating and releasing the Qi of the patient's lower body, believed to reside primarily in the kidneys.

The Six Subtle Movements of Unified Fitness allow the practitioner to experience the benefits touted by both Western and Chinese paradigms with a relatively small time investment. The six movements not only work the muscles, bones, ligaments, and tendons in ways similar to that of traditional Taiji and Qigong, but can also give the exerciser firsthand experience with the subjective validity of Qi. This sense of Qi is the previously mentioned reflective response: a tactile sense of the body's atmosphere, made possible by the subtle movement of the hands through the air.

As I mentioned earlier, the Six Subtle Movements take less than a half hour to learn, and reflective effects show up much sooner, especially when the six movements are combined with the Reflective Meditation exercise in the next chapter.

Repeating the Six Subtle Movements not only increases your reflective response, but also helps build lower musculoskeletal strength. To repeat the sequence, conclude the last of the sixth movements, then drop the hands from the High to the Low Center in the manner of the third position of the opening and begin the first movement to the left. Repeating the routine three or four times can yield a degree of the musculoskeletal and cardiovascular benefits Taiji has been shown to give, without forcing you to spend years perfecting dozens of complex movements.

## Margaret Overcomes Her Bad Knees and Back

Margaret joined a month-long reflective exercise class at the local senior center and was very anxious to get started. A prosperous lady in her middle sixties, Margaret had visited China and seen thousands of Shanghai residents rise at the crack of dawn to practice Taijiquan and Qigong. The only problem was that Margaret had bad knees and a bad back from a number of horse-riding accidents. At first, she was doubtful that the subtle movements were good for her.

Margaret turned out to be the star pupil of the class, often showing up early to help some of the less physically gifted students go over confusing transitions in the movements. The exercises were having a very good effect on her back and knees, though they still hurt from time to time. But, compared to the huge amount of pain and suffering they had caused her over the years, and the time spent with doctors and physical therapists who hadn't helped much, her problems seemed to be getting better. This encouraged her to practice outside class.

In the last few sessions of the course, I had the students begin meditating for about five minutes. To my surprise, Margaret reported experiencing what is, for me, the hallmark sensation necessary for achieving lasting immunological fitness: a gentle pulsing sensation just below the navel. Out of the hundreds I have taught, I can count on one hand the number of people who have gotten such profound results with such limited exposure to reflective exercise. When I told Margaret this, her eyes brightened and she left, assuring me that she would practice every day and keep me informed of her progress.

Because Margaret was affluent, I expected her to get distracted by a Pacific cruise or a month-long sightseeing tour of Europe. A couple of months passed before I heard from her again, in a phone call.

For a second, to my embarrassment, I had trouble placing the name but she not only forgave my slipped memory, but paid me an exceptional compliment. She said that she had been practicing reflective exercise faithfully, twice a day, every day since the course ended. Her back and knees felt better than they had in almost fifteen years, since her first serious horseback-riding accident. She happily reported being able to stoop and garden for hours—her favorite pastime, and something that would have been unthinkable before she began reflective exercise.

Because this was the only intervention she had been using, she attributed her renewed musculoskeletal health to what I had taught her. After expressing her deepest thanks, she said that learning reflective exercise was one of the greatest things she had ever experienced in her life.

## Ed Learns to Manage a Bad Back

Ed was a big, successful man in his middle thirties with a rich social life. By day he presided over a thriving advertising business and by night he led a local theater group and played in a popular band. The only complaint he had was that his back ached constantly, and whenever his stress level went up, the pain got worse. Having tried most treatments available, including acupuncture, Ed decided to try reflective exercise, based on the reviews he had heard from friends who had studied with me.

Unlike the senior program, which was really more "Reflective Exercise Lite," the program Ed enrolled in lasted ten weeks and required a commitment to two forty-five minute practice sessions a day. My goal was to get everyone in the class to experience what Margaret had attained, a pulse below the navel that traveled up a frontal pathway of the body to the nasal sinuses. This response effectively marks the ability to fight infection consciously.

Though Ed was intrigued by this possibility, he mainly wanted to be able to reduce the pain in his back, an effect I felt would be difficult to achieve if the problem were purely musculoskeletal, as it was for Margaret. She had spent years having her musculoskeletal misalignments redressed by professionals. But Ed's back pain was recent, and he had no particular trauma to attribute it to, as did Margaret. His limited time with professionals had produced vague conclusions and poor results, so given these confounding bits of information, I had no idea whether reflective exercise would make his back feel better.

Within two weeks, Ed reported an improvement in his condition. The subtle movements, he said, seemed to loosen his back substantially, as long as he didn't overextend on the turns. Encouraged by these results, Ed devoted himself to the demanding, twice-daily regimen, and by the third week, had attained the pulse below the navel and was able to move it to his sinuses.

The experience so astonished Ed that it changed his way of reacting to work, acting, and music. While at work, he found that he could instigate the pulsing sensation, which helped calm him in stressful situations, and it often reduced or eliminated his low back pain. Similarly, his performances in acting and music became more inspired and spontaneous, drawing unsolicited compliments from his colleagues. By the time the course came to an end, Ed was not only in the "driver's seat" of his immunological fitness, but was able to manage his low back pain so that it hardly affected him.

At this point, I encouraged Ed to develop flexibility and lower body strength through conventional fitness facilities, and that after achieving a period of consistent painlessness, he should incorporate cardiovascular exercise into his routine, always concluding with stretches and reflective exercise. At this writing, he appears to have sufficiently healed to incorporate such Phase 1 exercises into his routine.

## James Battles a Brain Injury

Prior to his learning reflective exercise, "battle" is an appropriate way to describe life for James, a forty-year-old man who had suffered a massive head injury during an automobile accident in the mid-1980s. The wreck also shattered his left leg in several places, including his knee, which, along with other bones and joints, had to be reconstructed. This, in turn, threw his posture out of alignment, so that he eventually ruptured a lumbar disc in his lower back.

James saw this as more of a minor setback compared to his other problems: a severely diminished speech and short-term memory capacity, much like that of a stroke victim. But his biggest concern, and what he aimed to remedy when he began learning reflective exercise, was an almost-paralyzed left hand—he could barely move one or two fingers, and only with exaggerated effort. The paralysis was due entirely to brain injury on his right hemisphere.

James had spent the last thirteen years of his life in various forms of rehabilitation that had run the gamut from physical therapy to energy healing. Though he had regained some competence in the first few years following his accident, he hadn't improved much since. Still, he tried his best to lead a normal life. Financially secure, he held a couple of part-time jobs, kept up a fairly busy social life, and maintained a daily physical fitness routine of stationary bike-riding and swimming, which provided an excellent opportunity to combine reflective exercise so that his routine could become "Unified."

But due to his weakened memory, he couldn't retain the subtle movements or the sequence of the steps that followed, so he could only practice reflective exercise in private sessions with me. These sessions, however, had a remarkable effect on him. The extra attention and encouragement I provided brightened his outlook. Within two months, he developed the lower abdominal pulse, and several weeks later, he was able to bring the sensation to his head, where the real healing had to take place.

By the end of five months, James was pulsing not only his head but his left arm as well. Not long thereafter, his fingers began to obey his will, moving with increasing range and freedom. The improvement inspired James to try to remember the subtle movements, so that he could follow his physical workouts with reflective exercise. Now able to do so, he gained even greater improvement.

After a couple of years of effort, during which he experienced a roller coaster of successes and setbacks, James could finally open and close all five of his fingers of his left hand. Compared to what he could do when we first met, his new dexterity represented a victory in his long battle. James was so pleased that he regaled anyone who would listen with the story of how reflective exercise helped him regain the use of his hand. Eventually, James' story made its way to brain injury specialists, who then contacted me about forming programs to help groups of brain-injured people. So far, the specialists have been pleased with the program results and now refer people to me on a regular basis.

## Melanie Cures Her Hemorrhoids

Melanie, in her late thirties, joined the first reflective exercise group I formed after returning to the U.S. from China. Though small in stature, she  was a tough, independent woman who worked construction for a living, trying to earn enough money to put herself through nursing school.

Aside from the physical difficulty of her job, Melanie had another problem that she refused to discuss with me until two months into her training. After class one night, she waited for the others to leave, then asked me if I thought reflective exercise could help her deal with a bad case of hemorrhoids. I admitted that I didn't have enough experience to answer her, but that the Chinese believed reflective exercises such as Taiji and Qigong could cure anything.

When I got home, I read up on hemorrhoids and learned that they are engorged veins in the rectum caused by strain. Internal hemorrhoids cause bleeding but aren't painful; the external variety tend to be painful. Melanie's discreet request implied that hers were painful. After giving the matter some thought, I decided that since hemorrhoids represented dilated and inflamed circulatory tissue, the pulse phenomenon could treat the problem, particularly on the exhale, when the pulse lingered in the Low Center.

From there, I reasoned that Melanie could direct the sensation to the rectum, where she could hold the pulse for a few seconds longer than normal before inhaling. Moreover, the inhale phase of Reverse Breathing involves contracting not only the lower abdominal muscles, but also the anal sphincter to a lesser extent. I suggested that she slightly exaggerate this co-contraction, effectively imitating an exercise called Kegels used to prepare pregnant women for the rigors of childbirth, an experience which often results in hemorrhoids.

After a few weeks of working with my suggestions, Melanie began to notice results. Within two months, her hemorrhoids cleared up.

## Katrina Relieves Postoperative Pain

Katrina enrolled in a Reflective Exercise Lite program I offered through a local fitness center that wanted to introduce its patrons to T'ai Chi. Katrina looked to be in her middle-to-late forties and seemed almost painfully shy compared to two or three other women who were quick to respond during question and answer time. Katrina always stood in the back of the room and said very little. I got the impression that she had been the awkward kid who was the last to get chosen to play kickball, and so was uncomfortable about the whole idea of exercise.

My suspicions appeared to be correct. In learning the first movements, she had more difficulty than the others, often pausing when I coached everyone to continue to move smoothly and without interruption. I prepared myself for the disappointment that Katrina would most likely be one of the few who don't respond to reflective exercise.

In spite of these reservations, Katrina showed up for class and stuck faithfully to the routine. By the end of the course, she was moving as well as the others. On the last day of class, I asked everyone to share what they had gotten out of the class. Oddly, the more assertive members of the class seemed to make the most modest gains. When Katrina's turn came, I was shocked to hear one of the strongest testimonials I had ever heard from a participant of such a short program.

As it turned out, Katrina had undergone surgery for breast cancer years before, and it had left her in such pain in the shoulders and neck that she could barely comb her hair. When she first began the class, just raising the arms to begin the subtle movements had been difficult. By the second week, she said that not only the movements, but also ordinary actions that were previously painful had ceased to be problems. Eventually, the pain in her shoulders and neck dissipated entirely, and with the diminishment of pain came a sense of serenity and confidence she hadn't known in years.

To this day, Katrina practices reflective exercise following her cardiovascular workouts and continues to report good results. Katrina's success makes a strong case for investing time in learning reflective exercise.

# Nellie Overcomes Hypertension, Arthritis Symptoms, and Raynaud's Syndrome

By the time I met Nellie, my reputation for being able to help people get miraculous results was well established, and one of our community's noted phases of indifference had set in, manifesting in the small turnout for a "Reflective Exercise Lite" class. Nellie was a pert, small woman in her late sixties who stood out among the other four seniors enrolled in the class, but such a small group hardly inspired me to muster the salesman's energy of my earlier days. Both my attitude and my expectations were low. Still, Nellie's enthusiasm and determination to get as much out of the class as she could lifted my spirits, and I found myself looking forward to the questions and comments she would make before and after each class.

In the course of these exchanges, I learned that Nellie suffered from a number of health problems, including hypertension (high blood pressure), osteoarthritis, and Raynaud's Syndrome, a tendency to experience cold and discoloration in the hands and fingers, a reaction often associated with osteoarthritis. Because of her hypertension, Nellie had trouble with Reverse Abdominal Breathing, which seemed to set her heart racing. Part of the problem was that Nellie wasn't relaxing adequately on the exhale; she didn't seem to know how. After a bit of coaching on this point, her heart stopped racing and she was able to practice with greater smoothness and coordination.

When the four weeks of class came to an end, Nellie was impressed by how much better she felt, and her physician enthusiastically endorsed Nellie's continued involvement in reflective exercise, based on the glowing feedback he was getting from Nellie. I encouraged her to practice twice daily, and she assured me that she would keep it up.

Almost nine months later, Nellie dropped by my school one day to cheerfully tell me that her arthritis hardly bothered her anymore and that the symptoms of Raynaud's Syndrome and hypertension had vanished. Her physician was at a loss to explain this improvement. Smiling broadly, Nellie conveyed how she felt about it with a story about a five-mile hike she had recently taken in the Blue Ridge mountains with her middle-thirties daughter. Though Nellie had never been the outdoors type, she kept up with her daughter the whole time. When they finished, her legs felt strong and pain-free, and she looked up to see a U.S. Park Service sign rating the hike she had just completed as "For Advanced Hikers."

"Not bad for a woman in her late sixties who had trouble walking around town six months ago," Nellie said. With that, she snatched up a handful of my flyers, said she was going to take them to her doctor, and was out the door.

## Ted Relieves Chronic Shoulder and Knee Pain

Ted joined my school along with a group of undergraduates from the local university who had read about my program in the local paper. Ted was a trim, intense young man who looked like he had little body fat. He confided immediately that he had pain in his shoulders and knees that was making it tough for him to carry out his normal student life. Upon further questioning, I discovered that Ted was an exercise overachiever, the most current of his accomplishments being the completion of a rigorous marathon that had left him stiff and pain-ridden. I also learned that he spent hours every day exercising as hard as he could. So far as nutrition was concerned, he ate a lot of calories, but they were mostly highly glycemic carbohydrates, such as pasta, the kind of diet advocated by runners over the past few years.

Rather than the hard-style martial arts form Ted wanted to learn, I insisted he take Taiji and work on his flexibility. The pain and discomfort Ted was experiencing made it hard for him to disagree, and he came almost every day to go through stretches and basic Taiji training.

Though Ted made some initial progress, his pain persisted to the point where he was growing frustrated, so I consulted one of my students who was a practicing physical therapist. Combined with the flexibility and Taiji routine he had gotten from me, the mobilizing and stretching exercises the physical therapist prescribed began to show better results for Ted. The physical therapist also backed up my insistence that Ted should rein in his tendency to overachieve.

In spite of these gains, Ted continued to experience bouts of tightness and pain following modest exertion, so I recommended he begin reflective exercise. Within weeks Ted felt significantly better, and the flexibility routine began having a more lasting effect.

This improvement encouraged Ted to go further in meditation, but here he quickly ran into emotional trouble. Unable to consistently feel the lower abdominal pulse, Ted consulted me to discuss what he might be doing wrong. Once I was certain he was doing everything correctly, I began asking him about his family background, which included divorced parents and a stern, nonempathic father who had basically refused to believe that Ted had been in pain for the past year. As he talked about his father's reluctance to believe there was a problem, Ted's eyes seemed to moisten. I interrupted and asked him to consider what he was feeling. Like his own emotionally restricted father, Ted tried to shrug off his sadness, but he agreed that it was likely he unconsciously absorbed, at a young age, his father's manner of expressing emotions. I encouraged Ted to discuss his feelings with a professional counselor, and Ted was open to the idea. He then confessed that his mother was a psychotherapist and had been after him for years to undertake counseling.

After that conversation, Ted's reflective exercise improved, and his muscular tightness and pain in the shoulder and legs—the original problem from which he had sought relief—were under control. The lower abdominal pulse appeared and disappeared, letting Ted know when he was "getting warm" on resolving the emotional pain behind the behavior that had driven him to be a physical overachiever. His progress was slow but steady, and Ted seemed to understand that his inclination to be emotionally reserved and his zeal for physical fitness were the two greatest forces shaping his development with reflective exercise.

A year later, Ted discovered to his astonishment that his reflective exercise practice had seemed to cause his pain to diminish, migrate, and dissipate. Though it returned during times of high stress, such as midterm or final exams, he could direct the abdominal pulse to a prob-lem site, then move, and dissolve the pain. If his problem were structural or tis-sue damage due to overexercising, these fluctuations were an anomaly, suggesting another factor.

The shifting behavior of Ted's pain in response to reflective exercise indicated to me that his excessive physical exercise and emotional reserve may have been secondary causes, making him suscepti-ble to another: a slow-working infection that was medically undetectable. If this was true, then there should have been other shifting immunological reactions, such as outbreaks of boils, muscular twitches, and itchy skin.

*Ted discovered to his astonishment that his reflective exercise practice seemed to cause his pain to diminish, migrate, and dissipate. Though it returned during times of high stress, such as midterm or final exams, he could direct the abdominal pulse to a problem site, then move, and dissolve the pain.*

Though I had mentioned these possible reactions to Ted before, he was so certain that his problem was structural or tissue damage from exercise that he had ignored them. But now he noticed them con-stantly. I asked him to watch for a relationship between these reactions and his fluctuating pain when he practiced reflective exercise.

Sure enough, immunological fluctuations such as skin rashes and muscle twitches followed changes in his pain. Eventually the pain and the skin and muscular reactions subsided, indicating that Ted was finally resolving an immunological problem.

# Chapter 5

## Day 9: The Door Opens Wider

### Exercise Series 3, A, B, C, and D: Reflective Meditation

Reflective Meditation is where the term "reflective" comes into play. In this phase, the hands begin to feel the body's complex interaction with the air most strongly, paving the way for blending the immune and nervous systems. This exercise series has four components:

A. Standing Reflective Meditation
B. Sensing the Middle Center
C. Closing Sculpt
D. Seated Reflective Meditation.

## Exercise 3A: Standing Reflective Meditation

Standing Reflective Meditation marks the beginning of Exercise Series 3. It should follow Exercise 2B, Six Subtle Movements, and is experiential, with very little you have to remember about it.

After completing the last of the Six Subtle Movements, bring the hands up to the Middle Center, as though gently embracing someone.

Keep the spine erect but not rigid, the legs straight without being taut. Allow the elbows to relax downward toward the rib cage. With closed eyes, hold the arms in the gentle embrace posture for five to seven minutes. Focus the mind on nothing but Reverse Breathing (tongue curled, lightly contracting the lower abdomen on the inhalation and relaxing it on the exhalation). If the arms become unbearably tired, shorten the time to two or three minutes. If dizzy or unable to stand, perform the meditation while seated.

## Exercise 3B: Sensing the Middle Center

After five to seven minutes of doing Exercise 3A, place the hands so that they face one another, as though holding a ball between the palms. On the inhale, slowly separate the hands, then exhale and bring them together, only a few inches apart. Repeat this two more times. Next, slowly begin rotating the right hand forward while keeping the left still. After completing six circles, reverse the circles of the right hand six more times. Next, hold the right hand still and repeat the circling process with the left, then circle the hands as though they were turning the pedals of a bicycle. Every now and then, reverse the direction of the circles. Also, you can compress and expand the hands as though playing the accordion. You may also hold one hand still and wave the other towards and away from the still hand.

You may feel a variety of things while rotating the hands. You may feel heat, tingling, or even a sense of two magnets repelling and/or attracting one another. At times you may feel as though a sphere of charged air has formed between the hands.

Day 9: The Door Opens Wider

Standing Reflective Meditation

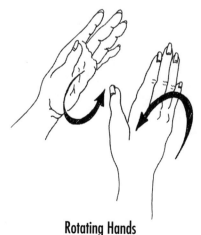

Rotating Hands

129

**Sensing the Middle Center**

At other times your sense of the sphere as warm, tingling, or magnetic air may abruptly shrink to a narrow column, expand to an asymmetrical shape, or vanish altogether. This chaotic aspect of Exercise 3B, Sensing the Middle Center, emerges more dramatically in later stages of reflective exercise (Chaosercise). But even at this more subtle stage it provides a lesson on body-air complexity, a subject discussed at greater length in a later section.

## Exercise 3C: Closing Sculpt

After at least five minutes of playing with the charged air, lower the hands to your sides. The hands may feel heavy and tingly. Then, on the inhale, perform Exercise 3C, Closing Sculpt. Bring the hands up over the top of your head on the inhale, then, on the exhale, direct them down the front center of the body so that they pass through all three centers. This action should be performed three times, once for each center, the hands "sculpting" a vertical line down the center of the body, connecting the Three Centers. On the last Closing Sculpt, bring the hands to rest over the Low Center. Men should begin the downward pass with their left hands on the bottom; women should have their right on the bottom.

## Closing Sculpt

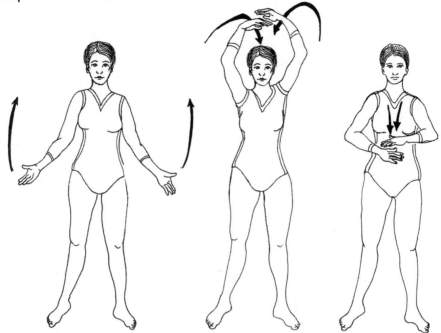

Such hand placement compensates for each gender's proclivity to rely to a greater extent on one side of the brain over the other. Men tend to favor the left hemisphere of the brain—which corresponds to the right side of the body—while women tend to favor the right, which corresponds to the left side. The left hemisphere supposedly accounts for logical, rational thought, while the right supposedly processes emotions and nonlinear thinking. Since each gender brings a socially determined predisposition to Reflective Meditation, men and women can balance out their predispositions by using their bodies to involve their less-favored brain hemispheres. The combined effect of these features of the Closing Sculpt encourages sensitivity in the Low Center.

After regular practice of the initial stage of Reflective Meditation, the hands may begin to feel permanently warm and magnetized. This is an indication that the practitioner's reflective response is increasing. The next step is to go further into even more passive states of meditation, which can lead to an opening of a blood pathway from the gut to the head, creating greater immunological fitness.

# Teresa Recovers from Heart Failure

Teresa was another woman in her late sixties who turned to reflective exercise for relief from a health problem. In Teresa's case, she had suffered a heart attack while climbing a steep flight of steps at the local university.

Teresa and her husband, a retired naval officer, weren't the sort of people I was used to teaching, but they weren't alone in the subtle movement class I had agreed to teach for a local parks and recreation program. About twenty people signed up because of a front page story in the newspaper, which included a strong endorsement from a prominent physician who had been studying with me for a year. This publicity catalyzed an already burgeoning interest sparked by a PBS show on Taiji and Qigong that had aired a few weeks earlier.

Though pleased with the turnout, I was prepared for the inevitable letdown. The kind of subtle movement I was slated to teach was traditional Taijiquan, highly demanding physical exercise that requires patience on the part of the practitioner, especially if the practitioner isn't gifted when it comes to learning physical movement. One by one, the students dropped from the ranks until Teresa and her husband were the only ones left, an elderly couple dressed in sleek sportswear and spotless sneakers. Teresa stood out even more because she wore a heart monitor on her finger that occasionally made high-pitched beeps, which prompted me to ask her questions about her health.

Though reluctant at first to say much other than that the monitor was gauging her blood pressure, Teresa finally told me the story of collapsing while climbing a steep flight of stairs and ending up under the surgeon's knife. She was given emergency bypass surgery, put on medication to lower her cholesterol and blood pressure, and given rehabilitation support, in which she was educated in the virtues of modest cardiovascular exercise and low-fat dieting. Her doctor knew the physician quoted in the newspaper article, and she had been impressed by the PBS show. So far, Teresa said, the Taiji was making her feel better.

From that point on, I made a special effort to give Teresa attention and to make sure she was getting the complex movements right.

Given her age and condition, Teresa's performance was more than adequate, and her dedication to daily practice was remarkable. Her husband's performance left a lot to be desired, but his support and willingness to do the exercises alongside his wife were important elements of getting Teresa to comply. The three of us got to the point where we enjoyed seeing each other on a weekly basis, and I always took time to sit with Teresa, to catch up on how she was doing.

Over the course of about three months, Teresa reported a number of remarkable improvements. Her blood pressure stabilized, her heart rate became strong and consistent, and her cholesterol readings normalized. Eventually, she was able to drop the finger monitor, and she told me she felt better than she had in years.

What was unusual about Teresa's case was that she had achieved substantial results merely by learning subtle movement; she had not yet been introduced to abdominal breathing or Reflective Meditation. Certain that she could enhance her already encouraging improvements, I suggested to Teresa that she and her husband try the deeper Reflective Meditation techniques. But as I described the desired effects of the training, a worried and confused expression appeared on Teresa's face. She said curtly that she wanted to talk with her doctor about it first. I shrugged off her concern and recommended that she have her doctor speak with my doctor-student to allay any fears.

It took several months of waiting, but Teresa and her husband finally decided to join a reflective exercise class, where they learned Reverse Breathing and Reflective Meditation. From the beginning, I could tell that Teresa was wary of meditation, but when she began sensing the charged air surrounding her body, her reluctance lessened. Still, she preferred the more complex and demanding Taiji to the comparatively simple subtle movements of the class, largely because Reflective Meditation enabled her to sense the air around her body with the Taiji movements. Because she already liked Taiji and its more complex movement, the movements in the reflective exercise class seemed redundant to her.

Though I tried to explain the greater benefits of deep Reflective Meditation, such as the ability to fight infectious disease, Teresa preferred to stick with what had impressed both her and her doctor. Implicit in Teresa's reaction, and in the reaction of her physician, was the conviction that exercise can only accomplish so much and should therefore merit limited investment. Also, at this point in time, evidence on the role of infectious disease in chronic health problems such as heart disease hadn't come to light, so my reasons for why someone in Teresa's condition should devote an extra twenty minutes to meditation exercise were unconvincing.

Nevertheless, Teresa gained a great deal by combining Reflective Meditation with Taiji movement. Together with the regimen laid out by her physician, the exercises she learned from me helped improve her heart condition a great deal. She came away satisfied, and that was good enough for me.

I now advocate simpler reflective exercise over the complex Taiji forms. Still, if all that is available is Taiji, the person willing to invest the time to learn the movements has at least as much to gain as did Teresa.

## Gabrielle Dissipates Chronic Fatigue Syndrome and Fibromyalgia

Gabrielle was one of twenty-five people who signed up for a Reflective Exercise Lite course offered through the YMCA of a nearby community. In the first class, Gabrielle stood out from the other participants, including several seniors, because she could do so little, having to sit down in a metal folding chair after only a minute on her feet. At the end of class, I asked her what was wrong.

With an expression that spoke of long years of debilitation and suffering, she explained she had been diagnosed with chronic fatigue syndrome and fibromyalgia, both of which caused severe exhaustion and pain in the legs, hips, and back. Both illnesses have thwarted conventional medical treatment, and both have shown a link to infectious agents. At one time, the Epstein-Barr virus was a chief causal suspect in chronic fatigue syndrome, though the current consensus acknowledges the virus as only one of many factors involved. The same virus, along with other immune actors, has been implicated in fibromyalgia (a chronic inflammation of the connective tissue below the muscles).

I had already seen reflective exercise deal effectively with these health problems in several people, so I was certain Gabrielle could improve her condition. When I told her this, her face seemed to brighten with hope before collapsing into a stoic expression as she got to her feet to leave.

The next class went only a little better. Gabrielle had to complete the subtle movement routine seated in a folding chair, and I had my doubts that the limited nature of the class could do much for her. Before she left, I encouraged her to practice the routine on her own, and she said she would.

The following week Gabrielle showed a noticeable improvement, able to stay on her feet for more than five minutes. When I congratulated her on her progress, she smiled broadly and said she had been practicing as she had promised. Then she grilled me with questions that showed she was serious about keeping up with her exercises.

The fourth time I met with the class, I made everyone stay on their feet for a half hour, and as time passed, I kept expecting Gabrielle to sit down. But she didn't. She stayed on her feet the entire time. When the class finished, everyone gave Gabrielle a round of applause for her achievement. She blushed, her spirits clearly lifted by the attention. Then I asked her to reveal the secret of how she had been able to improve her stamina by a factor of thirty in just four weeks. "I practice twice a day," Gabrielle said.

After class, I jotted down notes as Gabrielle gave her personal history. Somewhere along the way, I stopped writing, because there were too many problems, shocks, and illnesses to keep up with. Gabrielle's life read like a Greek tragedy, filled with disappointment and emotional pain. It was a small wonder to me that she suffered from mysterious autoimmune diseases, since emotional distress confounds immunity, an aspect of mental fitness taken up in a later chapter.

Even though Gabrielle's stamina had improved, she still had a lot of pain that got in the way of her willingness to exercise. I had seen this pattern before, and while I couldn't promise that Gabrielle could cure herself, I did have enough evidence to make the suggestion that management of her condition was possible, as long as she didn't give up. She needed to stick to her twice daily practices, and if the pain got too bad, I recommended she go to an acupuncturist.

Things seemed to level off for Gabrielle after that, and I didn't hear much from her for several weeks. Then one day she called to say that the pain had gotten so bad in her hands that she was worried. I asked her if the pain in her usual places—shoulders, hips, legs—had changed at all. She said she didn't feel much discomfort in those areas anymore.

"Good!" I said, to her surprise. How could her hands hurting be "good?" I explained that the absence of pain in her shoulders, hips, and legs suggested that she was affecting the source of her problem. She had dislodged it, so to speak, thus weakening its hold on her. I told her to keep practicing, even if the pain became unbearable.

Two weeks later, at the start of another Reflective Exercise Lite class at the same YMCA, Gabrielle showed up to repeat the program. When I asked her about the pain in her hands, she reported happily that it was gone. And, though she still felt a little discomfort in her usual places, she was enjoying greater freedom of movement and a greater sense of well-being than she could remember ever having before..

A few weeks after that, in the middle of her second pass through the Reflective Exercise Lite program, Gabrielle got the lower abdominal pulse, which led to a similar pulsation in her hands. With the emergence of this pulsing sensation, the symptoms of her diseases reached an all-time low, suggesting a relationship between the pulse and the immune system. For the first time in many years, Gabrielle could say she knew what it feels like to be healthy.

> *With the emergence of this pulsing sensation, the symptoms of her diseases reached an all-time low, suggesting a relationship between the pulse and the immune system. For the first time in many years, Gabrielle could say she knew what it feels like to be healthy.*

## Exercise 3D: Seated Reflective Meditation

After a session of the Six Subtle Movements and four tactile exercises, begin Seated Reflective Meditation. This phase of meditation provides the opportunity to build subtle connections between the nervous and immune systems already stimulated by the Six Subtle Movements, Standing Reflective Meditation, and Reverse Abdominal Breathing.

If the slow movements and hand-sensitizing action provoked peculiar sensations and feelings, then stillness is apt to have a similar effect. In fact, some people may have trouble sitting quietly and feel squirmy or irritable. If this is the case, don't force yourself to sit for too long. Abbreviate your stillness to a couple of minutes; then, as you get used to the behavior, increase the amount of time.

## Full Lotus, Half Lotus, Pretzel Legs, Chair

Stillness may be done in any of two seated fashions: in a chair or on the floor. In a chair, sit on the forward edge, away from the backrest, both feet flat on the floor. If seated on the floor, use a cushion to help make the experience more comfortable, which should be your first criterion. Relaxation is most important in the beginning. The half or full lotus positions are demanding postures and require a great deal of flexibility, so it is likely that in the beginning, you're better off in a chair or on the floor, seated on a cushion, legs crossed in a manner my son's preschool teacher refers to as "pretzel legs."

Keeping the posture erect without being rigid, head held up as though by a thin wire suspended from the ceiling, curl the tongue and begin Reverse Breathing. To keep the mind disciplined, hold your right index finger out in front of you at eye level and stare at it until everything else goes out of focus. Then bring the finger toward you, aiming at a spot directly between the eyes. Eventually your eyes will cross, at which point your finger should touch the center of your brow.

Next, look down, uncross the eyes, and trace an imaginary red line down the center of your face, throat, chest, and abdomen, following the contour of your body. Have the line pool in the superpubic area of the Low Center, about two inches below the navel. Closing your eyes, imagine on the inhale that the line ascends straight up the middle of your body to the center of your forehead. On the exhale, let the line fall back into the midst of the pelvic center. If thoughts enter your mind, don't drive them out. Allow them to linger for a moment, then, when their hold on you seems to abate, go back to the image of the red line.

This use of the eyes in meditation may help involve higher visual nerve centers of the brain, thus adding another neurological layer in the concerted effort to unite mind and body.

If you aren't used to sitting like this, begin with five- or ten-minute sessions. As your concentration and comfort levels increase, lengthen the time to twenty minutes.

If sitting upright proves to be too difficult, then try lying flat on your back. This position should make it easier to relax. You may even feel sleepy, in which case you should go to sleep. If you feel suddenly awake, then try returning to an upright, seated posture. Often the stillness phase of reflective exercise will allow the natural condition of the practitioner to emerge. The practitioner should surrender to, rather than fight against, these natural inclinations.

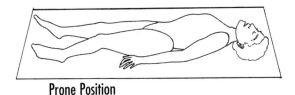

**Prone Position**

# *Harriet Pulses Away Her Rheumatoid Arthritis Symptoms*

Harriet was the oldest successful student I have ever taught, but she was remarkable in several other ways as well. Tall and dignified, Harriet seemed far younger than her age—eighty-five. This was, she claimed, the result of regular exercise, clean living, and strong genes. Even so, Harriet signed up for a Reflective Exercise Lite class because she suffered from rheumatoid arthritis, an autoimmune disease that inflames the joints.

The usual medical treatment for rheumatoid arthritis consists of attacking the disease with chemical poisons, much like chemotherapy in the treatment of cancer. Harriet was one of the lucky ones who had managed to somewhat stabilize her condition with the standard approach, but the disease still caused her problems, and she wanted to see if reflective exercise would have any effect.

With this class, I decided to be more aggressive than usual in introducing sitting meditation, so by the third week or so (we were meeting two or three times per week), the class concluded with everyone spending at least ten minutes seated in a chair, eyes closed, working with the imaginary red line. Sensing some discomfort in the students, all of whom were active seniors, I explained one day how the meditation helped promote the abdominal pulse and how it produced health benefits. As I talked, the blank faces suggested I wasn't getting through. But Harriet was smiling the whole time. She said, "I've felt that pulse."

"Really," I said incredulously.

"And I can move it up into my head."

My mouth hung open as I held back the urge to blurt out congratulations; I wanted Harriet to continue, and she did.

"It makes my rheumatism feel better, too," she offered, then stopped, aware that the other members of the class had turned to look at her.

"That's truly remarkable!" I interjected, drawing everyone's attention. "How did you manage to get such an advanced response?"

Harriet shrugged and said, "I practiced twice a day, like you told me."

When the class came to an end, I encouraged Harriet to continue training in the program for seniors, but she said she didn't need to. She understood the exercises and could use them to manage her health, which was what she had wanted in the first place. She promised to weave the reflective exercises into her other exercise routines, which included golf and walking. I asked her to call me if she had any problems. In four years, I received only one call from her, and that was to say her improved condition had impressed her doctor when she went in for a checkup.

Whenever anyone makes excuses for not being able to learn reflective exercise, I think of Harriet. If there ever was an example to follow, it is hers.

## The Theory of Reflective Exercise

For a minority of Westerners, ancient Chinese explanations for the healing effects of reflective exercise are fine. But those effects arise from a physically palpable ability to find and heal disease. This physical reality, plus years of stubborn opposition from skeptics and conventional medicine hard-liners, compelled me to search for a consistent, medically plausible theory that explains how and why reflective exercise works. My search turned up a great deal of information that points to the latent existence of a fascinating healing potential built into human biology. Though the full power of this healing potential generally manifests later in the program (around thirty days), phenomena that occur in the earlier stages of reflective exercise likely indicate subtle internal changes in the practitioner that lead to more developed levels of self-healing.

## What Are the Sensations in the Hands?

Most people describe what they feel during Exercise 3B, Sensing the Middle Center, as either warm, pulsing, electrostatic, magnetic, or all of the above. The Chinese call these sensations of Qi, a mysterious force that supposedly imbues all living things and is responsible for both health and illness.

Virtually all Western scientists and medical experts I have either spoken to or read insist that no such mysterious force has ever been recorded. But what they can all agree on and what the experimental record clearly shows is that the human body does radiate both heat and magnetism into the surrounding air. According to Dr. Steve Schnatterly, professor of physics at the University of Virginia, a human body at rest in a room with constant temperature heats the air up to several inches away from the surface of the skin, causing convection currents, or turbulence resulting from the heating and cooling of the surrounding air. Also, Dr. Schnatterly points out that both the heart and the brain produce measurable magnetic fields that project into the air. For many years, medical scientists and physicists have studied these magnetic fields with SQUID (Superconduction Quantum Interference Device) technology.

The body also generates electrical impulses measured by electro-cardiogram (EKG) and electroencephalogram (EEG) machines, but, unlike thermal and magnetic energy, the body's electrical charge remains on the surface of the skin. Even so, convection currents have the capacity to build static electricity, picking up a charge by moving over the skin, then carrying it into the body's atmosphere to join the silent swirl of thermal and magnetic energy (Schnatterly 2000).

In addition to heat, magnetism, and static electricity, the beating heart also produces a measurable vibration that resonates faintly in the surrounding air. When my student Tom measured my ability to send a pulse up and down the centerline of my body, the sensors, when held an inch or so from my chest and lower abdomen, could actually pick up the acoustic signals of my heartbeat.

Since warmth, static electricity, pulsation, and magnetism are commonly described reactions to Exercise 3B, Sensing the Middle Center, and since science can account for the presence of each in the air surrounding the body, we need look no further for evidence that there is something in the hands to feel. To be sure, the hands may be feeling more than what can be objectively measured, but we can say with confidence that the hands are at least sensing air that has been thermally, magnetically, and acoustically influenced. The possibility of electrostatic energy shouldn't be ruled out, but it originates from con-vection currents stirring outside the body.

Thermal, magnetic, and acoustic energies come from deep inside the body, and thus, when detected by the hands, can be considered reflections, energetic signals turned back toward their own source, the way an image bounces off a handheld mirror to the observer. Thus the appropriateness of the expression "reflective exercise" becomes clear: the air serves as a kind of mirror that the reflective exerciser uses to read the subtle projections of his or her own inner workings.

As previously mentioned, the hands' sense of reflections during Exercise 3B, Sensing the Middle Center, often seems chaotic, abruptly shifting from symmetrical, to asymmetrical, to empty impressions, indicating change in either the nervous system, the reflections themselves, or both. This protean aspect of sensing reflections is a process that one day may be explained by chaos theory, a subdiscipline of physics dealing with the way small variations in the many interrelated features of a complex system can generate unpredictable changes in the system as a whole.

Chaos theoreticians observe these changes in complex systems over time and develop equations to predict patterns that would otherwise remain bewildering or invisible in the midst of apparent chaos. A reflective exerciser is like a chaos theoretician, without the equations. The time a reflective exerciser spends with seemingly chaotic reflections can reveal order and relationships in the complex dynamic between the body and its surrounding atmosphere. The reflective exerciser's goal is to learn to recognize these structures and relationships and to manipulate them to serve immunological fitness.

The reflective exerciser's efforts to discover and manipulate patterns and relationships in the body's reflections focus on the three Centers, highlighted in Exercise 2B, Six Subtle Movements. Those three regions—the head, torso, and lower abdomen—contain substantial portions of the internal organs and systems that are, in a general sense, responsible for human healing: the nervous, vascular, endocrine, and lymphatic systems. Thus, spending time with reflections surrounding these areas is crucial to consciously accessing and managing their healing capacity.

The head or High Center houses the brain, which is riddled with a number of large blood vessels and lymph glands. The pituitary and pineal glands, embedded within the brain, and the thyroid and parathyroid glands, situated in the neck, represent the endocrine system in the High Center.

The heart and major internal organs, innervated by the brain stem and the thoracic region of the spine, dominate the chest or Middle Center. The spleen, thymus, and many nodes supply lymph, while glands and tissues inside the pancreas, gastrointestinal tract, and lung provide endocrine secretions (Wheater 1993).

The lower abdomen, or Low Center, is especially venerated in the Chinese fitness tradition, and for good reason. This area holds the descending aorta, which drops into the saddle of the pelvis, then splits off into the iliac vessels that supply the legs and feet with blood. Just above the pelvis, arteries and veins feed the kidneys, at the top of which lie the adrenal glands. These, along with the reproductive glands located further down, constitute perhaps the most crucial endocrine components of the immune system. In addition to intestinal lymph glands, a large concentration of lymph nodes sits where the iliac vessels leave the pelvis and begin branching into the legs. A complicated concentration of nerves radiates from the lumbosacral region and joins this complex vasculo-endocrine-lymphatic network.

Even more significantly, recent scientific investigations by Wolfgang Prinz of the Max Planck Institute of Psychological Research in Munich, Germany; Michael Gershon of Columbia University in New York City; and Benjamin Libet of the University of California have found a surprising neurological sophistication in millions of nerve cells surrounding the digestive tract. Their collective research indicates that these nerves act as a "second brain," not only regulating digestion and excretion but also controlling hormonal secretion and defending against harmful microorganisms. The "brain in the gut" can act independently of the "brain in the head," but it also shares the task of decision-making and negotiating stressful emotions (Luczak 2000).

The thermal, magnetic, and acoustic emanations of these three centers may be linked to the healing-related systems and organs of each region. Once detected by the tactile nerves in the hands and thus made a part of consciousness, those emanations become "reflections," registering first deeply, then more superficially, in the brain.

As strange or complicated as all this may seem, the basic mechanism behind reflective exercise is merely a special case of the general way we learn. Western and Eastern exercise relies on the same mechanism. When you stretch, run, or exert yourself in any way, you are pitting the body against the ground or an object such as a stretching bar, getting a variety of feedback, and learning the mechanics and limits of muscle, tendon, and bone. Similarly, we shape our personalities based on the reactions of those who surround us, and from these reactions we learn to see ourselves to a large (some would argue to the full) extent. Medical science uses our capacity to reflect when it employs biofeedback techniques, which rely on machines to help us identify with mechanical signals unconscious processes such as heart rate. Over time, people can use their reflective powers (under the banner of "feedback loops") to control such things as blood pressure, headaches, allergies, and a variety of symptoms that come with chronic illnesses. Recently, biofeedback has been used to help people suffering from neuropathy to improve blood flow to their feet. Reflective exercise is simply a low-tech version of biofeedback. It takes the capacity for "reflection" down to the primitive, tactile level.

## How Does Sensing Reflections in the Air Affect the Practitioner?

Nerves in the hands are extremely powerful tools in the tool kit of the human nervous system. As infants, our hands and sense of touch are primary sources of learning and experience. In *Why Zebras Don't Get Ulcers*, Dr. Robert M. Sapolsky presents strong evidence that touching and being touched during childhood encourages the production of growth hormones. By the time we reach adulthood, the sense of touch has been all but forgotten. Exercise 3B, Sensing the Middle Center, puts us back in touch (pun intended) with this basic sense and its collateral benefits.

Though using the hands for touch is a highly complex process that lights up neurons all over the nervous system, we can say for sure that it activates a deep center in the part of the brain called the brain stem, which transmits impulses to a higher level called the thalamus: the way station for all incoming sensation. The brain stem and thalamic tissues conduct electrical and chemical signals more easily than other, more superficial parts of the brain, such as the cortex. To be felt, tactile sensations must travel to this more superficial cortical layer of the brain, to a mid-lateral portion of the region known as the parietal lobe.

In connecting the hands to the brain stem, thalamic, and parietal tactile centers, Exercise 3B, Sensing the Middle Center, maximizes the sense of touch; at the same time it minimizes or limits the other senses. The eyes—the biggest source of potential distraction—are closed most of the time during reflective exercise. There should be no talking or listening to another person, unless, of course, you are following a teacher's instructions. This will limit and focus attention on the physical aspects of reflective exercise, such as body motion, hand positions, and breathing. Sustaining these quiet, undistracted conditions keeps the signal from the hands to brain stem-thalamic-parietal tactile centers active and dominant among the senses.

Another probable player in this neurological event is only a short distance away from the thalamic tactile center, farther down in the more primitive hypothalamus and brain stem, seat of the autonomic nervous system, which governs our most basic responses to life, such as fight-flight and rest-relaxation. There are two major subdivisions of the autonomic nervous system governing these opposing responses: the sympathetic and parasympathetic nervous systems. The sympathetic nervous system handles the fight-flight response, while the parasympathetic nervous system deals with the rest-relaxation response.

Reflective exercise is clearly more of a parasympathetic than a sympathetic experience, and the root of what amounts to almost seventy-five percent of the parasympathetic nervous system lies only a crucial centimeter or so away from the brain stem center. That important parasympathetic root is called the vagus nerve.

The vagus nerve plunges from its origin on the brain stem down into many of the major internal organs and terminates in the snaky confines of the intestines and lower regions of the body, including the upper portions of the genitals. Its primary function is to regulate the organs it touches, which include the heart, lungs, spleen, pancreas, liver, and gastrointestinal tract (commonly referred to as the "gut"). The vagus nerve performs a wide variety of functions, including slowing down these organs and their processes, and it does this largely by means of a neurotransmitter called acetylcholine. The sympathetic nervous system uses the neurotransmitters epinephrine and norepinephrine, or adrenaline, to perform its opposing function (Guyton 2000).

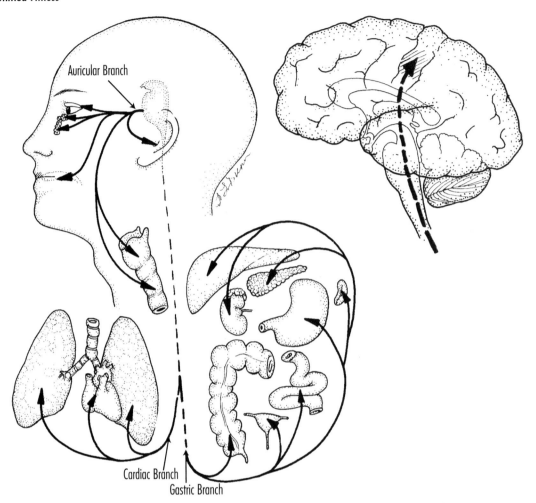

Auricular Branch

Cardiac Branch
Gastric Branch

**The Vagus Nerve's Internal Pathway and the Parietal, Thalamic, and Brain Stem Tactile Centers**

When looking for a medically known aspect of the body to account for the way a reflective exerciser gains a sense of his inner workings and reflections, the vagus nerve is a splendid candidate for a number of reasons.

First, there is the rather obvious connection between reflective exercise, particularly Exercises 3A-D (Standing Reflective Meditation, Sensing the Middle Center, Closing Sculpt, and Seated Reflective Meditation), and relaxation, a key function of the parasympathetic nervous system. The stillness and pleasure of sensing what appears to be an invisible force between the hands hardly excites a flight-fight response, while sitting still with eyes closed is as near to sleep as you can get without nodding off.

Second, the vagus nerve connects through the brain stem to nerves that innervate each sensory organ, which reflective exercise also engages in a variety of ways. Keeping the eyes closed most of the time—they are open only during Exercise 2B, Six Subtle Movements—effectively neutralizes them. The same can be said for the sense of hearing, to which the vagus nerve has a more direct connection. The quiet nature of reflective exercise lets auditory nerves lie in an unexcited state, simulating sleep. The vagus also has ties to the nose, the only aperture for breathing in reflective exercise, and the tongue, which continuously lifts to the upper palate, causing salivation, which, in turn, triggers pancreatic and digestive activity, another province of the vagus nerve. These actions with the nose and tongue occur continuously during all the exercises in the reflective series.

The third reason to suspect the vagus nerve as a primary factor in the effects of reflective exercise is the closeness of its root to the brain stem tactile center that reflective exercise, especially Exercise 3B, Sensing the Middle Center, stimulates and connects to the tactile center in the parietal lobe. This constant stream of tactile impulses between the brain stem, thalamic, and parietal centers, plus the parasympathetic-friendly involvement of the other senses, may help the vagus nerve achieve a tentative neurological connection first to the brain stem, then to the thalamic, then to the parietal, center.

If this were to happen, the vagus nerve might attain limited tactile ability that the practitioner could use to feel inside the body, a phenomenon reflective exercisers consistently experience. Over time, this ability grows stronger, perhaps linking the vagus nerve's enhanced sense of the internal organs to what the hands can detect in reflections surrounding the Three Centers, especially around the trunk, where nerve endings of the vagus communicate with the organs.

At this point, the practitioner can stroke the air around each Center and feel a corresponding internal reaction. Similarly, internal activity in each Center registers in the palms, hovering inches away from the body. Such a growth in ability marks an increase in reflective skill.

Continually exercising reflective skill helps strengthen the initial weak link between the parietal-thalamic-brain stem tactile centers and the vagus nerve, in much the same way that practicing scales over and over on the piano develops the connection between neuromuscular coordination of the hands and the listening capacity of the ear. Eventually, feeling the body's reflections, along with Exercise 2A, Reverse Breathing, triggers the vagus nerve, which ties internally to organs and processes, such as the heart (circulation) and brain (nervous system), that produce the external reflections. Thus, reflective exercise, especially Exercise 3B, Sensing the Middle Center, creates an internal/external sensory loop.

## What Makes the Pulsing Sensation Immunological?

Medical science understands the immune system as a broad function of two types of disease-fighting cells—lymphocytes and phagocytes—which are created in the bone marrow. Lymphocytes have many subclassifications and functions, but in the main they either tag and destroy disease-causing agents on their own, or cooperate with phagocytes to do the same. The subclassifications of phagocytes are not as numerous as those of lymphocytes, and their job is a bit simpler as well: to eat infectious entities and to assist lymphocytes in their more complex job of tagging and disseminating information about invading microbes. The workhorses of the phagocyte variety are called macrophages. While the bone marrow manufactures all of the phagocytes and many of the lymphocytes, the spleen, thymus, and lymph nodes also create lymphocytes (Wheater 1993).

The disease-fighting role of lymphocytes and phagocytes was presumably well understood until recent findings demonstrated that these prime movers of the immune system are more complicated than first thought. In *Molecules of Emotion*, author and researcher Dr. Candace B. Pert (1997) reveals the startling microbiology of lymphocytes, which have been shown to secrete and receive neurotransmitters, and neuropeptides, more complex chemicals similar to neurotransmitters.

As it turns out, lymphocytes have hundreds of sites on their surfaces where these molecules can attach themselves, and research shows that lymphocytes can and will migrate in the body in search of a variety of neurotransmitters and neuropeptides, which under extreme magnification resemble skinny snakes. When the relatively bald, globular-looking lymphocytes encounter these brain chemicals, the tentacle-like molecules attach to the lymphocytes' surfaces, giving the lymphocytes a hairy appearance. With this new look comes a new potential. The lymphocytes can now pass information along to any nerve or other kind of cell they encounter while circulating in the bloodstream.

According to Dr. Thomas Braciale, director of the Beirne B. Carter Center for Immunology Research at the University of Virginia School of Medicine, the lower body, measured from the diaphragm down, contains more lymphocytes than any other place in the body. Dr. Braciale cites as a reason for this distribution the legions of potentially devastating microorganisms that invade and colonize the body, especially the lower body, early in life. If our gut immunity weren't especially strong and plenteous, then we would likely perish. Microorganisms in food and water also make strong lower-body immunity advantageous. These conditions likely helped shape the evolution of lower-body immunity in humans.

An especially powerful concentration of lower-body lymphocytes resides inside dense, flattened lymph glands embedded in the walls of the small intestines. These glands are called Peyer's patches. Endocrine and immunological processes ordinarily provoke Peyer's patches to release their disease-fighting store into the intestine, where they enter the bloodstream via the venous pathway to the heart. Lactation in a nursing woman is one instance where endocrine signals cause disease-fighting cells from the Peyer's patches to migrate to the mammary glands, thus providing a nursing infant with some of the mother's strongest immunity. Potentially dangerous microorganisms ingested through the gastrointestinal tract are a common threat to which Peyer's patches respond immunologically.

Lymphocytes in the Peyer's patches, as well as those housed in the constellation of lymph glands filling the lower body, have another route to the bloodstream: the lymphatic system itself. All lymph glands take in infectious agents through openings called afferent ducts. Once the infectious entity is inside the lymph gland, lymphocytes manufacture a chemical imprint of the infection. These imprint-carrying lymphocytes then leave the gland by exits called efferent ducts and follow lymphatic vessels that lead to the thoracic duct, which dumps its contents into the heart, which in turn pumps the imprint-carrying lymphocytes throughout the body, including the head (Braciale 2000).

These vascular and lymphatic channels provide adequate means for gut-centered lymphocytes to leave their home sites and locate the brain chemicals for which they have a natural affinity. But the "brain in the gut" also offers on-site delivery of neurotransmitters and neuropeptides to the tissues of the gastrointestinal tract. The vagus nerve does the same, supplying the spleen, pancreas, liver, lungs, and heart as well. Still another source of neurotransmitters and neuropeptides is the vagus nerve's—or rather the parasympathetic nervous system's—complement, the sympathetic nervous system. In fact, research has confirmed the presence of histamine, an adrenal neurotransmitter, bound to the surface of lymphocytes (ibid).

In connecting the brain stem-thalamic-parietal tactile centers, the vagus nerve and the "brain in the gut" help a reflective exerciser sense the pulse rising and falling between the Low and High Centers. Then neurologically charged lymphocytes born of the increased local flow of neurotransmitters and neuropeptides from both the vagus and "gut brain" nerve endings may provide an additional source of sensitivity. As they navigate the circulatory and lymphatic pathways, these neurolymphocytes may boost the ability to feel the same pulse and expand it to other areas of the body.

Viewed from this perspective, the pulsing phenomenon that reflective exercise helps produce may constitute the beginning of a unique hybridization of the immune and nervous systems. Over time, the reflective exerciser develops an immune system that is more intelligent and a nervous system that is more immunological.

The immunological benefits of the pulsing sensation don't stop with creating an opportunity for lymphocytes in the lower body to bathe in brain chemicals. The rising and falling vascular and lymphatic currents may inadvertently sweep along benign bacteria and other microorganisms that flourish in the lining (lumen) of the intestines. Though these helpful microorganisms ordinarily stay put they would provoke a large immunological counter-attack if they leaked out—due to a cut in the intestinal wall, for example. Dr. Braciale concedes that some discrete amount of these bacteria could migrate up the venous or lymphatic pathway and reach the head (ibid). If that were to happen, two propitious things could occur.

First, the discrete flux of bacteria into the venous or lymphatic pathways might provoke a mild immune response, in much the same way that a vaccine strengthens immunity by introducing a weakened bacterium or virus. Second, the friendly bacteria that survive the journey to the head might colonize areas of the face, especially the nasal sinuses, where they would then help defend against hostile microbial invasions.

Reflective exercise could conceivably make all of the above possible. It might facilitate a union of the immune and nervous systems, constantly inoculate by introducing nonthreatening bacteria into the bloodstream, and draw tame microbes from the gastrointestinal tract to colonize the face.

If these theories are remotely accurate, then reflective exercise—that is, Exercise Series 2 (Reverse Breathing and Six Subtle Movements) and Exercise Series 3 (Standing Reflective Meditation, Sensing the Middle Center, Closing Sculpt, and Seated Reflective Meditation)—fills a substantial gap in the pantheon of health-promoting exercise. In my experience, and in the experience of hundreds of others whom I have taught, following a standard cardiovascular workout (i.e., twenty or thirty minutes of swimming or running, including preliminary and post-exercise stretches) with at least the same amount of reflective exercise is a powerful fitness experience.

## Neurovascular Pathways

Once reflective exercise increases the natural biochemical interaction between brain chemicals and lymphocytes in the gut, a greater abundance of neurologically enriched or "smart" lymphocytes roam circulatory and lymphatic pathways, connecting the

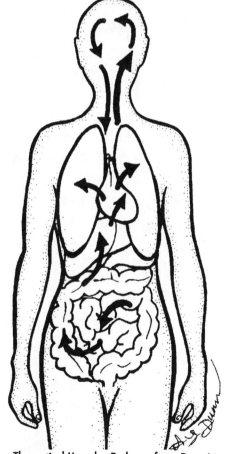

**Theoretical Vascular Pathway from Peyer's Patches to Liver to Heart to Nasal Sinuses**

**Surface Capillary
Pathway**

various systems of the body for sustaining health and fighting disease. Aside from the relatively large venous and lymphatic channels from the gastrointestinal tract to the heart, the rising, lymphocyte-saturated blood can ramify off into various strata of the skin, including surface layers, where smart lymphocytes could begin defining a network of vascular and lymphatic capillaries along the body's centerline.

I call this theoretical network of enlightened capillaries a "neurovascular pathway." When the reflective exerciser begins to sense such a pathway, his or her sinuses open, providing a strange sense of relief. The tissues and vascular vessels of the nasal sinus, long dried up and damaged by the continuous attacks of microorganisms and cauterizing air pollution, become suddenly invigorated. The reflective exerciser feels euphoric, in control, and grounded. In time, the sinuses develop a sense of opening and closing, similar to that of the lungs, a pulmonary liveliness they could not otherwise enjoy.

Once the neurovascular pathway becomes fairly strong—after about six months of twice-daily practice—the reflective exerciser can turn to the task of extending the pathway to include the back, so that the pulse can be directed, on the inhalation, up the spine to the back of the head, from where it descends on exhalation along the frontal pathway. Opening this dorsal pathway is far more difficult and should not be undertaken until the practitioner has spent six solid months scoring out the ventral pathway.

Even then, special exercises not covered in this book must be learned to help promote the dorsal pathway and to mitigate problems that can arise. The reason for these problems is that the blood pathway up the spine is much smaller than the ventral route. To make the situation worse, circulation in the spine tends to begin degrading somewhere in a person's mid-twenties, which is at least one of the reasons spinal injuries are far less common in the young. Attempting to extend the neurovascular network up the back prematurely is therefore most likely to yield disappointing results, but if a chronic or serious illness is involved, worse complications can arise. Tightness or pain may develop in the back, or disease symptoms may migrate and take on a new ferocity (a phenomenon discussed at greater length in chapter 12).

Nevertheless, with proper technique and instruction, the reflective exerciser can learn to use the dorsal pathway to gain greater immunological fitness. Expanding the neurovascular pathway to include the back helps distribute smart lymphocytes across a broader swath of the body, thus ensuring greater immunity. Moreover, the dorsal pathway allows the practitioner to sense the ebb and flow of cerebrospinal fluid contained in the spine, so that the rising sensation of the pulse becomes synchronized with the flux of the protein-rich fluid that bathes the brain.

Eventually, after approximately two years of devoted practice with the dorsal channel, the practitioner can open additional neurovascular pathways to the extremities, thus effectively recruiting the entire body for sensing and fighting disease. At this stage, the reflective exerciser can self-treat problems in the limbs, hands, and feet, whether the problems stem from injury or chronic conditions. In fact, by this point, the practitioner most likely will have already learned that infectious-based chronic conditions in the head and trunk can and will migrate to the extremities to escape heightened immune responses brought on by the opening of the ventral neurovascular pathway.

As in the case of the dorsal pathway, the whole-body pathway takes time, practice, and proper technique to open. Premature efforts to work with the whole-body pathway can produce complications similar to those that may occur when a chronically or seriously ill person tries to open the dorsal pathway ahead of schedule.

It would be inappropriate and irresponsible to introduce exercises and techniques for working with these more advanced pathways at this point. Such exercises and techniques are best reserved for another book. Besides, without opening the ventral pathway, the main biochemical engine that drives the eventual marriage of the immune and nervous systems never switches on, and Unified Fitness remains out of reach.

## Roy Conquers His Allergy

Roy took up Unified Fitness training in his late thirties. Born in upstate New York, Roy had primarily gotten his exercise by working with his hands, but since settling in the Virginia countryside, he had poured long hours into making a living with computers and gained a little extra weight. Even so, he still enjoyed robust health, with only one nagging complaint: a persistent allergy to ragweed pollen. Every fall and spring, his nose ran, eyes teared, and sinuses and throat burned.

Eventually, Roy took up Chinese martial arts to cultivate physical fitness, but his first focus was on reflective exercise. In about three weeks, he experienced the lower abdominal pulse, which he brought up a frontal pathway with muscular contraction, breath, and mental concentration. When the pulse reached his sinuses, the allergy symptoms faded, and, as a result, he became one of my strongest supporters.

Though happy for Roy, I warned him not to let down his guard and to abandon the vague idea of "allergies," a modern medical explanation for the immune system's inexplicable decision to go haywire. I suggested that the concept of an allergy, like the explanations for heart disease, begs the question of why the body breaks down and that some sort of infectious agent provides a simpler, more obvious explanation. I advised Roy to think of his condition as an infestation of termites, driven from a long-standing nesting place they would try to reclaim in due course.

Sure enough, within a few weeks the allergy symptoms came back, and I had to give Roy a number of pep talks to keep him from being discouraged. In time, he brought his symptoms under steady control and was able to see that other areas of his life—such as pressure at work or conflict at home or worry over finances—contributed greatly to his "allergy" gaining the upper hand.

Roy eventually learned that anxious, fearful, or irritated reactions to everyday problems provoked his allergy, helping him understand more clearly the need to respond to difficulties with a minimum of emotion. Without Unified Fitness, Roy wouldn't have been able to make the visceral connection between his allergy and his behavior. To this day, he prevails over his allergies and is relatively unaffected by ragweed pollen.

# Chapter 6

## Days 10–30: Going Through the Door

**Unifying Phases 1 and 2,**
**Exercise Series 4, A, B, and C: Gentle Chaosercise**

## Days 10–15: Unifying Phases 1 and 2

Once you've gotten through the first ten days of Unified Fitness, it's time to integrate Exercise Series 1 with Exercise Series 2–3. Let the numerical sequence set the order of the exercises.

You should integrate Exercise Series 1–3 every other day during this five-day block of time (3 times). The optimum time for these Unified practices should be one hour and a half. Your minimum time is 34 minutes.

Every day during this five-day period of the program, you should practice reflective exercise twice. Unified Fitness contains one reflective exercise practice, so you should do a second reflective exercise practice that same day. On the days you don't practice Unified Fitness, you should get in two reflective exercise sessions. Those practices have the same optimum and minimum time limits as described in Day 9 (35 and 19 minutes, respectively).

The five days you spend doing Exercise Series 1–3 (Stretching, Cardiovascular Exercise, Reverse Breathing, Six Subtle Movements, Standing Reflective Exercise, Sensing the Middle Center, Closing Sculpt, and Seated Reflective Meditation) give you the tools to enhance flexibility, range of motion, endurance, and control over the parasympathetic nervous system. Now, you're ready to begin Exercise Series 4, which expands your modest parasympathetic ability by building your sense of the other two Centers, starting with the lower one. Unlike the previous routines, however, Exercise Series 4 involves subtle movement that is more random, earning it the label "Gentle Chaosercise." Exercise Series 4 has three parts:

• Gentle Chaosercise of the Low Center (Days 16–22)
• Gentle Chaosercise of the Three Centers (Days 23–29)
• 16-Step Acupressure Massage (Day 30).

Gentle Chaosercise thoroughly immerses the reflective exerciser in the quest for complex order in the midst of seeming chaos. The discovery of this order marks a critical step in gaining the ability to develop immunological fitness consciously.

# Days 16–22. Exercise 4A: Gentle Chaosercise of the Low Center

Exercise 4A fits into the previous sequence just after ten or so seconds of Exercise 3B, Sensing the Middle Center. Lower the hands so that the palms face the Low Center (two inches below your navel), a few inches away from your body. Imagine that your hands hold a circle, with the thumbs marking the top, then use the hands to describe the circumference of that circle. Although the direction doesn't really matter, for consistency's sake, move the hands to the left (clockwise). You may or may not feel sensations similar to those you felt during Exercise 3B, Sensing the Middle Center.

Keep circling the hands as you slowly turn the waist to the left, stopping the waist when the navel is at forty-five degrees left of center.

Keep moving the hands to the left, however, all the while continuing to circle them.

When your hands reach the space beside your left hip, reverse the direction of the circling action of the hands and move them slowly to the right. When they line up with the navel, which is still forty-five degrees left of center, slowly move hands and waist together to the right. Stop moving the waist when the navel reaches forty-five degrees right of center, but keep going with the hands, continuing to circle in the opposite direction from which you started. Upon reaching the space beside the right hip, reverse the circling direction of the hands again so that you are back to your original leftward circling motion. Move the hands until they align with the navel, still positioned at forty-five degrees right of center, then move hands and waist together until you arrive at the center in your original forward-facing position.

During this preliminary aspect of the Gentle Chaosercise of the Low Center you are likely to feel thermal, magnetic, pulsing, electrostatic, or all of these sensations, as though the Low Center's reflections encircled the pelvis, like an invisible hula hoop. This is your sensory nervous system's impression of the energetic pattern of the air surrounding the lower body, generated by the physiology of the Low Center itself or by the brain and heart, extended to the Low Center.

**Gentle Chaosercise of the Low Center**

Next, use the hands to spin the apparent hula hoop clockwise (from left to right), just as you might start an actual hula hoop, only in slow motion. Then, in the exact fashion of slow-motion hula-hooping, begin rotating the hips. You may feel a portion of the entire spectrum of sensations fluctuate in the palms and fingers as the hips circle.

At this point, you should try to relax so that, in effect, you submit to the sense of revolving air, as though the hips were being moved by a slow-whirling, invisible ring. While doing this, enjoy the pure sensation of your body's impulse to indulge in this movement.

Your conscious mind will probably struggle against the impulse to chaosercise through feeling and movement, but you are likely to be encouraged by a pleasant sense of relaxation. There may be moments when the conscious mind lets go, and you'll feel fascinating subtleties both inside and outside the body, such as circles within circles, traveling up and down the spine in opposite directions, radiating out either end of the spine in tiny spirals. Though compelling, such sensations should not distract you from your focus on the Low Center and its surrounding reflections.

*Your conscious mind will probably struggle against the impulse to chaosercise through feeling and movement, but you are likely to be encouraged by a pleasant sense of relaxation. There may be moments when the conscious mind lets go, and you'll feel fascinating subtleties both inside and outside the body.*

After chaosercising the Low Center for about eight to ten minutes, take conscious control of the body and bring the circling to a halt, hands coming to rest at your sides. Then resume the former sequence, starting with Exercise 3C, Closing Sculpt, which you should always do three times, bringing the hands to rest in an embrace at the Low Center, two inches below the navel, as described previously. Conclude with Exercise 3D, Seated Reflective Meditation. At this stage, you should begin to devote an increasing amount of time to Exercise 3D, if you haven't already. Your ideal goal is twenty minutes.

## Days 23–29. Exercise 4B:
## Gentle Chaosercise of the Three Centers

After a consistent week of Exercise 4A (Gentle Chaosercise of the Low Center), you can move on to Exercise 4B, Gentle Chaosercise of the Three Centers, which takes the place of Exercise 4A in the routine.

After completing Exercise 2B and Exercise 3A (three sets of Six Subtle Movements and five minutes of Standing Reflective Meditation), maintain the Standing Reflective Meditation posture for two and a half minutes. Next, while exhaling, bring the fingers close together without touching. Then inhale and spread the hands apart. Repeat this two more times. Next, still in the Standing Reflective Meditation posture, rotate the hands. Both arms may feel thick with the Middle and High Centers' reflections. These sensations may strike you as different from and more intense than previous ones, perhaps a sign that the tactile and vagus nerve centers are integrating more thoroughly than in the earlier stages of reflective exercise. While continuing to rotate the hands, move them up to your face for several seconds, then above your head. You should feel changes in the sensations as you go, an indication that you have entered the field dominated

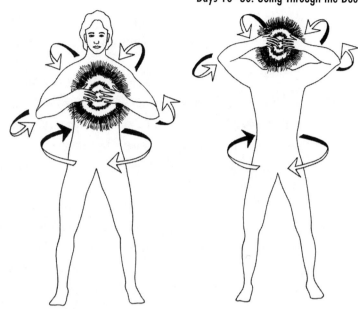

**Gentle Chaosercise of the Three Centers**

by the High Center. In addition to these external impressions, the inside of your head may respond to the motions of your hands, demonstrating a more advanced reflective skill: the ability to manipulate the inside of the body through external reflections in the air.

Next, lower the hands to the Middle Center position and begin moving your arms at the shoulders, which allows the hands to continue circling but makes the action a whole body movement. At this point, you may sense reflections coursing around the upper torso. As with gently chaosercising the Low Center, your movements should feel pleasant and natural. Relax and pay attention to the way your shoulders naturally rotate about the upper spine. At the same time you may notice changes in the surrounding reflections. Then close the eyes and let the hips hula-hoop as they did in Exercise 4A, Gentle Chaosercise of the Low Center.

As a result, your whole body may feel enveloped in a moving mass of warm, pulsing, magnetic, and electrostatic air. When your arms get tired, lower them and move as you did in Gentle Chaosercise of the Low Center. After the arms recover, move them up to feel reflections of the Middle and High Centers. Continue chaosercising like this for

159

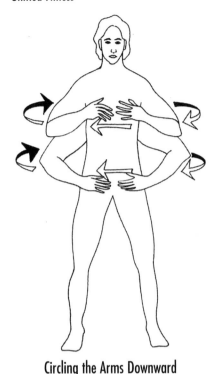

**Circling the Arms Downward**

eight to ten minutes, letting your impulses guide your hands to linger in or pass through each of the Centers.

At the end of the session, bring your arms into the Standing Reflective Meditation posture and begin circling the whole body clockwise, as though you were sloshing a basin full of water around in your arms. With each circle, lower the arms an inch or so until they drop to the sides. Close in the usual sculpting fashion, clasping the hands over the Low Center on the third Closing Sculpt.

This phase of the practice effectively makes conscious your sensory impressions of the reflections surrounding all three Centers. If you continue to feel these reflections for prolonged periods of time, they become increasingly real. At this point, connection between the vagus nerve and the thalamic-parietal-brainstem tactile centers has probably never been stronger, and other cortical centers have likely joined in as well, giving you a greater awareness of the body.

Each time the hands pass smoothly through the air surrounding the body, you may feel the subtly fluctuating reflections of heat, pulsation, magnetism, and static electricity emanating from the three Centers. In the beginning, these fluctuating reflections may seem disproportionate—weak in the Low Center but strong in the Middle and High Centers, and/or vivid on one side but feeble on the other. Eventually, with consistent practice, this sense of disproportion gives way to a greater feeling of symmetry.

As reflective skill progresses, your sense of the scope and fluidity of the reflections filling your personal space expands, and you may begin to feel and affect internal processes that produce the reflections. Awareness of both the inner and outer workings of the three Centers may reach the point where you can feel the entirety of your personal atmosphere, as if you were immersed in a pleasantly warm fluid.

Following Exercise 4B (Gentle Chaosercise of the Three Centers), you should begin Exercise 3D, Seated Reflective Meditation, which should be practiced for increasing amounts of time. At this point, if you haven't been meditating for twenty minutes, you should do so now.

Longer periods of stillness will likely enable you to begin feeling the pulsing sensation that moves from the Low to the High Center on the inhalation and falls back to the Low Center on exhalation. This phenomenon marks a sharp leap in immunological fitness.

If you begin to experience heat or a sense of fullness in the Low Center, then your practice is working. Approach each session with conviction and try to practice at least twice daily. Should you experience movement in the Low Center, such as a pulsing sensation, know you're on the threshold of opening the neurovascular pathway.

# Day 30. Exercise 4C: 16-Step Acupressure Massage

Massaging key areas of the body identified as beneficial by traditional Chinese fitness provides a relaxing and comforting follow-up to the physical and immunological aspects of Unified Fitness. In addition, the areas designated in the list below can and should receive stimulation throughout the day, especially the soles of the feet. Doing so works in concert with reflective exercise to open the whole-body neurovascular network, which allows for a thorough integration of the nervous and immune systems.

1. Eye Rolls: Roll your eyes straight upward without craning your head too much, then roll your eyes three times to the left, then three to the right. Make sure you flex the eye muscles in each direction during the eye rolls.

2. Eye Rub: Vigorously rub your palms together until you feel substantial heat, then press them into your eyes, circling the palms three times to the left, then three times to the right. Repeat this process in each direction.

3. Brow Rake: With the middle phalanges of your index fingers, press into the center of your eyebrows and rake them to the edges ten times.

4. Temple Rub: Place the proximal interphalangeal knuckles (the thumb knuckle closest to the nail) of your thumbs in your temples

and massage with a circular motion twenty times forward, then twenty times backward.

5. Mid-brow Rub: Place proximal interphalangeal knuckles of your thumbs in the middle of your eyebrows, then massage with a circular motion twenty times left, then twenty times to the right.

6. Nose Rub: With the proximal interphalangeal knuckles of your thumbs, rub down the sides of the bridge of your nose twenty times.

7. Ear Tugs: Grab your earlobes so that your index fingers are near your ear canal opening, with the thumbs on your earlobes, then tug downward ten times. Next grab your ears so that the index fingers are touching the upper back sides of the ears and your thumbs are touching the insides, near your ear canal opening. Then tug the ears upward and forward ten times.

8. Ear Rub: Place your index fingers behind each ear, with the middle finger resting on the front side, just in front of your ears. Then rub the index and middle fingers vigorously along each side of the ears twenty times.

9. Neck Rub: Dig your fingers into both sides of the back of the neck, then press down and out to either side. Start low on the neck, at or near the seventh cervical vertebra, then move up the neck to the cerebellum, then back down again for a total of twenty rubs.

10. Face Rub: Placing your open palms on your face, wipe from the forehead, down the checks, to the neck for a total of ten rubs.

11. Scalp Rub: Bending the fingers so that they resemble the teeth of a rake, run your fingers through your scalp, from the forehead, across the crown, to the back of the head, ten times.

12. Foot-to-Heart Massage: This exercise has two parts.

## Part One: Massaging the Front of the Leg from the Sole of the Foot to the Heart

Using your right index and middle fingers, held rigid and straight, rub the sole of your left foot thirty times, from the heel into the ball of the foot. Then massage each toe from the base to the nail; after which, grab all of the toes and bend them back and forth with both hands. Next, grab the big toe between your right index finger and thumb, and your second toe with your left index finger and thumb. Squeeze each toe from the nail to the base. Then, with the right fingers, massage from the ball of the foot into the middle of the arch, moving from there onto the front of the left ankle. Follow behind with the fingers of the left hand, massaging the top of the foot. Then with both hands, massage up the top of your left shin, knee, and thigh without breaking contact. Continue massaging into the groin, up the trunk, and finally to the heart, where the gender-appropriate hand (left for men, right for women) presses into the heart, capped with the other hand (right for men, left for women). With a circular motion, massage three times left, then three times right.

## Part Two: Massaging the Back of the Leg from the Sole of the Foot to the Heart

Dig your fingers into the middle of your left sole and massage toward your heel. Keep massaging up your Achilles tendon, into your calf, and back of the knee. Once you get to the thigh, massage up the left side with the left hand while simultaneously massaging up the inner thigh, into the groin, with the right hand. With the left hand, massage the left gluteal muscles up into the left lower back, while the right hand massages slowly up the lower abdomen. Follow the ribs on your back left side with your left hand around to your front, where it joins with your right to massage up the abdomen to the heart. With the gender-appropriate hand (left for men, right for women), capped with the opposite hand (right for men, left for women), press and circle three times left, then three times right.

Repeat parts one and two for the right side.

13. Arm-to-Heart Massage: This exercise has two parts.

### Part One: Massaging the Outside of the Arm

Extend your right arm in front of you with the palm facing away from you. With your left hand, squeeze the little finger of your right hand, then keep squeezing up to your hand, wrist, forearm, elbow, triceps muscle, shoulder, and trapezius muscle, then massage across your right collarbone to the heart, capping the left hand with the right, regardless of whether you are male or female. Press and massage with a circular motion three times left, then three times right.

### Part Two: Massaging the Inside of the Arm

With the right palm facing you, squeeze your right index finger with your left hand, then squeeze the space between your right thumb and index finger, then squeeze the thumb. Next keep squeezing up the inside of the right forearm, to the biceps and shoulder. Massage across the collarbone to your heart. Regardless of your gender, place your left hand over your heart, capped by your right hand, circling three times left, then three times right.

Repeat parts one and two for the left side, making sure to cap the right hand with the left when massaging the heart, regardless of your gender.

14. Low-Center-to-Heart Frontal Massage: With the gender-appropriate hand (left for men, right for women), capped with the opposite hand (right for men, left for women), press into the Low Center, then massage up the front of the abdomen to the heart. Press your hands into the heart, and with a circular motion, massage three times left, then three times right.

15. Hips-to-Heart Massage: Press your hands into either side of your hips, then massage up to the lower ribs. Massage the base of the

ribs to your sternum, then up to the heart, with the gender-appropriate hand (left for men, right for women) closest to your body, capped by the opposite hand (right for men, left for women). Press, and with a circular motion, massage three times left, then three times right.

16. Lower-Back-to-Heart Massage: Press your hands into the lower back, then massage up until you touch your ribs. Follow the base of your ribs around to the front until your hands converge at the sternum, then massage up to the heart. With the gender-appropriate hand (left for men, right for women), capped with the opposite hand (right for men, left for women), press, and with a circular motion, massage three time to the left, then three times to the right.

# Dianne Rehabilitates a Hip Replacement, Cures Colds, and Mends a Skull Fracture

Dianne began training in Taiji when she was in her mid-sixties in order to help recovery from surgery to replace her hip, which had become ravaged with arthritis. An avid skier her whole life, Dianne was already fairly well developed physically and disciplined enough to practice daily, an essential element in making the subtle movements of Taiji an effective form of rehabilitation.

After about six months of dedicated Taiji training and a series of glowing reports from her doctor, Dianne decided she wanted to give Reflective Meditation a try. She had heard good things from a number of my students and was anxious to obtain the immunological benefits. She taught high school and was constantly exposed to infection.

Within forty days, Dianne opened the neurovascular pathway, but she was uncertain of its value, until she managed to rid herself of a sore throat and head cold symptoms after two forty-minute practices. She went on to experience many more such triumphs over minor upper respiratory infections, which ordinarily laid her low for five to seven days. As a result, Dianne became one of my most vocal advocates, writing letters to the local papers to apprise them of the work I was doing. Though the papers chose to ignore Dianne's letters for the most part, her willingness to stand up and acknowledge things such as the neurovascular pulse and the immunological benefits of reflective exercise was an invaluable accreditation that helped earn me a place in our community. On several occasions, when I've been asked to address senior wellness programs sponsored by hospitals, Dianne has volunteered to give vivid, articulate testimony to encourage other seniors to turn to reflective exercise as a form of highly effective and rewarding self-treatment.

But Dianne's neurovascular ability proved even more surprising and handy than any of us expected when she used it to help deal with a serious injury. One day, while climbing around an outcropping of rocks in the Blue Ridge mountains, she lost her footing, fell to the ground, and struck her head on a rock. Dazed, she sat upright while her partner rushed to her side. Blood oozed from Dianne's ear, so they drove quickly down the mountain to the emergency room, where X rays showed a slight skull fracture. The ear that had oozed blood closed off from the building pressure.

The doctors were ready to drill a hole in Dianne's skull to relieve the pressure, but Dianne asked them to wait a while. Reluctantly, the doctors agreed, keeping her in the hospital under close observation for twenty-four hours. During this time, Dianne used her neurovascular and reflective skill to treat the site of the injury. Placing her palms a few inches away from her damaged skull, she began sculpting the reflections in the air surrounding the head, and at the same time, used the inhale portion of the reverse breath to bring the abdominal pulse up the neurovascular pathway, into the head, increasing the sense of pressure in the head. Then, on the exhale, she let the pulse drop back to its lower origin, guiding the sense of it with her hands, decreasing the pressure she felt in her head.

By the end of her twenty-four hour observation period, her condition had improved so dramatically—the sense of pressure had dropped off markedly—that the doctors decided to X ray again. To their surprise, the fracture they had seen in the previous X ray had healed.

If the doctors weren't completely sold on the power of reflective exercise, Dianne certainly was. She remains one of my most vocal and courageous students, ready to share with anyone willing to listen the numerous instances that have proven time and again that learning reflective exercise pays back in spades the time and effort required in learning it.

## "Smart" Germs

Perhaps the most startling immunological discovery I've made through reflective exercise is that microorganisms residing in the body have intelligence. One morning I woke with a sore throat, my right submandibular lymph gland swollen and painful to the touch. After a session of subtle movement and gentle chaosercise, I sat down and immediately drew the pulse in my lower abdomen up the neurovascular pathway to my throat, where I kept it by holding my breath for a few seconds longer than usual.

After a few minutes, the soreness in my lymph gland completely vanished and, at the same time, I felt something move under my skin to the left lymph gland, which immediately became sore. In retaliation, I concentrated the pulse on the left side of my throat. In a minute or so, the soreness subsided and again I felt movement, this time back to the right lymph gland, the soreness returning, though less than before. Using the pulse, I chased the soreness back and forth, from one side of my neck to the other. Each time, the pain lessened until a mere presence was all I could feel. Suddenly, the weakened presence moved up into my sinus cavity and lodged itself behind my right eye, where I directed the pulse until the presence dissipated.

Given the choice between labeling the presence an energy or a microorganism, most medical scientists would probably opt for the latter. I tend to agree, since microorganisms have been objectively identified and implicated in disease and the role of "energy" remains controversial. But I doubt many medical scientists would have predicted the way the microorganism responded, much less the internal physiological process by which I was able to elicit the response. Since then, I have had many such experiences, as have most of my students. Not all encounters have gone so nicely.

Sometimes the germ proves to be either too strong or too clever, spreading itself over such a vast area of the body or concentrating in a region where the neurovascular pathway is undeveloped. Even so, if the reflective exerciser keeps up the pressure—that is, practices at least twice daily—in time, the microorganism's presence weakens and apparently dissolves. Perhaps "smart" lymphocytes, bathed in neurotransmitters and neuropeptides, are smarter than most germs, better able to detect and destroy invading organisms by sharing their chemical intelligence with nearby cells and neurons, recruited for the purpose of stemming an infection.

*If the reflective exerciser keeps up the pressure—that is, practices at least twice daily—in time, the microorganism's presence weakens and apparently dissolves. Perhaps "smart" lymphocytes, bathed in neurotransmitters and neuropeptides, are smarter than most germs.*

If medical scientists could "feel" reactions between microorganic life and their immune systems, I'm certain much more attention would be paid to the notion of immunological and microorganic intelligence. As it stands, however, a new field of study seems poised to examine the issue most clearly, hovering on the edge of medical science, slowly gaining the attention and respect it deserves: evolutionary biology.

## The New Germ Theory: Evolutionary Medicine

In order to understand, much less acquire, immunological fitness, we have to look beyond the immune system to the entities it seeks to immunize us against: microorganisms.

The most compelling and forward thinker on microorganisms is Paul W. Ewald, a professor of evolutionary biology at Amherst College and author of two influential books: *Evolution of Infectious Disease,* and, most recently, *Plague Time.* In both his research and in his books, Dr. Ewald explores what is being called the "New Germ Theory," which sheds fresh light on the scope and the parasitic nature of infectious disease. Most relevant to immunological fitness is the New Germ Theory's thesis that what were presumed to be genetic or unknown-cause diseases—including heart disease, stroke, cancer, and diabetes—may be more virulent stages of infections that have evolved strategies that are radically different from the way conventional medicine has come to view infection. Ewald presents evidence that these so-called "stealth infections" possess special biochemical tricks that allow them to avoid our immune system's attack.

An important concept in understanding the stealth strategies of infectious disease is that of evolutionary "fitness," which differs sharply from the sense of the word as I've been using it. An infectious organism's evolutionary fitness is measured by its evolutionary success relative to its competitors within the same species. Ewald and his colleagues measure this success in terms of the relative frequencies of alternative genetic instructions in a species of infectious organism. These alternative instructions allow the organism to cope with changes in its environment. Infectious organisms with genetic propensity for mutation respond more effectively to potential conditions for transmission and immunological reactions of the host than do genetically limited infectious organisms. Thus, they make a better "fit" with the conditions of natural selection (Ewald 2000).

According to Ewald, conventional medicine's failure to incorporate a broad evolutionary foundation in its study of infectious diseases has led to a number of flawed assumptions about infection and its role in serious, chronic disease. He challenges these assumptions with the following assertions, based on large-scale observations and fundamental principles of natural selection:

• disease-causing parasites (both microorganisms and multicellular creatures such as worms) often do not evolve toward a benign relationship with their hosts;

• genetics and the environment (excluding infection) play only a partial, perhaps even a minor, role in determining health and illness;

• and human behavior, social conventions, and sanitation can help solve some of our most intractable problems, not just by reducing the numbers of people who are infected, but also by radically altering the evolution of infectious microbes.

This last assertion bears a bit more discussion because of the implications for immunological fitness and reflective exercise.

In *Evolution of Infectious Disease*, Ewald presents strong evidence that if human beings enhance, rather than impede, a microbe's opportunity to be transmitted from very sick hosts, the microbe tends to evolve in a virulent direction—a process that can occur in weeks, perhaps days. Thus, in developing countries, the absence of water purification technology and protection from biting insects (which carry infections such as malaria and dengue fever) can cause microorganisms to exhibit consistently greater virulence than in countries with pure water and insect-proof housing. HIV infections have shown a similar decline in virulence when protective measures make transmission more difficult.

In *Plague Time*, Ewald questions conventional medical wisdom on the causes of the diseases that quietly devastate the populations of developed countries. He gives particular attention to coronary artery disease, which several researchers have linked to a lower respiratory bacterium called *Chlamydia pneumoniae*, and to cancer of the cervix, now universally accepted as a disease caused by the human papillomavirus. He also presents evidence implicating viruses and bacteria as the primary causes of breast cancer, schizophrenia, and Alzheimer's disease.

Dr. Ewald isn't the only expert ready to point out a probable link between infectious disease and chronic, potentially lethal illness. Dr. Thomas Braciale, director of the Beirne B. Carter Center for Immunology Research at the University of Virginia School of Medicine, strongly suspects that infection may play a major role not only in all of the diseases Ewald discusses, but in stroke and Type I (so-called "inherited") diabetes as well. If Drs. Ewald and Braciale are correct, then the transmission of serious, chronic disease may occur either through the air, through direct contact with sick people, or through "vectors," such as insects or animals used by microbes to get into human hosts. This being the case, the pursuer of immunological fitness needs to ask him or herself: Where am I most vulnerable and what can I do to protect myself?

## Infection and Protection of the Nasal Sinus

While less immediately life-threatening than exotic or well-known tropical infections, such as the Ebola virus or malaria, common airborne disease accounts for the illness most frequently treated by primary care physicians. Since the 1970s, respiratory problems—ranging from allergies to severe bronchitis to asthma—have grown twenty-fold. This increase is attributed by some to the scarring effect of air pollution, which corrodes the mucosal lining of the air passages, particularly that of the nasal sinuses, creating an environment to catch particles and microorganisms.

An examination of the nasal sinus cavity shows the region's vulnerability to airborne disease. A natural chamber for collecting particulates and microorganisms, the nasal sinuses are bordered on the top and posterior by the brain. Separated from the sinuses by a thin, porous layer of bone, the olfactory bulb drops nerve branches down into the upper ceiling of the nasal cavity, creating a theoretical point of entry to the brain for nerve-oriented viruses such as herpes simplex, one of the most common human infections on the planet. From the olfactory bulb, it's a short hop to very deep, vascular nerve and endocrine centers, such as the hypothalamus and pituitary gland.

Though the nasal sinuses possess considerable immunity, medical statistics suggest the microbes are winning. More important, evidence continues to surface showing a connection between heart disease and respiratory infection. Recently, Austrian and Italian researchers examined more than 800 men and women over a five-year period, with a special eye on the prevalence of respiratory infection. The researchers found that those with chronic respiratory infections were nearly three times more likely to have developed new blockages in their blood vessels than those who suffered few such infections.

The suggestion of this research is that chronic respiratory infection increases the risk of coronary artery and other forms of heart disease (Fox 2001).

In addition to life-threatening heart disease, respiratory infection may play a role in many mysterious, multifactorial diseases. Fibro-myalgia, chronic fatigue syndrome, or even multiple sclerosis may have begun in some people as ordinary respiratory infections, such as the flu. Though genetic and environmental factors (exposure to toxic chemicals, for example) may be involved as well, there is more evidence to indict rather than to dismiss infectious disease as a primary cause in these cases.

Ewald's observations on the evolutionary processes governing infectious disease cover large populations and vast territories, but the lens of reflective exercise can provide a more discrete focus for the same logic. Just as governments can put environmental pressure on germs by purifying water and providing citizens with airtight houses and screened windows, so too can a reflective exerciser micromanage the host environment of a microorganism. Using the neurovascular pathway from the Low to High Centers, reflective exercise can alter the body's environment in at least three ways. It can help to transport lymphocytes from the lower abdomen to the mouth, nose, and eyes; it can constantly inoculate the body with discrete infusions of the bacteria that have colonized the gastrointestinal tract; or it can create an opportunity for gut-centered bacteria that survive the inoculation process to relocate, to colonize, and to help defend the nasal sinuses.

These internal, immunological manipulations of the host environment made possible by reflective exercise are analogous to the external manipulations that Ewald has shown can affect the evolution of infectious disease. The greater presence of both smart lymphocytes and host-friendly microorganisms makes it tougher for an invading infection to behave virulently. Aggression on the part of the invader is likely to invite a harsh response from an alert and sentient lymphocyte army. Furthermore, the relatively benign bacterial colonies that reflective exercise may encourage to dwell in the facial area will fight for their turf, thus providing a direct genetic pressure to evolve benignly.

In this way, the reflective exerciser's personal pursuit of immunological fitness may have larger social benefits. The microorganisms spread by reflective exercisers may tend to be more benign than those spread by people with no reflective skill.

In teaching reflective exercise, a number of cases and personal experiences have led me to embrace this prospect. After taking up reflective exercise, several married couples with small children reported that once they gained the ability to self-treat minor upper respiratory infection, their children, once constantly infected by schoolmates, seemed to get sick less often. When they did become ill, their symptoms were less severe. Other factors might be responsible for the changes in the health of these families. The parents may have taken up reflective exercise just when their children's immune systems were making a developmental leap, thus making their observations coincidental.

But my own experience suggests that the immunological benefits of reflective exercise can inadvertently redound to family members, regardless of whether or not they have reflective skill. When my two sons were being sent to preschool for a couple of hours during the weekdays, they frequently brought home infections that I immediately picked up and engaged with reflective exercise. On repeated occasions, their symptoms improved shortly after my success in taming the infectious invader. Before my oldest son turned six and my youngest turned four, they were keenly sensing their Middle Centers and now have a rudimentary ability to muster their immunity to self-heal.

This collateral benefit from practicing reflective exercise gives some cause for optimism, but Ewald's theories about the evolutionary behavior of infectious disease raise a number of other disturbing possibilities that complicate matters. Pets, once thought of solely as companions, may turn out to pose health risks. Hospitals, where attendants, much like mosquitoes carrying malaria, help already virulent germs spread from person to person, may have to be redesigned. The same evolutionary principles apply to childcare centers, nursing homes, jails, workplaces, shopping malls, airports, airplanes, and even health clubs and wellness centers.

These commonplace facilities recapitulate the problems faced by the nasal sinus cavity in a polluted, germ-ridden world: a chamber of air, ill-equipped to deal with what it has to let in. Since medication makes walking around with an upper respiratory infection standard practice, the potential for disease transmission, thus virulence, is greater.

## Personal Experiences of the New Germ Theory

The implications of this new theory of disease aren't going to bring about massive reforms in wellness centers, hospitals, shopping malls, airports, and airplanes anytime soon, and for a culture that makes jokes out of excessive concern for germs, Ewald's ideas may not get the hearing they should. As for me, the new germ theory is something I have very high regard for, and not simply because of my experience with reflective exercise.

On January 4, 1972, my younger brother died of mysterious causes in a hospital. He was only fourteen. Twenty-four hours earlier he had been admitted with a high fever that had dovetailed quickly into a coma, and the doctors were at a loss to explain it. My family—already a hornets' nest of despair over the breakup of my parents' twenty-year marriage the previous year—was devastated. Being only seventeen, and an immature seventeen at that, I was especially hard hit. Over the next several years, my family and I sank into separate corners of depression and increasing dysfunction. We never talked about my younger brother's death, terrified of reawakening the sadness that lay just beneath the surface.

The biggest cause of my despair wasn't my immaturity, but a question asked by the attendant physician in private conference with my older brother and me on the day my younger brother died. A thick-haired, brooding man in a white jacket, with deep furrows in his cheeks like scars from knife wounds, the doctor asked us if our younger brother had ever received a severe blow to the head. We both mentioned the time he had fallen at a football game and struck his forehead on a concrete step, a goose egg the size of a boy's fist welling above his right eyebrow. The doctor listened but didn't say anything.

What I failed to mention but thought about obsessively from that day forward was that I had repeatedly struck my younger brother on the head since childhood. With three years difference in our age, the violence I directed toward my younger brother began as unbridled sibling rivalry, enhanced by my own experience as the victim of my older brother's similar abuse. To top it off, the culture in which we were raised both tolerated and encouraged boy-on-boy violence, which is at least one of the reasons my parents probably didn't consider the hitting that went on between my brothers and me aberrant. By the time I reached young adolescence, whacking my younger brother across the noggin was something I did with what now seems an incredible lack of conscience. But on the day of my brother's death, one infamous episode overshadowed all other incriminating instances.

The previous year, almost to the day, my father took my brothers and me for a drive and informed us that he had divorced our mother and remarried. My younger brother burst into tears and didn't stop crying the whole time. Feeling bitterly betrayed, my older brother and I nonetheless remained stoic. Once we got home, our mother was gone, apparently unable to face us in our grief and confusion. My older brother left immediately in his car, leaving my still-hysterical younger brother and me in an empty house.

Desperate to get away from my brother's crying, I called my best friend who said he would drive over as soon as he could. When I hung up, I shouted at my younger brother to shut up because I didn't want my friend to know anything was wrong. My brother cried louder. "Shut up," I said, moving toward him with clenched fists. "No," he shouted back through his tears. "Shut up, shut up, shut up," I said, striking him on the top of the head repeatedly until he crawled under my mother's bed to get away from me.

To this day, any excuse I offer for what I did seems hollow, in spite of the mitigating circumstances I've already cited. My treatment of my younger brother was clearly, objectively reprehensible. Thus, given the doctor's question, it's easy to see how I might have accepted the blame for my brother's death and spent the next twenty years struggling with shame and guilt. Along the way, I survived by a handful of strategies that I hoped would either lead to redemption or at least help me cope.

One of those strategies was physical training. Another was to completely break off communication with my family for almost ten years.

The knot of guilt in which I had tied myself started to loosen when I went to China and discovered the immunological benefits of traditional Chinese healing practices. The knot unraveled further after I published the book on my discovery, which, in turn, gave me the opportunity to visit my hometown for a book signing that didn't turn out so well. What was supposed to be a triumphal return was greeted with only a handful of family friends and a tiny mention in the public announcement section of the local paper. It was only the third time I had been home in sixteen years.

Being around my family simply worsened my sense of letdown. My older brother and I got into a shouting match at dinner that ended with my having to leave the house. This greatly upset my mother, with whom my relations had been severely strained over the years. Just seeing her again seemed to make the knot retighten. But the publication of my book, along with the insight of several years of psychotherapy, gave me enough confidence, when I felt the time was right, to talk more openly about what I had been through over the years.

That time came late one afternoon, on a stunningly hot, deep-summer day. Inside, the den of my mother's house was dark and cool, the air conditioning purring. A physically sturdy-looking but emotionally fragile woman in her early seventies—about the same age as her own mother when my younger brother died—my mother sat in a chair across from the couch where I was sitting. The silence seemed to be making us both uncomfortable, so I finally spoke.

"Do you ever wonder why I've done things the way I have?"

"No," said my mother. "I gave up thinking about that."

"It was Andy's death," I said, my throat tightening. "I thought I killed him."

"That's ridiculous," she said, looking away, her grief surfacing. "He died of a strep infection."

I sat there for a few seconds, making sure I had heard right.

"Strep?"

She stared straight ahead and spoke in a level, unexaggerated voice. "Doctors said he was only the second person in the whole country to die from it."

"Second?"

"The first was a convict somewhere in Texas."

It was an astounding revelation for me, after so many years of assuming fault.

## My Brother Probably Died of *Streptococcus*

When I began to get used to the idea of my brother dying of strep, I started to recall the period just after my family moved from rural Alabama to the suburbs, where instead of woods my brothers and I had only vacant lots and concrete-sided aqueducts to play in. Once, while playing in the aqueducts—storm drains that fed into the public sewage system undermining all the houses—I was stung several times on the back by hornets and had a catastrophic allergic reaction to the venom. My face swelled and distorted like that of a monster, as did my bronchial passages, which posed a threat of asphyxiation.

After a day or so in the hospital, injected several times with whatever adrenaline compound they used at the time to treat bee stings, I returned to normal but was warned that if I were ever stung again, I might die. This puzzled me, since hornet and yellow jacket stings had been a way of life in the country, a sign, as it were, that summer was in full bloom. Why would I suddenly manifest an allergy? The doctors didn't have much of an answer, but one of them speculated that the hornets had extracted herbicides the city had been spraying in the aqueducts.

Around this same time, my brothers and I started coming down with strep infections, which brought high fevers as well as sore throats. It was a new disease for us, but we lived next to a pediatrician who paid house calls and prescribed lots of cold, sweet liquids. Still, the germ persisted, dogging my brothers and me like an angry bully. The doctor speculated that we were susceptible because, unlike the other children of the neighborhood, including her own children, we didn't go barefoot year round. Eventually, my brothers and I started going barefoot even in the cold weather. The strep would still come to visit us from time to time, but the frequency and duration decreased. Within a few years, a bout of strep was uncommon.

These incidences of infection seem to have little to do with my brother's death, but the appearance of those first virulent rounds happened around the time that my brothers and I began to follow the neighborhood children into the drainage ditches to play. *Streptococcus* bacteria are so abundant that the strain we contracted could have been living in the grass of our front lawn, but the ditches would have provided an even richer breeding ground. And if the ditch could foster hornets with above-normal venom, then perhaps it could do the same with *Streptococcus*.

Ewald's research suggests that water, especially untreated water, can encourage some waterborne diseases such as cholera to evolve in a more virulent direction. Though the water flowing through the suburban pipes of our neighborhood was treated with antibacterial chemicals, most of what filled the ditches behind the houses was untreated runoff. Moreover, whenever rains swelled the ditches to stream-sized torrents, there was ample opportunity for the ditch water to mix with sewage by backwashing into the drainage conduits, which were connected to the underground sewage pipes feeding into every household.

During the writing of this book, I contacted Dr. Ewald and asked him about the possible influence of water on the evolution of *Streptococcus*. He wasn't able to give a definite answer, presumably because there is either no or too little data on the subject. He offered the final opinion that he thought it unlikely that water would influence the "epidemiology of strep," but he speculated that *enterococcus*—another germ formerly classified as a form of *Streptococcus*—might acquire waterborne virulence. *Enterococcus* is associated with sewage, and could have caused some of my younger brother's symptoms, such as high fever and vomiting.

To double-check Ewald's speculation, I contacted Drs. Thomas Braciale, the immunologist, and William Petri, a specialist in infectious disease, both of the University of Virginia School of Medicine. After carefully listening to the story of my brother's death, both concluded that he had probably died of an acute strep infection, along the lines of the lately much publicized "flesh-eating strep," not *enterococcus*.

As a follow-up, I contacted my mother and with great discomfort asked her for more of the medical details surrounding my brother's death. To my surprise, she rifled through some old papers and found a letter from my late brother's attending physician, who said that he actually died of a brain "abscess" caused by a strep germ that had been growing in him for approximately sixteen days. The abscess grew to the size of an orange, which shifted for some unknown reason, pressing on crucial life-functioning nerve centers. The doctor's conclusion was that even if they had known about the abscess, any attempt to remove it would likely have rendered my brother a vegetable or killed him.

The only thing that seems certain about my brother's death is that he died of infection. Nonetheless, I remain steadfast in my conviction that his death portends a larger, deeper lesson beyond mere tragedy. In *Plague Time*, Dr. Ewald encourages his reader to use evolutionary logic to scrutinize pathological situations. He also advocates giving strong consideration to anecdotal evidence. Based on these two pieces of expert advice, I remain suspicious of the water in those ditches.

Even if water wasn't the evolutionary trigger that nudged such a strep infection toward virulence in my brother, the coincidence of my brothers and me coming down with chronic strep infections after we began playing in the ditches raises a red flag. Exclude our having played in the aqueducts, and there remains the possibility that proximity to the houses allowed the germs to spread up onto lawns and domestic fringes. Our more immunologically resistant playmates and the neighborhood pets provided another means for the infection to spread.

Once colonized by these strains, my brothers' and my immune systems may have spent a couple of years working out a living arrangement with our new parasites, until we achieved the same resistance as our friends. Though the infection that killed my brother may have been a new strain he inadvertently picked up in the yard, there remains the possibility that the lethal strep was already there, evolving, responding to the conditions of its host environment. If this were the case, then sadness over my parents' divorce, plus the stress of living in a semi-abusive family, could have combined to weaken my brother's immune system to the point where the strep, held in check up until then, took advantage of the opportunity to mutate a more virulent version of itself.

## Chinese Medicine, Evolutionary Biology, and Reflective Exercise

I first read about the New Germ Theory a few years ago while on a flight to Beijing. The purpose of my visit was to meet with officials of the China National Qigong Institute and the Beijing University of Traditional Chinese Medicine to explore ways to make traditional Chinese medicine and fitness more sensible to a Western audience. The New Germ Theory was a stunning revelation, and my mind caught fire with the idea that I was looking at the missing piece of an ancient puzzle. But the idea was too fresh and inarticulate for me to communicate to my Chinese hosts, so I spent most of my time pouring over impressive studies the two organizations conducted to prove the efficacy of traditional Chinese medicine and fitness.

In between meetings, my hosts arranged for sightseeing around Beijing. In the ten years that had passed since I had last been there, the city had undergone mind-boggling changes. Where old tile-roofed, single-story shops once lined the roads there now stood glittering high-rise buildings, computer stores, and fast-food restaurants. The formerly slow-moving river of bicycles had become a stagnant sea of bumper-to-bumper automobiles, spewing exhaust into the dusty air. Though the Mao-suited bureaucrats and drably dressed laborers still dotted the cityscape, an equal number of Chinese businessmen and women, dressed in elegant suits and sleek black leather, scurried around with digital mobile phones pressed to their ears.

My return flight was a crowded microcosm of what I had seen on the streets of Beijing. The Maoists tended to be older and modestly dressed, clutching cardboard boxes serving as suitcases. The business-people were mostly young, wore colorful clothes, and carried laptop computers. I sat between one man of each type, and as soon as we were aloft and the "fasten seatbelt" sign was turned off, both lowered their trays and began taking out small bottles and jars of traditional Chinese medicine. In fact, so many Chinese passengers were lowering their trays and taking out medicine that it raised an audible din, bringing the flight attendants out of hiding to see what was the matter. When I asked the young businessman next to me what his array of medicines were supposed to treat, he answered "rising fire," a traditional Chinese medical term for what a Westerner would call an ulcer of the mouth.

That moment on the airplane drove home for me the staying power of China's traditional medicine on its people, a power that Maoist communism inadvertently bolstered in its efforts to modernize. Before such efforts, eclectic shamans roaming the countryside or formally educated physicians bound to the aristocracy dominated traditional Chinese medicine. When the Maoists first began searching for a way to shore up the shamefully debilitated public health of the Chinese people, they hatched the "Barefoot Doctor" campaign, which created an army of roving healthcare practitioners trained in the rudiments of traditional Chinese medicine and a smattering of Western first aid. Eventually, this campaign gave rise to state-sponsored medicine that allowed both traditional Chinese and Western medicine to develop side by side.

This experiment most probably helped encourage and spread traditional Chinese medical thinking among the people, adding to an already considerably entrenched folk wisdom based on the same tradition. This augmented wisdom got passed on to the young, who, no matter how westernized, never let go of the traditional self-healing methods they learned from older family members or venerable teachers.

The number of Chinese people, old and young alike, who habitually self-treat with traditional Chinese medicine is enormous. Such broad acceptance and use in the face of rapid modernization in all areas, including medicine, suggests that traditional Chinese medicine is an effective treatment for a broad range of health problems. For the past few decades, Western critics have attributed this apparent efficacy to the placebo effect, healing that occurs simply because the persons being healed believe a particular treatment will be beneficial. More recently, a number of studies have suggested that traditional Chinese medicine gets the job done by means other than the placebo effect. But how? The traditional Chinese medical paradigm offers thorough explanations, but the language of this paradigm is pre-scientific, formed before the discoveries of the microscope, microorganisms, and the relationship between infection and disease.

*If Unified Fitness is to provide sustainable health, it must rise to the challenge of untying the semantic knot that keeps traditional Chinese and modern medical paradigms in a struggle for public attention that benefits no one.*

If Unified Fitness is to provide sustainable health, it must rise to the challenge of untying the semantic knot that keeps traditional Chinese and modern medical paradigms in a struggle for public attention that benefits no one. Conventional medicine, in a well-intentioned effort to protect the public from quackery, refuses to embrace healing methods whose mechanisms aren't well understood, even though the healing methods clearly work. Effective alternative therapies such as traditional Chinese medicine are lumped together with ineffective alternative modalities. In its growing frustration over not being recognized, the traditional Chinese medical establishment, along with practitioners of other effective alternative approaches, begin to feel persecuted and look for ways to discredit conventional medicine. Caught in the middle, the public, hungry for some say-so over their health, wanders around in chaos, not knowing who or what to believe.

This struggle between medical paradigms recapitulates a similar one that characterized the development of cosmology, or the study of the universe. Examining how cosmology resolved its philosophical differences sheds light on how medicine may resolve its paradigmatic conflicts. If the resolutions in cosmology are any indication, the prospect for the unification of medical paradigms looks promising. This philosophical unification may facilitate acceptance of sustainable health as the primary goal of medicine and Unified Fitness as an effective way to achieve that goal.

In primitive cosmology, theories about the structure of the universe tended to be geocentric, placing the Earth at the center and imbuing both the heavens and nature with anthropomorphic qualities. In the development of the healing sciences, traditional Chinese medicine, along with all pre-scientific medical approaches, most closely resembles the geocentric universe, which achieved its most refined expression in an elaborate scheme of concentric and overlapping circles to explain the movement of the heavens around the Earth. Similarly, traditional Chinese medicine relies on natural metaphors (especially the behavior of light and darkness) to predict the behavior of human health and illness.

Like geocentrism, traditional Chinese medicine places human experience at the center of attention. Subjective responses from the patient guide diagnosis and treatment. Improvements or failures are the result of a joint effort between patient and physician. In the case of Qigong, which traditional Chinese medicine regards as the highest form of medicine, the patient becomes the physician, maintaining absolute responsibility for and control over health and illness.

The fate of cosmological geocentrism was sealed with the advent of the Newtonian model of the universe, so called because of the influence of Isaac Newton's laws of gravity and motion. Aided by the work of predecessors Copernicus and Galileo, Newtonian cosmology moved human beings from the center of creation to an apparently arbitrary and insignificant location. In place of the comforting anthropomorphism of the Earth-centered view, the Newtonian paradigm installed cold mathematical formulas describing elegant natural and astronomical forces that acted indifferently toward and independently of human will.

A parallel development in health science is the emergence of the conventional medical view that reigns today. Like Newtonian cosmology, conventional medicine has grown out of a set of apparently objective principles that discredit other medical models and turn medicine into an offshoot of chemistry and physics. These principles, like those of its cosmological analog, often reduce the patient to helpless victim. The patient's health or illness is the result of microorganic, genetic, or environmental factors that act indifferently toward and independently of human will.

Rising up to oppose Newtonian cosmology in the early twentieth century was the relativistic model pioneered by Albert Einstein. This relativistic concept illuminated problems inherent in both the geocentric and Newtonian cosmologies, but at the same time demonstrated the limited legitimacy each possessed. Evolutionary medicine has the potential to do for traditional Chinese and conventional medicine what Einstein's model of the universe did for its cosmological predecessors: discredit the absolutism and highlight the elements of truth in each.

According to Einstein's theory, neither the geocentric nor Newtonian models had thought out in thorough enough detail the role the observer played in their respective cosmologies. Though the geocentrists were entitled to their view because humans did, in fact, observe heavenly events from the Earth, their failure to consider other perspectives limited their understanding of the mathematical laws governing the forces that caused events, thus preventing them from seeing the whole picture.

The Newtonians, on the other hand, understood the mathematical laws causing events to happen on Earth, but excluded the effect of the observer on the perception of motion, especially in space, away from Earth's gravity. Thus, the geocentric and Newtonian cosmologies are capable of explaining only limited truths, encompassed by Einstein's more general theory. The relativistic model extends to cover cosmological situations beyond Earth's perspective and its laws of gravity.

Evolutionary medicine's analog for the relativistic observer is infection, which traditional Chinese medicine judges from the overly subjective view of what an infection feels like in the body and which conventional medicine judges from the overly objective view of biochemistry. Like Einstein's cosmological relativism, evolutionary medicine may help sort out the flaws and reveal the elements of truth in each medical approach's understanding of infection, thus ushering in an era of unity in medical science.

The mistakes made by both earlier medical paradigms center around the causes and effects of infectious microorganisms. Traditional Chinese medicine doesn't account for the role of microorganisms and thus confuses symptoms for causation. Conventional medicine both underestimates the role of germs and overestimates genetics and the environment. But each medical approach got several things right, such as traditional Chinese medicine's insight into the primacy of the patient's power to handle infections and conventional medicine's short-term effectiveness in combating with antibiotics and vaccinations what appeared to be the pervading infectious threats of the day. Add to these correct perceptions evolutionary medicine's regard for germs as multidimensional, dynamic players in the struggle for sustainable health, and a clearer picture emerges.

The inclusiveness of Einstein's theory of relativity foreshadows the way evolutionary medicine can accommodate traditional Chinese and conventional medicine. Both evolutionary and conventional medicine depend on microbiology, but they disagree on which microscopic factors are the most crucial to the development of disease. With evolutionary and traditional Chinese medicine, the fit is comparable. Daoism, the ancient philosophy upon which traditional Chinese medicine relies, and Darwinism, the guiding rubric for evolutionary medicine, proceed from a very similar thesis.

Fundamental to each is the concept of life as a constantly changing struggle. Darwinian mutation of organisms and the contest between them resembles the Daoist restless ebb and flow of Qi, driven by the eternal interplay between yin and yang. Their key difference lies in the focus of their respective attentions. Evolutionary medicine's focus includes the microscopic; the traditional Chinese medical focus does not.

If the efficacy of traditional Chinese medicine isn't purely a placebo phenomenon, then it must be working with true medical principles that can be verified, at least in part. Why not the laws of evolutionary medicine? Just as the geocentric universe worked with principles the relativistic model could explain in more sophisticated terms, traditional Chinese medical concepts such as Qi and yin/yang could be pre-scientific, subjective, and generally accurate interpretations of the way infectious disease responds to both host immunity and secondary treatment.

Qigong throws the link between traditional Chinese and evolutionary medicine into sharper relief. At advanced levels, self-treatment with Qigong means controlling all of the "channels" that keep Qi moving throughout the body. Qigong practitioners struggling to overcome disease report feeling "sick" or "unbalanced" Qi moving along these channels, out of the body. Patients of traditional Chinese medicine undergoing treatments with herbs, acupuncture, and massage describe similar, less distinct feelings (their lack of Qigong training limits their sensibilities). If evolutionary medicine is correct in its hypothesis that infection drives most disease, then this sense of movement in the body might be firsthand impressions of the immune system fighting back an infection or pressuring it to evolve in a benign direction.

The theory of reflective exercise, which recasts Qigong in a language more acceptable to modern medicine, represents a piece of the puzzle evolutionary medicine could use in its struggle to unify medicine. The notion of neurovascular pathways created by smart lymphocytes roaming the body provides a tenable microbiological explanation for traditional Chinese medicine's mysterious acupuncture "channels," which conventional medicine has a tough time accepting. Thus, the theory of reflective exercise combined with evolutionary medical principles helps mitigate some of the conflict and encourages greater confluence between traditional Chinese and conventional medical paradigms.

With the help of the evolutionary medical perspective, conventional medicine may come to have the same high regard for reflective exercise that traditional Chinese medicine has for Qigong. Viewed as a method of generating an immune response to exert evolutionary pressure on an invading microbe, reflective exercise may achieve equal, if not superior, status among the preventive methods conventional medicine already embraces overwhelmingly: flexibility, strengthening, cardiovascular exercises, and proper nutrition. In my opinion, reflective exercise will likely join these recommendations as a low-cost, effective way to thwart a germ's survival strategy in the body.

With or without the support of evolutionary medicine and reflective exercise, Qigong, acupuncture, massage, and herbology continue to be enormously popular in China and are making headway in the United States. Millions of non-Chinese Americans are willing to attest that a good acupuncturist or Chinese massage therapist can literally rout pain and inflammation out of the site of an injury with remarkable speed and efficiency. Orthodox medicine threw its support behind this view when the American Medical Association acknowledged acupuncture as an effective analgesic.

But conventional medicine still holds traditional Chinese medicine in suspicion, largely, I think, because of the language differences between the two approaches. Evolutionary and reflective reinterpretations of traditional Chinese medicine offer a fresh beginning in what remains a long, frustrating effort to reconcile conventional and alternative approaches to health and healing. The next step will be to conduct research to test the hypotheses of evolutionary medicine and reflective exercise.

Dr. Braciale and I discussed how such research might be carried out. In his opinion, the hypothesis that reflective exercise bolsters immunity is fairly easy to test. He recommends skin testing two sets of people—those who practice reflective exercise and those who don't—with a highly reactive form of yeast. At least two reactions would signify enhanced immunity in the reflective exercisers: one, a large skin response to the yeast, and two, the rapid disappearance of such a skin response. The same test could be conducted to examine other traditional Chinese modalities, such as acupuncture, massage, or herbal treatments.

If either or both of these reactions occur, then the next experiment should test the hypothesis of "smart lymphocytes": whether or not the lymphocyte cell surfaces of reflective exercisers (or people treated with traditional Chinese medical modalities) have more (and possibly different) neurotransmitters and neuropeptides than those of nonreflective exercisers. In this test, blood drawn from reflective exercisers (or participants using traditional Chinese medicine) and another random group could be examined for differences in the cell surfaces of both sets of lymphocytes. In the case of reflective exercise, all the reflective exercisers should be able to sense and affect the nasal sinuses with the rising and falling pulse, which can be objectively measured with the same device that indicated a pulse in the middle of my forehead.

Medical science usually follows this second level of study with an effort to pinpoint the exact biochemical mechanisms in order to develop a drug that can effect the same result. Such an effort may prove fruit-less, since no drug is likely to match the body's immunological power. But the search for a drug that works with the body's natural mechanisms in the same way that effective herbal treatments operate might lead down a path that allows conventional medicine to join on its own terms with natural, alternative approaches to health. Instead of each form of medicine being demonized as "allopathic" or "New Age," the fresh insight into the holistic way that the molecular biology of the immune system can alter and tame parasitic infections could lead to clearer principles of effective treatment and the unification of medicine itself.

# Chapter 7

## *Days 31–32: Taming Germs*

**Optional Exercise 4D:**
**Rigorous Chaosercise**

The last few days of Unified Fitness involve learning how to exercise when you've come down with a cold, flu, or some other minor ailment, or when you suffer from chronic illness. Doing the Exercises 2B, Six Subtle Movements; 3A, Standing Reflective Meditation; 4B, Gentle Chaosercise of the Three Centers; and 3D, Seated Reflective Meditation, can help in such cases, but there is an even more effective way to speed things along. Eastern traditions have a variety of names for this method. The Chinese, for example, apply the euphemism "automatic movement." Certain sects of Tibetan Buddhism are more straightforward, calling it "crazy movement." I call it Rigorous Chaosercise.

When I lived in China in the late 1980s, it was common to walk through a public park and see scores of people doing Rigorous Chaosercise that ranged between what seemed to be schizophrenic or autistic behaviors to epileptic seizures. Such sights never bothered me; I had been engaging in similar, though more structured, behavior since my teacher introduced it during the first few months of my training. Though these "automatic movements" were presented to me as part of a well-understood tradition, I have since learned that they were really more of a fad, inspired by charismatic Qigong masters who supposedly summon cosmic Qi to drive out the "sick" Qi inhabiting the bodies of their students. Since that time, a more scientific Qigong coalition has tried to de-romanticize public attitudes toward these "crazy" movements, encouraging instead quieter, softer approaches to self-treatment.

The fad issue notwithstanding, I have found Rigorous Chaosercise to be quite useful in helping the body tame the effects of infectious or chronic disease. The Chinese approach emphasizes total randomness in the movements, but I find that hard to justify. My approach to these movements is more structured than many traditional practitioners would probably like, effectively turning them into a form of exercise—essentially a kind of aerobic flailing.

The purpose of Gentle Chaosercise is to help the practitioner sense reflections in the air around the three Centers. Rigorous Chaosercise functions differently. Driven largely by rapid gyrations of the waist and bending and straightening the legs at an equally fast

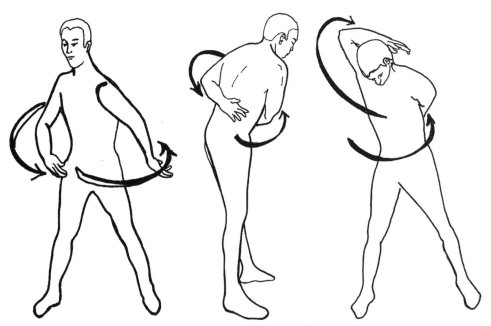

**Rigorous Chaosercise: Pivot-Slap-Bounce**

pace, these hard, chaotic movements are a kind of scatter-shot acupressure massage/aerobic workout rolled into one. While the legs push continuously against the floor and the pelvis pivots vigorously, the arms and upper body relax, so that the arms swing around and strike the lower abdomen in front and a parallel spot on the lower back. Then the arms travel up both the front and the back of the body and then down again. The blows combined with the pelvic gyrations stimulate circulation in the skin and churn blood and fluids throughout the torso and extremities. The bouncing motion connects the legs to the actions of the torso in a manner similar to a style of Chinese martial art called *Tongbeiquan* (literally "penetrating fist").

An even more effective but painful movement involves rapidly shaking the body from the hips so that the arms are forced out to the sides as Elvis Presley did in his heyday. In fact, the "Elvis" is a fitting moniker for the action. As a result of doing the Elvis for several minutes, your body may seize up with cramps and aches, especially if you are ill. The pain may focus in the liver (right ribcage), kidney (lower back), or abdomen.

These cramps are generally different from those incurred during ordinary aerobic exercise, which considers cramping something to be avoided. Rigorous Chaosercise cramps run deeper than the superficial muscles typically worked in aerobics. A movement such as the Elvis jostles the vital organs so that the mover is able to feel his or her insides in a way that would not otherwise be possible. Cramps signify constriction and a lack of suppleness in the organs, which may indicate an unhealthy state. One major contributing factor to organ constriction may be visceral fat. A large concentration of visceral fat around internal organs, especially the liver, is associated with chronic illnesses such as heart disease, cancer, and Type II diabetes.

If evolutionary medicine's assertions are correct, then visceral fat may be either the direct or indirect result of stealth infections. In stirring up, moving, and eventually eliminating deep cramping sensations, Rigorous Chaosercise may represent one of the few ways the body can burn excess visceral fat around the vital organs.

Rigorous Chaosercise runs contrary to current fashions in exercise, which are not based on intimate, profound connections between mind and body. By today's standards, a person can have a healthy body and an unhealthy mind. In fact, most health clubs demonstrate their disregard for the mind by offering their patrons exercise diversions, such as television, music, or both.

Not so for the Rigorous Chaoserciser. Like a psychotherapist working with a patient, the chaoserciser must struggle against his or her own "resistance," a general tendency to fight progress because of the short-term unpleasantness encountered. When the harder movements become intolerably painful, the conscious mind resists. Then, the slower movements can take over until recovery, whereupon the hard movements begin again. Because painful cramps in the viscera and in muscles and tissues may indicate the location of an infection or a chronic condition, the striking movements should be used to break up the cramping sensation; or, if the cramps are in the lower trunk, which is often the case, the striking movements can help drive the cramps up into the shoulders, where the brachial blood vessels and nerves can disperse the sensation.

Total time for practicing Rigorous Chaosercise should be eight to ten minutes, beginning with a period of flailing, followed by slower, softer movements. In terms of a whole routine, Rigorous Chaosercise should follow Exercise 2B, Six Subtle Movements. After moving hard for eight to ten minutes, the slower reflective movements are next, including Exercise 4B, Gentle Chaosercise of the Three Centers. This should take from five to seven minutes, followed by at least twenty minutes of Exercise 3D, Seated Reflective Meditation.

As I mentioned earlier, Rigorous Chaosercise, despite its apparent formlessness, can be performed as a structured exercise. Though unorthodox, even compared to reflective exercise, I have both experienced and witnessed it effectively drive out low-grade illness and get at pockets of chronic trouble, often causing disease symptoms to change in ways that conventional medicine might not expect. For the most part, the changes in symptoms mark improvement, and even when symptoms appear to grow more severe, persistence with Rigorous Chaosercise usually turns the tide.

The effect of Rigorous Chaosercise on disease symptoms makes perfect sense from an evolutionary medical perspective, which holds that the primary or significant cause of the disease is an infectious microorganism. Rigorous Chaosercise unquestionably produces an immunological flooding effect in the body, which can pressure the microorganism to evolve. With lightweight infections, such as upper respiratory infections, a single session may do the job. With chronic diseases, especially asthma, fibromyalgia, chronic fatigue syndrome, lupus, and rheumatoid arthritis, the pressure must persist over several months, perhaps years. In these cases, Rigorous Chaosercisers must have patience and respect the limits of their pain thresholds and musculoskeletal systems. People hampered by chronic pain, as is the case with many suffering from fibromyalgia, and seniors whose bodies lack resilience, should employ a modified version of Rigorous Chaosercise, which consists largely of bouncing in place without lifting the feet off the floor.

*The effect of Rigorous Chaosercise on disease symptoms makes perfect sense from an evolutionary medical perspective. Rigorous Chaosercise unquestionably produces an immunological flooding effect in the body . . . With lightweight infections, such as upper respiratory infections, a single session may do the job.*

When performed with these precautions in mind, Rigorous Chaosercise can assist in pressuring an infectious agent to either evolve or surrender to a persistent flood of immunity that would otherwise not occur. In addition to this effect, Rigorous Chaosercise encourages the development of the ventral neurovascular pathway, facilitating integration of the immune and nervous systems and further enhancing a person's ability to keep pressuring the infectious agent to evolve in a more benign direction.

## The Structure of Rigorous Chaosercise

By counting breaths, you can structure Rigorous Chaosercise into five intervals of each of the following movements: the Elvis, Pivot-Slap-Bounce, and Recovery Movements, which are less intense than either the Elvis or Pivot-Slap-Bounce and are not measured by counting breaths, but are sufficiently vigorous to keep the body moving and the heart rate elevated. Repeat each of the movements in five intervals, like boxing rounds, the lengths of which are determined by counting exhalations: ten for the first, fifteen for the second, twenty, twenty-five, and finally thirty. Remember that counting exhalations only applies to the Elvis and Pivot-Slap-Bounce portions of the intervals, not to the Recovery Movements, the lengths of which are subjective and meant to help you move from one interval to the next.

You will need this help because the intervals become increasingly long and demanding, pushing you toward exhaustion or collapse. Though every instinct in your body may tell you to remain on your feet, occasionally collapsing during the most rigorous movements of the later intervals might be the right thing to do. This phenomenon bears some commentary.

Ancient Chinese tradition views the collapse during Rigorous Chaosercise as an act of humility that encourages heavenly Qi to enter and promote healing in the body. Evolutionary medicine makes another explanation possible, based on the notion that parasitic disease-causing microbes and human beings have greatly influenced each other's evolution. If natural selection has helped teach microbes to take advantage of human behavior that benefits their survival and propagation, then natural selection may have also imparted the lesson of learning to read internal biological distress signs that either encourage or discourage virulence. These distress signs may indicate to the microbe that the host is experiencing severe trauma, such as that inflicted by the jaws or paws of a large predator.

If such mechanisms exist, then the physical paroxysms of the Elvis or Pivot-Slap-Bounce probably produce similar internal distress signals, and collapse on the floor may send an even stronger message that the vitality of the host is on the verge of being lost and should either be parasitized to the maximum or preserved at all costs. If the microbe becomes virulent, then the heightened immune response induced by Rigorous Chaosercise, followed by the even more powerfully directed focus of Exercise 3D, Seated Reflective Meditation, will likely prove especially effective. The virulence of the germ flags the immune system's attention, then the immune system kills the germ. If the microbe opts for a more benign strategy, then the host benefits immediately. In most cases I've observed, such a change toward benignity in a chronic or debilitating infectious agent is gradual, taking months, sometimes years. Thus, the virulent reaction is most likely to occur in the early stages of using Rigorous Chaosercise to tame disease.

As strange as these explanations may seem, my observations of the effects of Rigorous Chaosercise on others and myself corroborate the effectiveness of occasionally collapsing when movement becomes too painful or exhausting. An evolutionary medical explanation could provide some basis for these observations, which are further supported by the collective observations of the ancient Chinese tradition.

## Rigorous Chaosercise in Action

Rigorous Chaosercise should be inserted in the exercise routine immediately following Exercise 2B, Six Subtle Movements. Then bring the hands into the Exercise 3A, Standing Reflective Meditation, posture, but instead of holding the arms in place, begin circling them counterclockwise as though you were swirling a basin of water in your arms. Gradually lower your hands until they drop to your sides, then begin moderately pivoting and striking the trunk for no more than a minute, speeding up near the end of the minute until you dovetail into the Elvis for as long as it takes for you to exhale ten times. Then follow up with Pivot-Slap-Bounce for ten exhales as well.

Afterwards, use Recovery Movements such as bouncing or shaking the body in a less demanding manner until you are ready to do the Elvis again, this time for fifteen exhales, followed by Pivot-Slap-Bounce for the same duration. After that, continue moving at a moderate rate so as to regain the strength to do the Elvis again, this time for twenty exhales, followed by Pivot-Slap-Bounce for an equal number of exhales. Do Recovery Movements until ready for another round of Elvis and pounding gyrations for twenty-five exhales each. After Recovery Movements, do the Elvis and Pivot-Slap-Bounce once more for thirty exhales apiece.

The numbers used to mark exhales during intervals of hard movement serve one purpose: to help structure the chaos. What matters most is that the vigorous movements be kept up for a period of about eight minutes, possibly as long as ten. During this time, you may find it impossible to keep up the Reverse Breathing. That's okay. As your skill in Rigorous Chaosercise increases, you may find it easier to do Reverse Breathing, even during the Elvis.

As I mentioned earlier, seniors and people with injuries or chronic musculoskeletal problems should modify Rigorous Chaosercise to flat-footed bouncing and arm shaking. However, pain does not necessarily signify structural problems. According to evolutionary medicine, a stealth infection could be a primary cause. The best test for structural versus infection-based pain is to have a thorough examination by both an orthopedist and a physical therapist. If neither can identify a clear structural problem, then you have a right to be suspicious of other causes of the pain, and stealth infection is as good an explanation as you are likely to find.

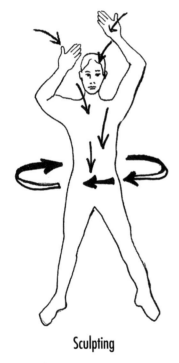

**Sculpting**

So, if you feel you can handle collapsing when you feel pain, don't be shy about it. Go down on the floor during any point in the interval, but don't just lie there. Keep moving by rocking from side to side or by rolling around. When the urge to get up comes, rise to your feet, proceed to the next interval, and do battle with the pain again, as though you were trying to drive it out of your body. Sometimes the pain will move from the lower or middle abdomen to the upper chest and shoulder area. If this happens, consider an important milestone crossed.

Generally, the movement of pain from one area to another, especially if the movement is from the abdomen to the shoulders, foretells a leap in your ability to use the neurovascular pathway effectively. If the pain remains stagnant, try collapsing again, then when you get up, start the next interval. Rigorously chaosercise in this way until you complete the five intervals, which should take from eight to ten minutes.

The next phases of Rigorous Chaosercise involve recovery from the severe shake-up your body has experienced. Begin by simply rocking from side to side, shifting the weight from one leg to the other by using the waist, letting the arms swing like pendulums. Do this for about two minutes. Next, start hula-hooping the hips as in Exercise 4A, Gentle Chaosercise of the Low Center. At the same time, reach high overhead and begin "sculpting." Bring the hands slowly down through the air and brush them an inch or so across each bisymmetrical feature of the head and trunk. Begin with the face—brows and cheek—then move down to the chest—breasts and ribcage—finally arriving at the Low Center, then return the hands overhead to repeat the sculpting process. Do this continually for about two minutes.

Next, begin Exercise 4B (Gentle Chaosercise of the Three Centers). First engage reflections of the upper Centers, but when the arms tire, let them fall and play with the waist reflections. Do this for at least two minutes.

By this time, you have been moving continuously for almost twenty minutes. You are ready to end the exercise. Bring the arms up to the Exercise 3A, Standing Reflective Meditation, posture and close in the manner you began, circling the arms laterally. You should feel warmth, pulsing, magnetic, or electrostatic sensations fluxing in the circle of your arms. With each circle, slowly lower the arms until they rest at your sides. Then do the Closing Sculpt down the centerline, hands passing through the fields of each Center. On the third pass, bring the hands to the Low Center in an embrace. Men should have their left hands closer to their bodies, women their right. Follow this immediately with Exercise 3D, Seated Reflective Meditation, using the imaginary red line and Reverse Breathing to focus the mind on the breath and body.

# Summary of Optional Exercise 4D

1. Exercise 2B (Six Subtle Movements: one set, approximately 4 minutes)

2. Begin Optional Exercise 4D (Rigorous Chaosercise: modest Pivot-Slap-Bounce, approximately 1 minute)

3. Begin 5 Intervals of Exercise 4D, Rigorous Chaosercise

10 Elvis exhalations, 10 Pivot-Slap-Bounce exhalations, Recovery Movements

15 Elvis exhalations, 15 Pivot-Slap-Bounce exhalations, Recovery Movements

20 Elvis exhalations, 20 Pivot-Slap-Bounce exhalations, Recovery Movements

25 Elvis exhalations, 25 Pivot-Slap-Bounce exhalations, Recovery Movements

30 Elvis exhalations, 30 Pivot-Slap-Bounce exhalations, Recovery Movements

4. Cool Down: 2 minutes

5. Sculpting: 2 minutes

6. Exercise 4B (Gentle Chaosercise of the Three Centers, 2 minutes)

7. Exercise 3D (Seated Reflective Meditation, 20 minutes)

8. 16-Step Acupressure Massage

## *Fred Banishes Gastroenteritis*

Fred was a retired navy chief who began studying reflective exercise with me after experimenting with a Taiji class. In his early sixties, Fred was wry and thin, a man who seemed the easiest-going fellow you could hope to meet. But during his Taiji training, he confided that he suffered from a mysterious upper gastrointestinal condition—broadly classified as gastroenteritis—that had him and his doctors worried. His symptoms included difficulty swallowing, a burning sensation in the upper gastrointestinal track, and occasional heartburn. The doctors were afraid it might be an ulcer or cancer, yet all the tests had proven inconclusive.

Being independent, Fred didn't like the idea of being a helpless patient, so he eagerly accepted my invitation to join a reflective exercise program. Sensing his body's relationship with the air and gaining the abdominal pulse came easily for Fred, but he didn't achieve a big breakthrough until he began Rigorous Chaosercise. He was particularly masterful with the Elvis movement. Within a couple of weeks, Fred's gastrointestinal symptoms vanished. After a few checkups, his doctor said he was out of the woods.

Subsequently, Fred became one of my keenest students, and he took an interest in Chinese martial arts. To this day, he remains free from his former illness, and can fight infectious disease at will.

## Hank Overcomes His Asthma

Hank was in his early thirties when he came to study Taiji with me. Although he had run cross-country in college, Hank had a number of fitness strikes against him: he worked a sedentary job as a newspaper editor, smoked cigarettes, and drank alcohol. On top of it all, he suffered from chronic asthma and had to use an inhaler several times a day. He also tended to be a magnet for every upper respiratory germ that wafted through the recirculating air of his office building.

During the course of about six months of Taiji training, I persuaded Hank to stop smoking and drinking and to get back into running and stretching. Once he got settled into this routine, I recommended he graduate from Taiji into pure reflective exercise. Within forty days, he opened the ventral pathway and began to control both his asthma and his susceptibility to upper respiratory infection. Eventually he used his inhaler less, and he seemed on track to enjoying all the benefits of Unified Fitness.

Predictably, however, Hank suffered a couple of setbacks, which necessitated a number of intimate conversations wherein I learned quite a bit about the complexity of his problems. For one, he drank a lot of coffee, as much as twenty cups a day, which along with his medication, helped to keep his asthma symptoms in check. (Caffeine helps blood vessels in the lungs dilate. Asthma encourages those vessels to constrict, thus causing difficulty in breathing.) He was also ashamed of his compromised health, for which he had learned to compensate with a hardened, sarcastic manner, stimulated by massive infusions of caffeine and sustained by his work as an editor.

Our discussions and continued reflective practice encouraged Hank to seek some professional counseling, which helped him become even more aware of the pathological links in his life. Eventually he began weaning himself off coffee with milder, more beneficial teas, but then his asthma flared up, making him especially vulnerable to upper respiratory infection.

Refusing to return to the vicious cycle of using coffee to control his symptoms, Hank began fighting back with Rigorous Chaosercise, which produced prodigious cramping in his liver and kidneys. With me coaching him to persist through what I was certain was temporary distress, he kept it up every day until the cramping diminished. With each session, whatever upper respiratory symptoms he was experiencing would abate. Soon he was able to control many of the upper respiratory infections that would have previously overwhelmed him.

Not long after that, his asthma symptoms lessened, much to the amazement of his doctor. Simultaneously, an odd rash broke out on Hank's skin, which his doctor diagnosed as "contact dermatitis," a broad category that includes poison ivy rashes. But the rash appeared in the dead of winter, and other than the usual upper respiratory infections he was incessantly picking up at work, there was no obvious source of the problem. Moreover, the rash would come and go according to the extent to which he practiced reflective exercise and Rigorous Chaosercise. Twice-a-day practices wiped out symptoms, whereas scattered or missed practices saw a return of the rash.

As Hank got more competent in using reflective exercise and Rigorous Chaosercise to combat his condition, he began to notice a clear connection between the appearance of skin rashes and the abatement of both asthma and upper respiratory infection symptoms. There are a number of ways to interpret this apparent relationship between symptoms. Conventional medicine would likely dismiss the relationship as coincidental. Traditional Chinese medicine would view the rash as a sign that the symptom-causing imbalance is working its way from a more severe internal condition to a less threatening manifestation on the body's surface. The combined perspectives of evolutionary medicine and reflective exercise allow the traditional Chinese medical observation to pass over into the language of conventional medicine: the relationship between disease symptoms indicates a stealth infection under pressure to evolve.

Traditional Chinese medicine would trace Hank's symptom-causing imbalance back to his early years, when his problems first surfaced. Since traditional Chinese medicine considers the skin and lungs related systems, the imbalance could have begun in either place. In fact, Hank does remember having mysterious skin rashes around the time his asthma symptoms surfaced, but he doesn't remember which came first. Even more telling, however, is that his family owned several dogs which they kept indoors because they lived in a large urban area, two factors—indoor pets and urban environments—that conventional medicine recognizes as possible triggers for asthma.

From the evolutionary medical perspective, dogs represent potential vectors for disease transmission, and keeping them indoors merely increases the risk of transmission. This bit of information was important in helping Hank because he had always owned dogs and kept them indoors. While he wasn't prepared to give up his dogs, he could at least take some action to improve the situation, such as putting the dogs outside more often or cleaning or arranging his living quarters to reduce microorganic opportunity. These kinds of efforts eased the struggle to keep the disease from reasserting itself and helped make his reflective exercise more effective.

It took about two more years of learning that he couldn't go back to coffee, verbal aggression, neglect of reflective exercise, or oblivion toward the potential influence of his pets on his condition before Hank was able to stabilize his condition and control his asthma without medication. No longer constrained by the threat of having his lungs seize in mid-stride, he was able to run regularly and follow up with reflective exercise. When the problem returned, he responded with Rigorous Chaosercise, and by this he was able to control his health.

# Pathological Reflections

If a reflective exerciser can enhance the body's health by manipulating his or her reflections with the hands, as Exercises 3A, Sensing the Middle Center; 4A, Gentle Chaosercise of the Low Center, and 4B, Gentle Chaosercise of the Three Centers demonstrate, then wouldn't the same thing happen if a reflective exerciser were to manipulate the reflections of someone else? The answer isn't simple, because the nature and behavior of reflections are complex. They constitute a chaotic system; therefore, mingling two or more such systems should result in a more unpredictable conglomerate. Under such circumstances, problems are just as likely as benefits.

When two sets of reflections come together, both complex systems probably run together to form a larger, more amorphous one, like raindrops that get too close to each other. Within this combined system, some innately stronger or willfully asserted reflections can transfer to the weaker person in the form of warmth or a vague sense of fluid-like energy. But other reflections possess a different kind of strength, the kind associated with internal pathologies.

These reflections range from wholly palpable to barely noticeable. Palpable reflections of internal pathologies often feel cold and prickly, and are easy to predict because people emanating such reflections will usually show clear signs of sickness, whether the sickness is a bad cold or cancer. Problems arise, however, when people show no overt symptoms of disease but emit pathological reflections, a situation that stealth infection helps to explain.

But how about the possibility of vague or undetectable pathological reflections that may also be the work of stealth infections? Then feeling someone else's stronger reflections asserting themselves into your weaker ones becomes a riskier proposition, raising doubts about the benefits for both people. The possibility of stealth contamination by stealth reflection is especially daunting. Such reflections may act like a weak-looking supervillain who, when struck in the face breaks into a thousand pieces, only to reassemble when the superhero is off-guard or preoccupied with subduing a more obvious threat.

They may behave like a colony of deer ticks that coast inside your home on the back of your faithful companion Fido, then leap onto you to nest in your armpit and infect you with Lyme Disease. The telltale signs of subtle pathological reflections are hard to pin down because, by definition, they fly beneath our radars. At this stage, acknowledging the possibility of their existence and impact on health is about all that can be done.

The effects of pathological reflections mimic the chaos and unpredictability of the reflective systems. Reflections from a person with cancer, for example, can mingle with those of an apparently well person and deplete the health of the well person in a number of ways that have nothing to do with cancer. Sore throats, skin rashes, boils, arthritic pains, edema, urinary tract inflammation, and tight, painful muscles are just a few standard complaints I've both witnessed and experienced over the years from seemingly healthy people who impart their reflections to someone with an obvious chronic disease.

While the causes of this phenomenon defy absolute explanation, there is one intriguing possibility that harkens to evolutionary medicine. The body swarms with ordinary infectious microorganisms, such as *Streptococcus* and *Staphylococcus*, which could cause many of these reactions. This suggests that pathological reflections probably work indirectly, perhaps exciting indigenous germ colonies to "misbehave."

If these possibilities aren't off-putting enough, then how about this even more likely threat? Viruses, bacteria, and fragments left over from immunological warfare travel on exhalation or from the pores of the skin into the immediate airspace where they have a brief window of opportunity to springboard to another host. Interfacing reflections with another person probably opens that window wider and longer, thus actually facilitating infection. The possibility that the infection may be of the stealth variety makes deliberate interpersonal reflective exercise all the more dangerous.

If pathological reflections are transmittable, then sitting next to someone on a plane, in a movie theater, or on a public bus shouldn't be regarded as entirely without risk. Indeed, reflective exercisers report a greater sensitivity toward the reflections of others, but this sensitivity simply serves as an early warning system for ongoing pathological transmissions that occur with or without reflective exercise. The ability to detect inadvertent pathological reflections from others gives the reflective exerciser a preventive leg up. For those with no reflective ability, the situation is at least as chaotic and unpredictable as in deliberate interpersonal reflective exercise, probably more so. But without the intentional effort to sense another's reflections, conflated reflections are unlikely to produce noticeable symptoms of any significance.

Traditional Chinese fitness recognizes similar side effects in Qigong and echoes similar warnings to those who practice on others. It is also very strict and demanding in identifying the kinds of skills needed to counter potentially harmful consequences. Thus, Qigong practitioners must spend a number of years building their skill in order to treat others. Qigong theory holds that a practitioner's Qi must be sufficiently strong to brook the problem of "unbalanced" or "sick" Qi.

*But the theory of reflective exercise recasts the process of building Qi as the development of greater control over a nexus of neurovascular pathways that span the body, so what begins as mere sensitivity—to both the pathway and to bodily reflections in the surrounding air— becomes part of the practitioner's living tool kit.*

But the theory of reflective exercise recasts the process of building Qi as the development of greater control over a nexus of neurovascular pathways that span the body, so what begins as mere sensitivity—to both the pathway and to bodily reflections in the surrounding air—becomes part of the practitioner's living tool kit. The skin, which is embryologically related to nerve cells, becomes increasingly sensitive to both neurovascular flow and reflection, feeling farther into the surrounding air, which comes to act as a second skin, both to protect the practitioner and to enhance the practitioner's ability to sense outside of his or her body.

When this happens, the potential to reflect into the airspaces of other people and living creatures goes up, but the practitioner must be fully capable of controlling his or her own health before even thinking about taking on the health problems of others. Usually, this takes a couple of years. During that time, the practitioner learns a number of important lessons. For example, Hank's case demonstrated the complex impact both infection and deep emotion have on sustaining health through reflective exercise. Such lessons are not learned overnight.

Reflective exercise is merely a tool and sustainable health is more of a process than a goal. The Chinese tradition counsels that persistence is a key factor in your ability to use that tool and to make that process successful. But, in the first couple of years, reflective exercise should be used for self-development and self-healing only, not for imparting to a passive recipient or for experiencing passively at the hands of another.

## Maxine Learns the Hazards of Healing without Protection

Maxine had been a massage therapist with fifteen years experience before she began studying Taiji with me. A tall, affable woman in her early forties, Maxine exuded a warmth that, while admirable, suggested she might have trouble maintaining boundaries with her clients, thus opening her up to contamination through the indirect routes of reflection. When I warned her of this possibility, Maxine assured me that she was well aware of the phenomenon and had her own methods of dealing with the problem. These included imagining thick bands embedded in her wrists which blocked the flow of unhealthy energy from clients.

My insistence that the situation was more complicated than that did little to faze her confidence. She belonged to a group of therapists, sponsored by a local millionaire who was herself a massage therapist, and all of them felt certain that they had nothing to worry about.

To avoid unpleasantness, I dropped the matter until Maxine became a reflective exerciser, at which point the Reflective Exercises sharpened her ability to sense the extent to which she interacted with her clients, especially during a massage technique known as craniosacral therapy. One day Maxine described how she had felt a strange, sickly energy surge from her client's lower back into her hands and arms before she had time to launch a counterstrategy. I warned her to expect a health problem in the next day or so. She developed upper respiratory infection symptoms and an ulcer inside her mouth within twenty-four hours.

Though she was able to self-treat with reflective exercise and chaosercise, the experience rocked Maxine's world. She confided that the other members of her massage group suffered from a variety of ailments that seemed to worsen when they worked on clients. One therapist confessed to Maxine that her spine ached so relentlessly that she was afraid she had cancer, yet she continued with her work, stubbornly refusing to entertain the possibility that the mechanisms permitting her to affect symptoms in a client might also work in reverse, creating symptoms in her.

# Mental Fitness

# Chapter 8

## Days 33–34:
## Stress, Stealth Psychosocial Pathologies

### Optional Exercise 4E: Prone Relaxation Meditation

The first steps toward achieving mental fitness involve understanding the physiological effects of stress and identifying hidden pathologies that affect us on both personal and social levels. The pursuer of mental fitness must deal with each of these facets one at a time.

Understanding the physiological mechanisms of stress underscores the crucial role the mind plays in overall fitness. Both physical and emotional stress excite the sympathetic nervous system, which, you may recall, governs fight-flight responses. In the case of physical stress, movement or static exertion causes the adrenal glands to secrete so-called stress hormones such as norepinephrine and cortisol into the bloodstream. Whereas norepinephrine provides a boost in energy, cortisol is an anti-inflammatory chemical, whose job is to clean up cellular damage, like that produced by infection or contusion. Along with this heightened sympathetic response, however, comes an increase in heart rate, blood pressure, and lymph flow, which in the short run puts the sympathetic secretions to good use.

With emotional stress, the absence of physical movement or exertion leaves the sympathetic chemicals floating aimlessly in the bloodstream. This can be bad news for the body, especially in the case of cortisol, whose prolonged presence leads to a kind of internal corrosion. Research shows that people who suffer from continuous emotional stress tend to accrue visceral fat around the internal organs, especially the liver, a condition associated with a high risk of heart disease, cancer, and Type II diabetes (Gaessar 1996).

Though most of us tend to block out the sense of what stress is doing to us, strong emotional shocks, such as the loss of a loved one, are harder to ignore. It is no figure of speech to characterize emotional damage in terms of being "heartbroken." Anyone who has lived long enough to be confronted by loss and sadness knows the heavy, even painful, sensation in the chest that occurs when tragic news arrives. Similarly, when we receive love or recognition, we may feel light, even ticklish in the chest.

Such experiences show how emotion affects the physiological mind and underscore the need to be vigilant regarding less apparent forms of stress. In many instances, practicing Unified Fitness provides a means of both sensing and remedying covert stress reactions. Exercise Series 1 (stretching and moving) is a natural response to the sympathetic nervous system's fight-flight chemical mandate. Afterwards, Exercise Series 2 and 3 (reflective exercise) stimulate the parasympathetic nervous system, which further counteracts sympathetic excitations. Eventually, the practitioner carries the calming effect of reflective exercise on the mind's physiology into ordinary life, allowing the practitioner to recognize even subtle stress reactions. When this happens, the reflective exerciser must identify the causes of the stress and either alter his or her perception of these causes or avoid them, which may take time.

Unfortunately, stress reactions aren't likely to accommodate anyone's schedule and often show up at times that make practicing the full range of Unified Fitness inconvenient or unwise: tense traffic conditions, person-to-person confrontations, and worrisome nights when you should be sleeping but can't because you're wound up about something. Stress in traffic can best be handled by practicing Exercise 2A, Reverse Abdominal Breathing, which is especially effective if the practitioner is able to feel the abdominal pulse rise and fall. Instead of getting upset because of a long red light or backed up traffic due to someone else's careless driving, put the car in park, place the hands over the Low Center, lift the tongue to the upper palate, and breathe through the nose, gently contracting the lower abdomen on the inhalation and relaxing it on the exhalation. If you can't feel the abdominal pulse, focus on the image of the red line moving up and down your centerline with your breath. You'll feel better, and you will have spent time cultivating rather than undermining immunological fitness.

With personal confrontations, practicing any aspect of reflective exercise may be immediately impossible, especially if the confrontational person is speaking harshly to you. But once such a conflict passes, reflective exercise can help calm your nerves. Sensing the body's reflections, for example, invokes the parasympathetic nervous system, which helps counter the adrenal reaction provoked by the confrontation. Following a disturbing argument with one round of Exercise 2B, Six Subtle Movements, and a little bit of Exercise 3B, Sensing the Middle Center, helps tone down physiological stress reactions and creates an opportunity to build reflective skill.

Of all the inconvenient times for reflective exercise practice, periods of insomnia probably prove the least troublesome. Though in rare cases the insomniac might benefit from a full Unified Fitness workout, several nights of poor or nonexistent sleep can lead to physical as well as emotional exhaustion, making cardiovascular exercise inadvisable. Moreover, you may be too tired for Exercise 3D, Seated Reflective Meditation. In that case you should conclude with the following optional exercise, which can deliver a deeper sense of calm.

# Optional Exercise 4E: Prone Relaxation Meditation

Lying flat on your back, with arms at your sides, slowly begin using relaxation abdominal breathing, which, you may recall, involves distending the abdominal muscles on the inhalation and relaxing them on the exhale. As you inhale, imagine that the top of your head becomes an open hole, through which you are drawing your breath. Think of what you're breathing in as something purely benign—energy, spirit, or God—filling your abdomen to maximum capacity. Then on the exhale, picture the pure goodness you've taken in through your head driving all the anxiety and bad feelings out through the legs and the soles of the feet. Continue this meditation until you feel better. If necessary, repeat the reflective movements and do the meditation again. Then follow up with the 16-Step Acupressure Massage (See pages 161-165).

## Recognizing Stealth Psychosocial Pathologies

Altering the body's response through reflective exercise is only part of the solution to dealing with emotional stress. Learning to recognize the mental and emotional triggers of emotional stress is equally important, especially in the long run. These triggers are often both personally and socially endemic, with lives of their own. I call these living instigators of stress "psychosocial pathologies." They are the mental equivalent of the evolving microorganisms the immune system faces.

Like infections that may cause lethal diseases, such as atherosclerosis (coronary artery disease), cancer, stroke, and diabetes, and chronic debilitating illness, such as fibromyalgia, chronic fatigue syndrome, lupus, and arthritis, unhealthy psychosocial conditions either abide in individuals or hide in the social landscape, waiting to seize the unsuspecting and unprepared. Many of these pathologies are thrust upon people in childhood and thus appear beyond individual control. Still, the ability to discern such mental pathologies shapes the course of effective action, just as understanding that one's heart condition is caused by infection rather than genetics is bound to alter the treatment. Recognizing pathologies lurking in the psychosocial terrain is the tricky but necessary business of Unified Fitness, which, as in the cases of physical and immunological fitness, finds support in expert findings and opinion.

Expert opinion on mental pathology is even more rife with disagreement than it is for physical pathology. Many experts will take issue with my use of the term *pathology*, because of its severe connotations. In general, the mental health profession views mental dysfunction along a spectrum, ranging from fairly common and supposedly harmless "personality disorders" to extremely debilitating "pathologies." Some mental health experts, perhaps the majority, tend to shy away from hypothesizing about the relationships between divisions of the spectrum. For them, depression is marked by distinct characteristics that separate it from other disorders, such as anorexia nervosa.

Still other authorities look for relationships between divisions of the mental disorder spectrum, seeing the seeds of pathology in what is roundly believed to be ordinary and nonthreatening. These experts are doing in mental health what Paul W. Ewald is doing in medicine: identifying stealth pathologies, chronic degenerative conditions that lack the acute signature of the commonly accepted notions of pathology. My sympathies are with both the mental and medical "stealth" pathologists.

Over the years I have identified three proponents of the mental stealth pathology position whose ideas assist recognition of hidden psychosocial pathology. The first of these experts is Alfred Korzybski, a Polish mathematician and philosopher, and founder of General Semantics, an effort to describe human behavior in terms of the structure of the brain. Though Korzybski wrote in the first half of the twentieth century, and some of his concepts are dated, his basic idea still holds true: the overall structure of the brain shapes everything we feel, think, and do, and thus needs to be understood and factored into our thinking about health.

A zealous student of brain anatomy, Korzybski observed that core biological drives that motivate us to eat, avoid pain, seek pleasure, and reproduce are all located in a deep center of the brain called the hypothalamus, which itself is underpinned by deeper, more primitive layers. At the deepest level lies the brain stem, the seat of so-called involuntary reflexes. The next layer up from the hypothalamus is the thalamus, which relays signals from the more primitive levels to the next layer of gray matter known as the limbic system, which is in turn wrapped in the cortex, the most superficial layer, responsible for voluntary reflexes, as well as language and abstract reasoning.

**Neural Pathway between Hypothalamus and Cortex**

This layered structure, Korzybski reasoned, creates an inherent link between the cortex and hypothalamus, effectively mixing the neurology of verbal opinions and constructs with that of biological drives. In this way someone can learn to associate a deep biological urge such as sex with a comparatively abstract notion such as being thin or to associate eating with being loved. This general structure of the human nervous system, Korzybski believed, lays the groundwork for the manufacture of phobias, obsessions, and neuroses.

Though more recent findings on the brain have shown neurological sophistication and interactions that were beyond the reach of science during Korzybski's time, his basic understanding of how the brain's structure can thwart clear thinking is accurate and represents an important, liberating step in learning to recognize stealth psychosocial pathologies. It demonstrates that our passion and zeal for how we think things are or ought to be may be the arbitrary result of the brain's structure.

Adhering to such arbitrary thoughts in the face of continuous contrary evidence or uncontrollable circumstances produces frustration and stress, and with repeated failure, depression. As children we learn lessons such as these over and again. We think we can't be happy unless we have a certain toy, item of clothing, or companion, yet we find other toys or interests that end up making us reasonably satisfied. Unfortunately for many, these lessons continue well into adulthood. If we don't make certain grades, or graduate from school by a certain time, or achieve the material or social status we feel we deserve, the disappointment and stress that register in the physiological mind can be devastating. In extreme cases, such continual frustration and stress can lead to suicide or homicide.

To brook this built-in problem, Korzybski recommended that people accept the fact that most ideas, especially unscientific opinions about politics and philosophy, inherently lack the rigor and detail necessary to be considered "truthful." Quietly and unemotionally observing and collecting as much data as possible before forming judgments was Korzybski's first rule to live by. Though sound enough advice, such unflaggingly scientific and empirical prescription was typical of a scientist in Korzybski's day, when inordinate faith in the ability of science to solve all problems was fashionable, perhaps a stealth psychosocial pathology of the very European, very male society to which Korzybski belonged.

Even so, his observations offer the Unified Fitness practitioner a glimpse into how stealth psychosocial pathologies can develop in individuals and why they persist socially in the face of sometimes overwhelming evidence to the contrary. In place of Korzybski's ultra-rational solution to the brain's structural tendency to blur feelings and ideas, Unified Fitness substitutes a coherent set of exercises that turn health into a sustainable resource. The practitioner's growing awareness of the nuances of health becomes Korzybski's "data," quietly observed and collected. In this way, Unified Fitness can create a more complete sense of fitness as a value, which often has to compete with other, health-draining values, linked to stealth psychosocial pathologies.

## Addiction

Addiction is one widespread psychosocial pathology whose stealth strategy is now well understood. The person addicted to smoking or alcohol or prescription drugs or food or sex or abusive relationships is at the mercy of a complex chemistry hard at work in the physiological mind. The addicted person's nervous system secretes natural opiates (classified as neurotransmitters), which have a powerful stimulating or calming effect on the body. After those chemicals dissipate, the addict repeats the behavior to regenerate the same secretions, self-medicating as it were. In the case of smoking, alcohol, and drugs, however, the mood-altering chemicals in the substances consumed magnify the work of natural opiates and complicate the addiction.

Because Unified Fitness, and reflective exercise in particular, affects the physiological mind in a way similar to that of addiction (that is, by enhancing the flow of neurotransmitters), it sometimes proves effective in helping people overcome their addictions. Though the addicted individuals I have worked with tended to need a lot of support, including psychotherapy, they have also fought the good fight and blazed for themselves a clearer path to sustainable health.

## Travis Triumphs over Alcoholism

The first day Travis, a former karate black belt, entered my school, his shoulders were thrown back in a defiant posture, but his face seemed filled with pain and sorrow. Travis had seen a public demonstration I had given a few years back and he was finally satisfying his curiosity.

> *Because Unified Fitness, and reflective exercise in particular, affects the physiological mind in a way similar to that of addiction (that is, by enhancing the flow of neurotransmitters), it sometimes proves effective in helping people overcome their addictions.*

Leery at first, I told him that I wasn't interested in teaching black belts unless they were willing to "empty their cup," that is, leave behind assumptions based on former training. Travis accepted this condition and began several years of what would be life-changing training.

Because of his background, Travis quickly learned the martial arts aspect of my program, and within nine months I felt comfortable introducing him to reflective exercise. By this time, I had learned that Travis was a talented, sensitive man who had been brought up in a violent urban setting in the Northeast. He worked by day as a home builder, but his passion was painting, and on several occasions he brought in his work for me to examine.

The drawings and paintings were realistic, composed in fine, sharp lines, but also exaggerated, full of gore and tenderness. One in particular told me a lot about Travis: a portrait of a sad older man, sitting in a chair; deep facial lines and shadows suggested a life of torment and disappointment. On a hill behind the old man stood the three crosses on which Jesus and the two criminals were crucified. Behind them were skyscrapers enveloped in flames. Blood poured from the three crucified figures and formed red rivers which flowed around and past the old man. The picture was called *Portrait of My Father*. It was a kind of memorial to the source of his problems.

The blend of violence, spiritual concern, and pain I saw in the painting were characteristic of Travis's life. The image of his father bespoke the self-hatred Travis had picked up in his early years, and the constant tension between his desire to paint and the need to provide a living for his family fed those self-destructive impulses. Karate had given him a way to express this tension through violence, but it had taken a toll on his physical and mental health. It also encouraged aggressive behavior in general, which threatened to spill over into his domestic life.

Compounding these psychological problems was Travis's use of alcohol, a habit he acquired as a teenager and allowed to persist into adulthood. Though he frequently quit, he was never able to stick with it for more than a couple of months. His habit was to drink on week-ends, but soon he found himself taking a drink on weekdays. The next thing he knew he was drinking every day.

One of the requirements for learning reflective exercise is that the practitioner abstain from alcohol during the training period (35 to 100 days, depending on the frequency of classes), because alcohol and all recreational drugs, upset the neurological integration between the tactile centers and the vagus nerve. Travis was anxious to get the healing effect of reflective exercise so he readily complied.

During the early stages of his training, Travis had a number of important psychological breakthroughs, most of which involved releasing sadness. But when he got to Rigorous Chaosercise, the damage he had done to his liver through alcohol abuse and living in a state of nervous tension, made itself clear. The cramps Rigorous Chaosercise produced under his right ribcage brought Travis to his knees many times. It took several months of dedicated reflective exercise for him to develop the sense that he was healing. Eventually the discomfort in his liver—he had learned to recognize it without having to move at all—faded away.

Once his reflective exercise skill was established, he took up Unified Fitness, adding a cardiovascular workout to help regain his stamina. He felt better than he had in many years, and that good feeling was a powerful incentive to stay away from the things that had taken away his health.

In spite of this, the built-in tensions of Travis's life (especially his unsatisfied urge to paint full time) produced problems from time to time. Squabbles with his wife over money, conflicts with coworkers, and his defeatist mentality pulled him back into destructive ways, including drinking. But the habit of reflective exercise was too compelling, and each time he practiced he was able to feel the losses inflicted by even slight indulgences. At this point, he bade alcohol goodbye, it was to be hoped, forever.

Soon Travis was able to understand how his emotions could weaken him just like alcohol did. He learned that reacting to adversity with rage was tantamount to taking a drink, so far as his liver was concerned, and so he experimented with other ways to express disappointment. He began to channel his anger and frustration through painting and sculpture. If someone made him mad, he might sit down and draw a cartoon, satirizing or ridiculing the individual. One of his achievements was a sculpture with a hand holding a hammer mounted on a massive spring. Once the spring was set, he placed delicate handmade figurines representing particular frustrations on a target-like platform, which the hammer would strike when the spring was released, smashing the little figurines to dust. Eventually these devices lost their appeal, and Travis's knee-jerk angry reactions to disappointments became ever less frequent.

## Elaine Escapes Abuse and Drug Addiction

Elaine bore one child out of wedlock and another in an unhappy, semi-abusive marriage from which she fled, only to end up in an even more abusive relationship with the leader of an American Indian cult. A former hippie and follower of several other Eastern cults before she had children, Elaine was attracted, as were many who lived through the 1960s and 1970s, to the romantic notions of American Indians as portrayed in movies such as *Little Big Man* and the more recent *Dances with Wolves*.

The reality of the group she fell into was one of drug, alcohol, and physical abuse, combined with powerful psychological experiences such as vision quests and sweat lodges conducted by both authentic and phony shamans. Though there was obviously much to dislike, the group afforded a great deal of high drama and excitement that kept the members stirred up, interested, and locked in. I came across this sad group after returning from China, so I was rather naïve about the impact of reflective exercise on emotions. As a result, I was unprepared to deal with many of the problems the group presented.

In the course of my association with Elaine, I learned a number of disturbing personal things that indicated to me she had been running from an unhappy childhood her whole life. Born out of an adulterous affair her mother had had with a man who was also married, Elaine wasn't treated as well as her other, legitimate siblings, despite the fact that she outshone them physically and mentally. At an early age, her alcoholic and abusive father left her mother, whose compulsive and undisciplined behavior exerted its influence over the home.

Elaine's treatment went from bad to worse, and to gain attention she resorted to the usual "bad girl" behavior of the time, such as wearing short skirts and staying out past her family's curfew. Her mother responded to these acts of defiance with violent punishment that included beatings with a belt. Small wonder that Elaine ended up with men who violently punished her.

After struggling to teach Elaine reflective exercise for a couple of months, I told her that if she didn't break free from her current circumstances, she would never succeed. To my surprise, Elaine listened. She left the cult and returned to mainstream society.

The first job she took was cleaning rooms in a hotel, a task far below her skills, but given the depression and addiction she struggled with daily, it was a miracle she stuck to it. One night she and another man who had distanced himself from the group sat down and wept in each other's arms over how badly they wanted to get high. Unfortunately, he lacked Elaine's resolve; a few months later he was doing drugs again. Elaine, on the other hand, had reflective exercise as a substitute, and she used it every day to reaffirm the importance of staying healthy.

Eventually, Elaine left the area to get away from the group, which continued to try to drag her back in. She went to school and then went into business for herself. During this time, reflective exercise and psychological counseling for both her children and her became centerpieces in Elaine's life. It took approximately three years, but Elaine emerged from a long nightmare into the light of a healthy existence.

## Depression and Addiction

Outlining the stealth psychosocial pathology of depression and addiction requires two other experts whose views reflect the thinking of the mental stealth pathologist. The first is sociologist Francis Fukuyama, whose book *The Great Disruption* extensively examines world social patterns over the past fifty years, when many social taboos and proprieties seemed to come apart. The second expert is psychotherapist Terrance Real, director of the Gender Studies Research Project at Harvard University and author of *I Don't Want To Talk About It: Overcoming the Legacy of Male Depression*. The combined insights of Fukuyama and Real illuminate both the cause and effect of a widespread stealth psychosocial pathology that stands in the way of any effort to achieve mental fitness.

Fukuyama's analysis of the Great Disruption focuses on the period from the 1960s through the 1980s, when the world saw an unprecedented rise in alcohol and drug addiction among the young. The same period also marked a time of social disintegration, when most of the traditions of the earlier part of the century, such as the nuclear family and community-based society, fell apart. Interestingly, this broad-scale breakdown wasn't just limited to the U.S. or even developed nations. It happened across socioeconomic boundaries.

In the U.S., the spread of substance addiction and soaring divorce rates were joined by the civil rights movement, the Vietnam war, and a number of public scandals to create a high level of cynicism toward once-respected institutions. Large numbers of people left the traditional churches, and state and national politics became the butt of jokes by late-night television comedians. Mistakes and failures by formerly crowning scientific achievements such as the nuclear power and chemical industries drew increasing public scorn and suspicion, as did such previous wonders of medicine as life-prolonging surgeries and treatment by antibiotics. For a long time, nothing substantial followed in the wake of this vast disillusionment, leaving only a great void. Now, according to Fukuyama, new social institutions and interpersonal relations are emerging to replace what was lost.

Though some aspects of the aftermath of the Great Disruption may have brought necessary and positive change (the civil rights movement), others such as family strife, divorce, and substance abuse have caused great harm. A recent study on the effect of divorce on children of the Great Disruption shows that most remain emotionally troubled into adulthood. Children from troubled or divorced families tend to have high rates of substance addiction, suggesting that given the opportunity, people will turn to addictive substances to alleviate sadness, a connection that the cases of both Travis and Elaine certainly bear out.

The Great Disruption in the U.S. may have spread a cloud of unacknowledged chronic sadness across the social landscape, a thesis supported indirectly by Terrance Real. Real identifies an epidemic of what he calls "covert depression," distinct from "clinical depression," which can include such signs as loss of appetite, lethargy, and insomnia. Covert depression is marked by psychosocial pathologies that have no apparent relationship to classic depression. Covertly depressed people might eat too much or too little. They might work too much, then have long bouts of lethargy or feckless irritability. They may abuse alcohol and drugs or manifest puritanical disdain for mood-altering substances, the main reason being they are already altering their mood by their excessive behavior, again "self-medicating," as it were.

According to Real, traditional notions of masculine virtue provide the greatest bastion of covert depression in American culture. In the twentieth century these notions stemmed from the aptly-named Great

Depression of the 1930s. Real infers that the Great Depression, with its sense of impending doom and manic work ethic, spawned a generation of covertly depressed people. If he is correct, then he may also have inadvertently uncovered an important source of the Great Disruption.

The Great Depression may have created a covertly depressed condition in his own father which was in turn passed on to Real and his brother. In describing his situation and comparing it to a number of other case studies, Real provides a window on how the two great social catastrophes may be related.

Dominated by a father who flew into inexplicable, violent rages, Real's growth to adulthood illustrates the Great Disruption. After drifting from drugs to failed romantic relationships, he finally discovered psychotherapy, which allowed him not only to restore his emotional health but to unravel a secret in his father's past during the Great Depression, one that was at the seat of his covert depression. As it turned out, Real's father was not only abandoned at a young age but was almost killed by his own father in a suicide attempt. This piece of information Real unearthed only after a dogged effort to heal his emotional wounds and to reach out to his father.

In addition to seeing much of the same forces at work in many of the people I've worked with, the story of my family accords with Real's thesis. My maternal grandmother earned my enmity when I was a child due to the beatings she was quick to administer for seemingly minor offenses. She was bossy and invasive of my privacy. The only thing I knew about her was that she ran a hotel during the Depression and that she lost her husband to heart disease before I was born. When I got older, I began to suspect that her annoying, aggressive behavior was probably linked to dismal experiences growing up on a Georgia farm. Though she was reluctant to talk about it, I remember her muttering angrily about "men" and what they did to "young women who tried to go out and make a living." Running the hotel during the Depression instilled in her a terror of poverty such that she never got over it, even though she died well off.

My paternal grandfather appeared to be a different story. We had what I considered a loving and trusting relationship. He also grew up on a Georgia farm and lived through the Depression, but, so far as my limited judgment was concerned, he showed no signs of abuse. Then one day, after gorging ourselves on my grandmother's Sunday dinner, we retired to the den where we customarily discussed the Bible and the breakdown of society. Though I secretly scoffed at many things my grandfather said, I enjoyed his taking the time for me. It gave me the chance to talk about confusing choices I faced, which in turn prompted him to remember his youth, which he rarely discussed. That day, my grandfather launched himself on an extraordinary description of how and why he had run away from home at fourteen.

One night, when everyone was asleep, he and a couple of his older brothers slipped out the window and made their way through the Georgia countryside into town, where a traveling carnival had set up. After observing what the carnival had to offer, they returned home. My grandfather was the first to climb back into the open window, where he was met with a broom handle, swung with such force it broke in half. He landed outside on his back, the wind knocked out of him. His brothers scattered. Framed in the window, brandishing the broken broom, was his father, cursing and trembling with rage. My grandfather got up, touched the goose egg that was beginning to form on his forehead, then walked away from home for good.

Years after my grandfather died, my father mailed me a photocopy of a letter my grandfather had written in the 1930s. For a man with little education, it was graceful and detailed. It told a story of a man who loved his family and worked hard to support them, but then found himself in such debt to the bank that he could see no better way to provide for his family than to drive his automobile off a bridge so that his family could then live off his life insurance policy. The letter concluded with the revelation that the man of the story was my grandfather and that Jesus had come into his life and helped him see that he need not die for his family.

Touched by this letter, my thoughts wove together three details: the boy who left home at fourteen; the near-suicidal man he would become thirty years later; and his son, my father, who at approximately the same age had also come close to killing himself so that his family could live off his life insurance policy.

My father had related his brush with suicide during the height of my alienation from him and the rest of my family, so I was unsympathetic and incapable of thinking through what his story said about me. Like my grandfather, my father pulled back from the act for religious reasons, claiming that he and another businessman, both distraught over failed enterprises, had been on the verge of throwing themselves out of the window of their hotel room. What saved them both was that Jesus intervened and encouraged them to go on with their lives, he told me.

I dismissed my father's confession as the ravings of a man reeling from multiple emotional shocks. It would take a great deal of healing for me to realize that, in spite of everything, my father was not much different from me and that the more I knew about him, the more I would learn about myself.

I was in the midst of such a realization when I returned home for my failed book signing. Just as I had decided to mend fences with my mother, so was I determined to do the same with my father, in spite of feeling that he had emotionally abandoned me years before he divorced my mother. I was also still smoldering with contempt for the poor judgment he showed in the way he told us about divorcing our mother.

The day before my mother revealed that my brother had died of a strep infection of the brain, my father and I drove from the suburbs to the swampy environs of the small town in which we had all been born. I tried not to notice the signs of my father's poor health. He was overweight, his complexion was mottled; stiffness around his shoulders and neck screamed that he was in pain. I talked instead of my divorce and my fears that my two small children were going to be affected by it. That kept us busy until we arrived.

The town had changed very little since we had lived there. My father opened up about his childhood. He said that during his fiftieth high school class reunion, he felt disconnected from those who extolled the "good old days." He had so hated high school that he couldn't wait for it to end so he could leave.

"Why?" I asked. "What was so terrible?"

"Work," he answered. "All I ever did was work for Daddy."

"How old were you when you started working?"

My father paused for a few seconds, then began to describe having to get up at four in the morning at the age of four or five to start a coal fire in the furnace. If he failed or was late doing the chore, his father beat him.

"Beat?" I asked.

My father nodded. "Once I thought he was going to kill me. He just went crazy."

As my father was telling me this, I felt inconsolably sad, and when I returned to my home and could lower my guard, I wept bitterly. With the help of psychotherapy and Real's book, I was able to make out the pattern of covert depression that began at least as far back as when my great-grandfather broke a broomstick across my grandfather's forehead. I understood why my father remained aloof, terrified that he would do to my brothers and me what his father had done to him. My father beat me only a handful of times, but I recall almost every one of the times, so traumatic were the experiences. My father's inherited depression, together with a similar condition my maternal grandmother had inadvertently inflicted on my mother, probably contributed to the violent behavior my older brother showed toward me, which I then dished out to my younger brother.

The combined insight of Fukuyama and Real suggests covert depression is a stealth psychosocial pathology, deeply rooted in American culture and possibly in others as well. Without an understanding of the way this problem resonates in the generations and our society as a whole, mental fitness, and fitness in general, will remain elusive. Virtually every person I have taught, and possibly everyone I have met, has shown some sign of having been touched by the Great Disruption, and most of those betray traces of covert depression. The people outlined in the previous case studies involving chronic illnesses showed even more blatant signs.

So what can the pursuer of sustainable health do about such a widespread, endemic stealth psychosocial pathology? A recent medical study suggests that simply looking into and acknowledging the link between emotion and disease can improve health. The study showed that when people suffering from asthma and rheumatoid arthritis wrote about an intense emotional experience, their disease symptoms decreased. Asthma and rheumatoid arthritis are chronic diseases found to have some association with troubled emotions.

These findings suggest that unresolved emotional distress may affect the physiological mind the way stress does. While reflective exercise can reverse the harmful biochemistry of stress hormones by activating the parasympathetic nervous system, buried feelings over past traumas represent a more complex problem. Buttressing reflective exercise with an understanding of stealth psychosocial pathologies such as covert depression and of how the structure of the brain makes us vulnerable to them provides part of a solution to the problem. The other part of the solution comes from taking action to structure a healthy balance between the constant, sometimes conflicting, needs of the mind.

## Greg Breaks the Drug Addiction-Depression Cycle

Greg was twenty years old when he began studying reflective exercise with me. At first Greg seemed a quiet and mature young man, but later I would learn a different story. A heavy marijuana user from his early teens, Greg was a charismatic man who had stayed in such perpetual trouble that his parents sent him to college as far away from the influence of his hometown as they could afford. Since arriving at the university, Greg had used his charisma to get in with student athletes and other powerful "lords" of the collegiate underground.

Unlike his newfound partners in debauchery, Greg had been punished enough by his drug experiences to respect the need for health. In his class with me, it took a long time for Greg to respond, but eventually he was able to use the lower abdominal pulse to combat infectious disease and to ameliorate a lower back injury he had sustained while playing lacrosse in high school.

The following two years went well for Greg, though he fell into depression and mild drug use whenever his hometown girlfriend, Amy, came to see him. Eventually he talked to me about his relationship with Amy. During high school, Greg had gotten Amy pregnant a couple of times, and each time she had secretly gotten an abortion. These were traumatic events, made worse, according to Greg, by Amy's Catholic upbringing. The experiences bonded them in a way that was as terrible as it was firm.

In his senior year at the university, Greg dropped out of my program for several months, then returned one day with his head hung contritely. He reported that in an impulsive fit of rebellion he had decided to give up pursuing health and resume partying and using drugs. One day, high as a kite, he rode his bike down a steep hill and cracked up. He woke in the hospital, his right leg encased in bandages, aching as though it had been cut wide open. As he lay there, he generated the lower abdominal pulse and sent it down his leg to the aching spot.

About a half hour later, a team of nurses and doctors entered the room and seemed shocked that Greg was awake. They told him that he had gashed open his leg in the bike wreck and that the wound had become severely infected. If they didn't open the wound at once and clean it, there was a danger they might have to amputate. Greg continued to send the pulse to the site of wound, and when the lead doctor examined the area, he couldn't find any trace of the infection, even though a series of blood tests had indicated it was present only a few hours earlier. Greg tried explaining what he had done, but they smiled patronizingly and ignored him. Out of gratitude for what he had learned, Greg returned to class and finished his senior year in relative peace.

## Gertrude's Struggle with Endometriosis and Low Self-Esteem

Gertrude walked into my studio with a shaved head and an unpronounceable Indian name. A tall, big-boned woman fifty to eighty pounds overweight, Gertrude worked as a nurse when she wasn't involved in her sect which used group meditations for healing. Prior to joining the sect, Gertrude had been a follower of a man who claimed to practice magic in the medieval tradition of the Cabala.

Nervous about the psychological problems Gertrude presented, I explained to her that I only worked with people who could put their commitment to reflective exercise first. Gertrude sat with an odd grin spread across her face. Fine, she said. She would quit the sect and drop the Indian name.

Though shocked by this sudden easy compliance, I was encouraged by her apparent willingness to cooperate, and I accepted Gertrude into a Taiji class, where I could teach unambiguous movements. Gertrude proved a difficult person to teach because she required a lot of attention, but she showed such determination to succeed that I didn't give up on her.

As her training progressed, Gertrude confided that she suffered from a number of health problems, from recurrent skin rashes to a strange flu-like illness that struck her down at least once a month during menstruation and whenever else she was under stress. The flu-like illness, she believed, was linked to endometriosis, with which she had been diagnosed several years previously. Endometriosis is a chronic gynecological problem marked by womb-lining tissue growing outside the womb. The condition is associated with menstrual cramps and non-uterine menstrual bleeding.

In Gertrude's opinion, stress was her big problem, but she also remarked that she could detect other people's "sick energy," which she believed contributed to her problem. Because of her job as a nurse in pediatric intensive care, stress was a given in her life. But her comment about "sick energy" made me suspicious that she might have been applying the methods of the mystical orders she had previously been involved with. When I pressed her on this, she revealed that over the years she had practiced energetic healing such as Reiki (a Japanese version of Qigong) and therapeutic touch (an approach that has gained popularity among nurses) on sick babies. There was little doubt in my mind that Gertrude's health problems and her efforts to effect magical healing on suffering infants—many of them in the throes of death—were related.

It took several months of conferencing and reflective training for Gertrude to become a believer in the approach, but once she did, reflective exercise became the center of her life and her health problems got better. She learned to swim and used brisk walking to reduce her weight. Her reflective exercise—especially Rigorous Chaosercise—began having an impact on her endometriosis. On the whole, Gertrude appeared to be on the upswing.

Nonetheless, Gertrude continued to demand an exorbitant amount of my time, both in class and in private conferences. One day I told her she needed some counseling to get a better handle on her health. Gertrude blinked as though I had scolded her, so I reiterated how pleased I had been with all her progress, but that I was concerned she might lose ground if she didn't get to the heart of what I saw as unresolved emotional issues.

*It took several months of conferencing and reflective training for Gertrude to become a believer in the approach, but once she did, reflective exercise became the center of her life and her health problems got better.*

"What issues?" she asked.

"Are you happy with yourself?" I responded.

Her answer amounted to half an hour of shrugs and evasive counter-questions, but finally I got her to admit that her relationship with her father, who had treated Gertrude distantly and unlovingly since childhood, was an unhappy one. Feeling as though I was at last getting somewhere with Gertrude and the problems blocking her mental fitness, I urged her to enter counseling and explore her feelings about her father.

I felt certain that Gertrude's former involvement with healing mystics, as well as her endometriosis and weight problem, had something to do her father, and that a little honest work in therapy would help her face and deal with both her troubled emotions and the health problem they had helped bring on. But my hopes faded when Gertrude's father passed away, making direct reconciliation impossible and any sort of critical thought about him unlikely.

A year passed, and Gertrude's progress crept to a halt. She began complaining that her reflective exercise practice had become ineffective. One day, when I was feeling out of sorts, I pulled Gertrude aside and told her that her practice had degenerated because of her unresolved emotional trouble. Gertrude blinked incredulously and pointed out that she had been in counseling for a year. When I refused to take the bait, she began a stream-of-consciousness monologue about her therapy. It was as though I wasn't there.

"How about your father?" I interjected at one point. "Have you dealt with your feelings for him?"

Gertrude shrugged, expressing in my view, a child's reluctance to face a simple but harsh truth. I backed away from giving Gertrude any more advice other than to keep working with her therapist, and dutifully she did.

I started paying less attention to Gertrude, who continued to complain regularly of the inefficacy of her practice. At the same time, she developed a keen interest in Christianity, deciding that all the time and energy she had devoted to Eastern methods were ill-spent. To my surprise, she began an earnest preparation to enter a nunnery. She showed up less and less for class. One day I received a letter from her, describing the peace she had found by becoming a novice. She thanked me for all I had taught her and expressed undying gratitude and best wishes for my students, family, and me.

Though a year later I learned that Gertrude had dropped out of the novice program—she had a personality conflict with the director—I still believe she is better off than she was prior to training in Unified Fitness. Her physical and immunological fitness improved, giving her a degree of control over a serious health problem, without the use of conventional drugs or surgery. Moreover, she gained insight into her mental problems. She dug deep down in herself and came close to facing a big source of her emotional turmoil, and she started a quest to get back to her spiritual roots, an inevitable phase in the pursuit of Unified Fitness.

# Chapter 9

## Exercise Series 5, A and B:
## Mapping the Mind and Using the Map

## The Parable of the Six Couples

Once upon a time, there were six couples who set sail together on a south Pacific cruise. Somewhere between the U.S. mainland and Hawaii, a storm drove the ship off course into remote waters. The ship sank and its captain and crew perished.

The six couples survived, however, and swam to safety, three to the south and three to the north. Each group landed on islands on either side of the shipwreck, with about two hundred yards between them. From the shore, the couples could see that the others had pulled through, but just as they were making plans to rejoin one another, hundreds of shark fins broke the surface of the water between the southern and northern islands where the ship had gone down.

Deciding to make the best of things, each couple set about exploring their new homes. Lush jungles covered both islands, and spectacular waterfalls cascaded from steep cliffs deep in their interiors. In spite of these similarities, each island had its own peculiar food sources. The southern island was rich in coconuts and mangoes. On the northern isle, papayas, bananas, and pineapples grew abundantly. Between the islands, seaweed flourished, but it was most abundant in the shallow water at one end of the southern island.

In time, the couples adapted to their island homes, but began to show marked differences in their food choices. On the southern island, one couple ate only coconuts. Another chose mangoes. Still another preferred seaweed and fish, which they managed to catch with primitive traps. On the northern island, one couple became papaya eaters, while the other two consumed bananas and pineapples.

The couples also began to behave in distinct ways. The coconut couple became focused on getting off the island, which they believed would happen only if a large signal fire were maintained on the beach. A few years earlier, the coconut couple had been trained in survival techniques, including primitive methods of making and maintaining fires. They spent most of their time gathering up driftwood to feed the fire and coconuts to feed themselves. Retrieving coconuts from the trees and then cracking them open took a lot of effort, but this helped to make them stronger, an effect they considered desirable in the event that circumstances ended up driving the couples against one another. But the main reason the coconut couple worked hard was because they wanted to be reunited with their loving family. Moreover, they believed the other couples felt the same about their loved ones and would be eternally grateful once everyone was rescued.

The mango-eating couple took a different tack on island life. A passionate couple to begin with, the mango eaters spent most of their time making love under the exotic waterfalls and among the beautiful pungent plants and trees. Aside from eating mangoes, they did little else. A serene sense of fulfillment enveloped them whenever they entered the foliage to make love. Amused by the coconut couple's devotion to building and maintaining a signal fire, the mango eaters were happier than they ever had been and couldn't imagine wanting to leave their island paradise.

The seaweed and fish couple spent most of their time watching the sea and their fish traps. They had chosen fish and seaweed as their primary foods because of their high nutritional value, particularly with respect to the brain. They wanted to keep their thinking clear at all times because they felt that their survival, as well as everyone else's, depended on it. Unfortunately, the sharks ate or scared away most of the fish, so the couple consumed a lot more seaweed than fish. They spent a great deal of time discussing this problem, along with how best to communicate with the other couples, especially the ones on the northern island, since their fellow southerners were absorbed with either love-making or fire-tending.

Eventually the seaweed-and-fish couple became determined to cross the shark-infested waters to connect with the couples on the northern island, but their progress was slow because they spent most of their time fishing. Their efforts were further slowed by the coconut couple's unwillingness to sacrifice part of their supply of driftwood so that the fisher couple could build a raft. The mango-eating couple provided no help because they were always making love.

On the northern island, the papaya-eating couple was similar in mind to the seaweed-and-fish couple, but the papaya eaters didn't have to worry as much about their food supply because it was so abundant. In fact, they had so much they constantly brought papayas and papaya juice to the other couples on the northern island. Even then, they had more than they could give away, so they began to turn their attention to the others on the southern island, who, from their two-hundred-yard perspective, appeared to be working fairly hard to get their food, especially the couple who stood on the shore and stared constantly across the water between the two islands. Filled with concern and having a great amount of free time, the papaya-eaters roamed the northern island in search of materials for a raft. They figured once the waters had been safely crossed, the six couples could work together effectively for the good of all.

The banana-eating couple didn't worry much about food because bananas were second in abundance only to papayas. They spent their spare time roaming the northern island where they built small camps. They established twelve campsites and spent a week at a time at each. During their stays, they developed art materials from the clay and plants, such as dyes and canvases woven from grasses. Once they had assembled these, they painted pictures of their campsites and of one another. They also worked with clay to make sculptures, and began to depict their companions in paint and sculpture. Though they tended to keep their distance, preferring each other's company, the seclusion of their campsites, and their painting and sculpting, the banana couple finally decided to lend their talents to the papaya couple's efforts to build a raft. The banana couple examined the raft's design and made suggestions that helped make the raft more seaworthy.

The pineapple couple also had no problem getting their food, so they had time to make a study of native plants and mushrooms for their healing effects. This interest arose because the man was suffering from a stomach ailment when the ship had gone down. Once ashore, the woman in this couple found a pineapple grove and fed some fruit to her feeble mate, who recovered in hours. The apparent healing effect of the pineapple put them on to an idea that plants, roots, and fungi growing around the pineapples might have similar properties. They spent much of their spare time testing this hypothesis.

The couple also devoted two hours a day to exercise and meditation, jogging along the beach or sitting with folded legs in the shade, ignoring the offerings of the papaya eaters or the artistic attentions of the banana couple. Because of these devotions, they learned to thrive on the island, achieving levels of health they had never before known. Eventually they developed ways to combine tropical plants with their pineapple diet to cure illness and injury, and discovered a mushroom-pineapple combination that retarded the effects of aging.

When they noticed that the raft-building efforts were taking a toll on the banana and papaya couples, the pineapple couple made an effort to teach the banana and papaya eaters how to take better care of themselves. The papaya couple was reluctant to devote so much time to themselves because they felt sacrifices had to be made for the sake of the south islanders. The banana couple also resisted spending a lot of time on their health because they wanted to complete the raft project. The pineapple couple argued that only by managing personal health could there be assurance that the escape operation would go smoothly . . . .

## Exercise 5A: Mapping the Mind

Before reading any further, try this exercise: get a sheet of paper and, without giving too much thought to the above story, label the couple

234

you liked or identified with the most on a scale of 1 to 6, with 1 being the best and 6 the least. Even if you liked more than one couple the same amount, make the tough choice of putting one ahead of the other. Write one number (1–6) beside each of the following: the coconut couple, the mango couple, the seaweed and fish couple, the papaya couple, the banana couple, and the pineapple couple.

Now read on to find out how to interpret your choices.

# The Six Themes of Mental Fitness

Each couple in the Parable of the Six Couples represents one of six themes that affect our psychological makeup. When I first began using these themes to help students think more deeply about themselves, I didn't rely on a story to soften the impact of the ideas. Gradually, I began to work with the symbolic approach to disarm deeply felt prejudices toward the names of the six themes.

I adapted the Parable of the Six Couples from a simpler story told to me by a traveling salesman when I was twenty. The salesman never revealed his source, yet when he finished sharing the story, along with the interpretation, I was startled by how well it unveiled human nature.

Over the years of teaching Unified Fitness, I began to combine the salesman's story with ideas taken from works of philosophy by Plato, Aristotle, Immanuel Kant, John Locke, Arthur Schopenhauer, John Stewart Mill, Friedrich Nietzsche, Bertrand Russell, and John Whitehead; from psychological essays and books by Sigmund Freud, William James, and B. F. Skinner; and finally from poems, plays, stories, essays, and novels that span the literary spectrum, from classical Greece and Rome to mid-twentieth century Britain and America. Works by William Blake, William Butler Yeats, Eugene O'Neill, Norman Mailer, and Walker Percy had particular influence on my thinking.

From this rich pool of authors, I sifted out what appeared to be six recurrent life themes that color all that is said and done. Expanding the salesman's parable to include the six themes provided a method of unobtrusively illuminating the mind and facilitating progress toward sustainable health.

The six themes represented by the six couples affect us with differing degrees of intensity, each tending to predominate at a particular time of life. Even so, all six coexist and can interact with one another at any given moment, making it hard to figure out what's going on. The two islands and the ensuing conflicts help dramatize these interthematic relationships. The southern island themes stem from deeply rooted impulses that dominate us in our youth. The northern island themes are more refined, related to the more basic themes of the south island, but achieving their fulfillment in later, more adult stages of development.

Of the south island themes, the coconut couple stands for *empowerment* or the need for a sense of control. While an ongoing concern throughout life, empowerment is especially crucial in early development. Infants struggling to become toddlers expend tremendous effort trying to move about, to travel across a room and get their hands on some object that captures their fancy. This is a simple power that able-bodied young and middle-age adults take for granted (elderly and disabled adults know better). In addition to the physical limits imposed by childhood, parents and caregivers constantly remind children that they are helpless. Loving assurances of adult guardians can soften the often frustrating, sometimes heartbreaking experience of childhood fecklessness, thus giving children a sense of security and a foundation upon which to build a sense of empowerment. A lack of nurturing assurance may lead some to have an inordinate or unslakable thirst for power in later stages of life.

The mango couple represents *sexuality*, another key determinant of psychological development. The ages of twelve through fourteen usually mark the onset of puberty, the beginning of hormonal and social tyranny of sex over the teenager, shaping identity and self-esteem before completion of high school. The degree to which teenage sexual worries are negotiated may determine the role sexuality plays in later life. The sexually blocked or unsuccessful teenager may find future choices driven either directly or indirectly by sex, leading to relationships that can either satisfy or sadden, depending very often on pure luck. Sex dominates well into middle age, and as the infidelities, promiscuity, and divorce rates that characterized the Great Disruption seem to suggest, social boundaries prove a poor match for an unrequited libido. But if given their due, successful sexual relationships provide deep satisfaction and bolster well-being on virtually every level.

The seaweed and fish couple constitutes *intelligence,* or our drive to make ourselves understood by others. The drive for intelligence may in fact be a natural outgrowth of earlier struggles with power and sex, a maturation that stems from trying to make sense out of the chaos of less articulate drives. But once into our teens, the acquisition of intelligence and intelligence symbols such as grades and test scores can profoundly affect self-worth and quality of life. In adulthood, academic degrees become even stronger determinants of social worth.

Though intelligence covers a broad swath of possible subjects, communication is the common denominator, from the most basic level involving salesmanship to the upper reaches of high-energy physics and applied mathematics. However intelligence is applied, failure to come to successful terms with it can, like sexuality, linger into stages of life long after the grades have been given out.

The more refined themes of the north island affect life most dramatically in the middle and later stages, though they can and do exert themselves in the younger stages as well. The papaya couple represents *altruism*, which typically manifests as a consistent behavior in the late twenties to mid-thirties, a time when most people think about settling down, if not with a family, then with a significant other or with a career that accomplishes a larger sense of purpose. This is not to say that altruism doesn't play a part in early development. In fact, learning at an early age to sacrifice personal desire on behalf of another may determine success or failure regarding the theme of altruism.

The banana couple symbolizes *creativity*, which not only includes the self-indulgent finger-painting acts of youth but also the weightier acts of imagination that creative geniuses often display in their middle years. Most famous painters, novelists, and thinkers of almost every type who had to struggle to produce in their early years gain a newfound facility of expression in middle age that often leads to their most significant work. Unfortunately, most people experience a slow decline in creativity in their middle years. Jobs that were once a challenge or altruistically driven become rote and unsatisfactory. Marriages seem similarly stifling and unfulfilling. Psychosocial pathologies such as alcohol and drug addiction or compulsive behaviors such as fanatic work, travel, or consumerism may crest as well.

These bleak experiences may be the oblique result of languishing creativity, needing a final good challenge to justify an increasingly ominous sense that the end of a long struggle is coming into view. When the sense of stagnation grows too oppressive, buried creativity may find expression in the much-discussed "midlife crisis," an outburst that shakes apart habits, routines, and even self-concept, sometimes to the detriment of the person in crisis. Thus, discovering a wholesome outlet for creative urges that carry well into midlife is especially crucial to mental fitness.

The theme of *health*, represented by the pineapple couple, exerts such an influence on our lives that it's fairly easy to see why the philosopher Plato (or his mentor Socrates) considered it the greatest human virtue. Unfortunately, most of us take health for granted, rarely if ever understanding that all energy expenditures draw upon this most precious resource. Even if our health is threatened, we go right back to ignoring it once the threat passes. We maintain this carefree attitude at our own peril. If we're fortunate enough to make it to old age, then what might be a small accident for a teenager or even a middle-aged person, such as slipping and falling on an icy sidewalk, can mean the beginning of fast-track degeneration and monstrous healthcare costs. Thus, sooner or later, we all come to see Plato's point or pay a heavy price for our blindness.

The chronological and developmental relationship between the six themes can be illustrated with an elliptical diagram, in much the same way the phases of the moon are depicted.

This schematic permits the illustration of another broad division between the themes. Themes on the left side of the ellipse—namely *empowerment* and *health*—are *self*-oriented, while themes on the right—*intelligence* and *altruism*—are *other*-based. The themes of

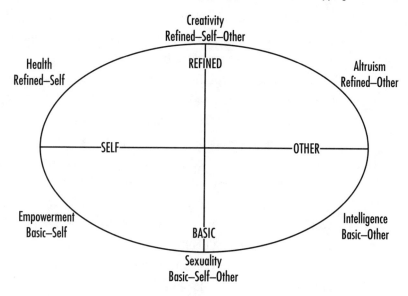

Creativity
Refined–Self–Other

Health
Refined–Self

Altruism
Refined–Other

REFINED

SELF

OTHER

Empowerment
Basic–Self

Intelligence
Basic–Other

BASIC

Sexuality
Basic–Self–Other

## Map of the Six Themes

*sexuality* and *creativity* can swing either way, which is to say sexual and creative acts can fulfill either the self or others, depending on the influence of the other four themes. Perfectly balanced sexuality and creativity register on both sides of the thematic spectrum between self and other.

Combined with the other two broad categories under which the six themes can be grouped—"basic" versus "refined" drives—the "self" and "other" categories provide a means of further decoding thematic patterns that can be visually depicted in the elliptical diagram as triangulations. To examine your particular triangulations, write the number of each couple you rated in Exercise 5A, Mapping the Mind, beside the corresponding themes depicted in the diagram. Next, connect numbers 1, 2, and 3 with a triangle, then do the same with 4, 5, and 6. Numbers 1, 2, and 3 represent a triangulation of themes that most likely dominates your mental outlook, while numbers 4, 5, and 6 generally exert less influence.

The lines you trace provide nonjudgmental geometric pictures of the psychological forces at work in your life. For example, if your first three choices are the coconut couple (empowerment), the fish and seaweed couple (intelligence), and the banana couple (creativity), you should draw a triangle connecting the three themes on the ellipse. If your second three choices are the pineapple couple (health), the papaya couple (altruism), and the mango couple (sexuality), then you should connect those three themes with a similar triangle. Such a set of triangulations shows a balance between "basic" and "refined" drives, as well as between "self" and "other" orientation.

On the other hand, if your choices are either all basic or all refined, a flatter, less comprehensive triangulation is established, an image for the impact such a clustering of themes is likely to have on your life. Taller triangles, conversely, signify diversity and dimension, which may be just the thing you need to broaden and liberate your mind from stultifying habits.

There are 120 triangulations possible among the six themes, and they are presented at the end of this section as twenty different matrices, which can be further broken down in terms of "basic" and "refined" drives, as well as "self" or "other" orientations. The number of these thematic combinations gives us an idea of the complex psychological possibilities at work in our lives.

Laying out the six themes shows us the full range of our own psychological potential, and it permits a degree of evaluation in what is essentially a non-evaluative process. For example, a triangulation between only "south island" themes (empowerment, sexuality, and intelligence) suggests these more basic themes might overshadow the more refined themes of the "north island" (altruism, creativity, and health).

Moreover, primary triangulation between south island themes bodes for a mindset that is likely to be more self- than other-oriented, because self-concern is more basic than concern for others. Replacing south island behaviors and thinking patterns with new activities, persons, places, and even ideas that involve the north island themes would help remedy the imbalances suggested by this basic, self-oriented triangulation. The problem lies in accurately matching themes with action and behavior.

# Possible Triangulations among the Six Themes

On page 242, the matrix of potential triangulation among the six themes provides a fast way to decode your response to the Parable of the Six Couples in terms of the level (basic-refined) and orientation (self-other) each theme signifies. These four level-and-orientation categories give you additional understanding of the function of each theme and help you see balances and imbalances in triangulations. Also, decoding themes according to level-and-orientation categories proves useful in the next mental exercise, which examines what themes permeate your daily routine.

After locating your particular set of triangulations, use the following level-and-orientation key to reclassify each theme:

- Empowerment: Basic-Self (BS)
- Sexuality: Basic-Self-Other (BSO)
- Intelligence: Basic-Other (BO)
- Altruism: Refined-Other (RO)
- Creativity: Refined-Self-Other (RSO)
- Health: Refined-Self (RS)

## Exercise 5B: Using the Map

The daily planner lends strong support to the maxim that actions reflect the inner life, and using a daily planner can give you an objective expression of how and what you think. Exercise 5A, Mapping the Mind, can help you interpret the themes motivating that expression.

Exercise 5B, Using the Map, requires that you purchase or create a daily planner, with any given day divided into thirty-minute intervals. Begin the schedule with waking up, and end it with going to bed. Fill in each interval of one full day with brief descriptions of your typical activities. No matter how mundane or obvious, interpret each half-hour interval with one or more of the six themes. Look for thematic pairings, triangulations, and even quadrangulations across basic, refined, self, and other boundaries of the mental ellipse depicted on page 239.

241

# The Six Themes of Mapping the Mind—In Various Combinations

| | | | | | |
|---|---|---|---|---|---|
| Empowerment<br>Sexuality<br>Intelligence | Empowerment<br>Intelligence<br>Sexuality | Sexuality<br>Empowerment<br>Intelligence | Sexuality<br>Intelligence<br>Empowerment | Intelligence<br>Empowerment<br>Sexuality | Intelligence<br>Sexuality<br>Empowerment |
| Empowerment<br>Sexuality<br>Health | Empowerment<br>Health<br>Sexuality | Sexuality<br>Empowerment<br>Health | Sexuality<br>Health<br>Empowerment | Health<br>Empowerment<br>Sexuality | Health<br>Sexuality<br>Empowerment |
| Empowerment<br>Creativity<br>Health | Empowerment<br>Health<br>Creativity | Creativity<br>Empowerment<br>Health | Creativity<br>Health<br>Empowerment | Health<br>Empowerment<br>Creativity | Health<br>Creativity<br>Empowerment |
| Empowerment<br>Sexuality<br>Creativity | Empowerment<br>Creativity<br>Sexuality | Sexuality<br>Empowerment<br>Creativity | Sexuality<br>Creativity<br>Empowerment | Creativity<br>Empowerment<br>Sexuality | Creativity<br>Sexuality<br>Empowerment |
| Empowerment<br>Sexuality<br>Altruism | Empowerment<br>Altruism<br>Sexuality | Sexuality<br>Empowerment<br>Altruism | Sexuality<br>Altruism<br>Empowerment | Altruism<br>Empowerment<br>Sexuality | Altruism<br>Sexuality<br>Empowerment |
| Empowerment<br>Creativity<br>Altruism | Empowerment<br>Altruism<br>Creativity | Creativity<br>Empowerment<br>Altruism | Creativity<br>Altruism<br>Empowerment | Altruism<br>Empowerment<br>Creativity | Altruism<br>Creativity<br>Empowerment |
| Empowerment<br>Intelligence<br>Altruism | Empowerment<br>Altruism<br>Intelligence | Intelligence<br>Empowerment<br>Altruism | Intelligence<br>Altruism<br>Empowerment | Altruism<br>Empowerment<br>Intelligence | Altruism<br>Intelligence<br>Empowerment |
| Empowerment<br>Intelligence<br>Creativity | Empowerment<br>Creativity<br>Intelligence | Intelligence<br>Empowerment<br>Creativity | Intelligence<br>Creativity<br>Empowerment | Creativity<br>Empowerment<br>Intelligence | Creativity<br>Intelligence<br>Empowerment |
| Empowerment<br>Intelligence<br>Health | Empowerment<br>Health<br>Intelligence | Intelligence<br>Empowerment<br>Health | Intelligence<br>Health<br>Empowerment | Health<br>Empowerment<br>Intelligence | Health<br>Intelligence<br>Empowerment |
| Empowerment<br>Health<br>Altruism | Empowerment<br>Altruism<br>Health | Health<br>Empowerment<br>Altruism | Health<br>Altruism<br>Empowerment | Altruism<br>Empowerment<br>Health | Altruism<br>Health<br>Empowerment |

| | | | | | |
|---|---|---|---|---|---|
| Sexuality<br>Creativity<br>Health | Sexuality<br>Health<br>Creativity | Creativity<br>Sexuality<br>Health | Creativity<br>Health<br>Sexuality | Health<br>Sexuality<br>Creativity | Health<br>Creativity<br>Sexuality |
| Sexuality<br>Intelligence<br>Creativity | Sexuality<br>Creativity<br>Intelligence | Intelligence<br>Sexuality<br>Creativity | Intelligence<br>Creativity<br>Sexuality | Creativity<br>Sexuality<br>Intelligence | Creativity<br>Intelligence<br>Sexuality |
| Sexuality<br>Intelligence<br>Altruism | Sexuality<br>Altruism<br>Intelligence | Intelligence<br>Sexuality<br>Altruism | Intelligence<br>Altruism<br>Sexuality | Altruism<br>Sexuality<br>Intelligence | Altruism<br>Intelligence<br>Sexuality |
| Sexuality<br>Health<br>Altruism | Sexuality<br>Altruism<br>Health | Health<br>Sexuality<br>Altruism | Health<br>Altruism<br>Sexuality | Altruism<br>Sexuality<br>Health | Altruism<br>Health<br>Sexuality |
| Sexuality<br>Intelligence<br>Health | Sexuality<br>Health<br>Intelligence | Intelligence<br>Sexuality<br>Health | Intelligence<br>Health<br>Sexuality | Health<br>Sexuality<br>Intelligence | Health<br>Intelligence<br>Sexuality |
| Sexuality<br>Creativity<br>Altruism | Sexuality<br>Altruism<br>Creativity | Creativity<br>Sexuality<br>Altruism | Creativity<br>Altruism<br>Sexuality | Altruism<br>Sexuality<br>Creativity | Altruism<br>Creativity<br>Sexuality |
| Intelligence<br>Altruism<br>Creativity | Intelligence<br>Creativity<br>Altruism | Altruism<br>Intelligence<br>Creativity | Altruism<br>Creativity<br>Intelligence | Creativity<br>Intelligence<br>Altruism | Creativity<br>Altruism<br>Intelligence |
| Intelligence<br>Creativity<br>Health | Intelligence<br>Health<br>Creativity | Creativity<br>Intelligence<br>Health | Creativity<br>Health<br>Intelligence | Health<br>Intelligence<br>Creativity | Health<br>Creativity<br>Intelligence |
| Intelligence<br>Altruism<br>Health | Intelligence<br>Health<br>Altruism | Altruism<br>Intelligence<br>Health | Altruism<br>Health<br>Intelligence | Health<br>Intelligence<br>Altruism | Health<br>Altruism<br>Intelligence |
| Altruism<br>Creativity<br>Health | Altruism<br>Health<br>Creativity | Creativity<br>Altruism<br>Health | Creativity<br>Health<br>Altruism | Health<br>Altruism<br>Creativity | Health<br>Creativity<br>Altruism |

Activities that appear to involve triangulations and quadrangulations cover more of the mental map, and therefore should be considered more balanced than activities that seem inspired by only one or two themes.

For most adults, work represents the predominant waking activity, and as such it must be carefully examined for possible "multiple-angulations." At first blush, work seems to be a straightforward empowerment and/or altruistic issue: what we have in lieu of survival, the means by which we feed, clothe, and house our families and ourselves. It can provide us with a supreme sense of self-worth and social standing, or it can be a source of shame and isolation. But work can also involve creativity, health, intelligence, and sexuality at different times of the day.

A ten o'clock meeting may require that you show more intelligence and/or creativity than at other times. Health may govern your choices of food during breakfast at home, but lunch at work may be more of a social affair (intelligence or altruism), when you sacrifice good nutrition for the camaraderie and atmospherics of a nearby diner. Later in the day, from two o'clock till quitting time, may be less demanding than the morning, limited to rote tasks that allow you to indulge in idle thoughts or gossip with coworkers. Sexuality may influence this relative down time, but altruism, intelligence, and empowerment may operate as well. Thus, any accurate thematic assessment of work behavior must be both specific and brutally honest.

Work isn't the only activity requiring specificity and honesty. For example, you may tell others that attending a dance class is for health, empowerment, and creativity, but an important but unmentionable reason may be because the teacher or a classmate is sexually titillating. You should also be able to recognize which theme predominates in apparent pairings and multiple-angulations. For a person employed by a nonprofit organization, for example, work may appear to fulfill empowerment and altruistic themes, but the main impetus may have mostly to do with job security, clearly an empowerment issue.

Once you've scheduled and thematically interpreted a full day, proceed to do the same for the rest of the week. In the case of most adults, there will be a lot of repetition. If your score on Exercise 5A is accurate, the majority of activities on your weekly schedule should reflect your first, second, and third choices of themes. Circle intervals of time with thematic activities that repeat every day or that you feel you can do without.

On a separate sheet of paper, list activities you feel reflect at least one of the thematic choices that would help you achieve a taller, more inclusive triangulation on the elliptical map of Exercise 5A. Start modestly. Don't overload yourself with activity changes you know you can't sustain. Then refer back to circled intervals of time on your schedule where you can realistically substitute the new activity. Once a new activity gives a theme greater expression on a regular basis, you can substitute additional activities to support the new theme or to introduce another, neglected theme.

If your weekly calendar doesn't match with your results from Exercise 5A, Mapping the Mind, your task is a little more difficult. First you have to face the possibility of a disparity between the way things are and the way you wish they were. For example, someone with a deep yearning to feel powerful might perceive the socially admirable behavior of the papaya couple (altruism) as something that could bring praise and attention from others, turning what is supposed to capitulate selflessness into self-service. Thus, such a person may have ranked the papaya couple in the first group of choices, yet in his or her personal life there is little altruistic activity. Such disparities between Exercises 5A and B suggest a life destined for confusion and dissatisfaction.

In such cases, the first step is to ferret out the source of the confusion. A stealth psychosocial pathology could be the culprit, but its roots may run far back into childhood while its thorns and prickly leaves thrust into the present through a bad marriage, covert depression, or substance addiction. Whatever the source, clearing up the confusion may take some time, as well as some professional counseling. But, once the actual thematic meaning of the predominant behavior is clarified, the person can use Exercises 5A and B with greater efficacy. If the disparity resolves with little trouble, then the person can reconfigure the triangulations on the elliptical map and see more clearly what thematic changes are needed for greater mental balance.

The inherent subjectivity of mental fitness permits yet another disparity that may escape detection in either Exercise 5A or B. In this case, basic themes can disguise themselves as refined, and vice versa, probably to maintain a stealth psychosocial pathology. For example, mistreatment in childhood could cut an individual off from satisfying the empowerment theme, but, like a stream of water following the natural slope of the land, the need to feel powerful may assert itself covertly, perhaps through passive-aggressive behavior.

Imagine such an individual finding her way into working with the poor and underprivileged. On the outside, she may appear to be living by the theme of altruism, but on the inside, the real motive is to feel superior to or hold power over essentially powerless people. In such a case, the disparity would only show up in the nuances of daily life, such as contemptuous statements toward or mistreatment of the ones supposedly being served. Supervisors, coworkers, or those on the receiving end of the contempt and mistreatment might help illuminate the problem with evaluations or direct confrontation, but it is unlikely that anyone except the person generating the disparity would be motivated to resolve it.

The friction that such stealth disparities are likely to produce usually ensures that the person with the problem suffers in some way, probably in the form of stress. When the stress becomes great enough, the impetus to seek help and improve the situation increases. Failure to stop the stress leads to illness, forcing the theme of health into the center of attention. Unfortunately, at this point health becomes more than a physical and immunological issue. Imbalances in the six themes must be clarified. More often than not, this means confronting the nature of the stealth psychosocial pathology. Without the assistance of a professional counselor, such a situation is very unlikely to improve.

## A Guide for Daily Mental Balance

Apart from Exercises 5A and B, the six themes can serve as a kind of psychological menu for daily living. Each day, try to think and act in ways that touch on each theme. Make an effort to insure that your drives for self-assurance, sexual satisfaction, effective communication, helping others, ingenuity, and good health find some sort of outlet, which in turn can help balance the tension between the demands of self- and other-oriented themes. If daily fulfillment is impossible for some themes, make a commitment to nurture those neglected themes at a later time. If at a loss as to how to meet such a commitment, talk with trusted friends or seek professional help. You may find that another perspective reveals more of a particular theme than you realized. You may think your life is filled with a particular theme and yet others see it differently.

Not surprisingly, most people I work with tend to prioritize health in their responses to the Parable of the Six Couples. After all, they've come to me seeking improved health or athletic performance. The majority have arrived at such a high opinion of health because for many years they have neglected it. Regardless of why they chose to neglect health, all of them benefited from familiarizing themselves with the six themes and their influence on the quest for Unified Fitness.

On page 249, the sample of Exercise 5B, Using the Map, offers an ideal work-oriented day, with Unified Fitness sessions (thus, the theme of health) serving as bookends. During work, abbreviated reflective exercise provides a way to constantly build immunological fitness. The schedule presumes several lifestyle factors you may have to adjust. First, the schedule includes activities with either a family or romantic partner. Second, the work itself is generically office- and information-based, thus bringing into play the intellectual theme. If your job involves more physical activity, you can adapt the schedule by either substituting or adding the themes of health and empowerment to the thematic interpretations of working intervals.

Because generating information requires at least two vital stages—individual creation of ideas and the sharing of those ideas with peers and supervisors—creativity, intelligence, empowerment, and altruism are thematic constants in the sample schedule. While both stages of information generation draw on creativity, the solitary and primary nature of the individual creation stage suggests the self-oriented theme of empowerment. Other-oriented altruism is more of a driving force behind peer and supervisory review.

The two stages have a chronology (individual creation followed by peer/supervisory review) that matches the thematic order (empowerment first, intelligence second, altruism third), which suggests each information-generating activity is best suited to particular times of day. As the first part of the day, and an analog of the mind's early struggle with empowerment, morning is probably the best time for individual creation, whereas the afternoon, the day's equivalent of a more mature, socially interactive mind, is best spent in group efforts to sharpen, refine, and edit raw ideas.

If the above logic seems unconvincing, try thinking on a more practical, experiential level. Take the "morning person," for example, whose exuberance early in the day may get squandered in rambling conversations and gossip sessions with coworkers. Having that high energy focused on creating job-related ideas is probably a better use of both the morning person's and everyone else's time. By the same token, spending the morning hours puzzling through assignments alone, rather than negotiating social pressure from peers or supervisors, probably serves the best interests of the non-morning person.

If you don't reserve the morning for individual creativity and the afternoon for peer/supervisor discussion, give it a try and see for yourself. If you don't have this sort of fine control over your work schedule, suggest this thematic schedule arrangement to management. Chances are such an arrangement is likely to make you and everyone else with such a schedule change more productive and make work less of a health drain.

# SAMPLE DAILY SCHEDULE

| TIME | DAILY ROUTINE | PRACTICE | THEMES |
|---|---|---|---|
| 6:30 AM | rise, drink green tea, go to bathroom | Unified Fitness | RS, BS, RSO |
| 7:30 AM | shower | | RS, BS, BO |
| 8:00 AM | eat breakfast, | | RS, RO, BSO, |
| | converse with family or companion, | | BS, BO, RO |
| | prepare for work | | |
| 8:30 AM | drive to work | Exercises 2A and 3B | BO, RS, BS |
| 9:00 AM | work | Exercises 2A and 3B | BS, RSO, BO, RS |
| 9:30 AM | work | Exercises 2A and 3B | BS, RSO, BO, RS |
| 10:00 AM | work | Exercises 2A and 3B | BS, RSO, BO, RS |
| 10:30 AM | | Exercises 2B, 3A, 3B, or 4C (for a total of 15 minutes) | RS, BS, RSO |
| 10:45 AM | work | Exercises 2A and 3B | BS, RSO, BO, RS |
| 11:00 AM | work | Exercises 2A and 3B | BS, RSO, BO, RS |
| 11:30 AM | work | Exercises 2A and 3B | BS, RSO, BO, RS |
| Noon | lunch | | RS, RO, BO |
| 12:30 PM | read or relax | | RS, RSO, BO |
| 1:00 PM | work | Exercises 2A and 3B | BO, RSO, RO, RS |
| 1:30 PM | work | Exercises 2A and 3B | BO, RSO, RO, RS |
| 2:00 PM | work | Exercises 2A and 3B | BO, RSO, RO, RS |
| 2:30 PM | work | Exercises 2A and 3B | BO, RSO, RO, RS |
| 3:00 PM | work | Exercises 2A and 3B | BO, RSO, RO, RS |
| 3:30 PM | work | Exercises 2B, 3B, or 4C (for a total of 15 minutes) | RS, BS, RSO |
| 3:45 PM | work | Exercises 2A and 3B | RS, BS, RSO |
| 4:00 PM | work | Exercises 2A and 3B | BO, RSO, RO, RS |
| 4:30 PM | work | Exercises 2A and 3B | BO, RSO, RO, RS |
| 5:00 PM | work | Exercises 2A and 3B | BO, RSO, RO, RS |
| 5:30 PM | work | Exercises 2A and 3B | BO, RSO, RO, RS |
| 6:00 PM | drive home | Exercises 2A and 3B | BO, RS, BS |
| 6:30 PM | eat dinner, interact with family | | RS, BO, RO |
| 7:00 PM | clean up after meal | Exercises 2A and 3B | RO, BO, RS |
| 7:30 PM | rest, entertainment | Exercises 2A and 3B | RO, RSO, RS |
| 8:00 PM | rest, entertainment | Exercises 2A and 3B | RO, RSO, RS |
| 8:30 PM | prepare family and self for bed | Exercises 2A and 3B | RO, BO, RS |
| 9:00 PM | | Reflective exercise: 2B, 4B, 3C, 3D, and 4C (for approximately 30 minutes) | RS, BS, RSO |
| 9:30 PM | intimate time with companion | Exercise 2A | BSO, BS, RO, RS |
| 10:00 PM | | Exercises 2A, 3C, and 3D (for 10 minutes) | RS, BS, RSO |
| 10:10 PM | rest, entertainment | Exercises 2A and 3B | RSO, RO, RS |
| 10:30 PM | sleep | | |

| | | |
|---|---|---|
| RS – Health | Exercise 2A: Reverse Abdominal | Exercise 3B: Sensing the Middle |
| BS – Empowerment | Breathing | Center |
| RSO – Creativity | Exercise 2B: Six Subtle Movements | Exercise 4B: Gentle Chaosercise of |
| BSO – Sexuality | Exercise 3A: Standing Reflective | the Three Centers |
| BO – Intelligence | Meditation | Exercise 4C: Acupressure Massage |
| RO – Altruism | | |

# *Marybeth Gains a New Appreciation for Health*

Marybeth had once been a minor movie star and stage performer who gained the attention of a wealthy and successful architect. She married the architect and took his last name, settling into the role of dutiful wife and mother with only a modicum of discomfort. Then her husband was struck down by a mysterious autoimmune disease that crippled him, and in spite of all the advantages of wealth, Marybeth's life grew increasingly restrictive and emotionally painful.

By the time I began working with her, she had been through several years of psychotherapy, in which she had worked out sexual abuse issues. A number of alternative healers had prescribed massage and herbs for a condition she had that was similar to her husband's autoimmune disease: muscular aches, pains in the back and shoulders, and an intermittent numbness in the extremities.

Marybeth insisted that we work out of her home, and she was enthusiastic about learning reflective exercise. After our third session, she invited me to have dinner with her husband and her so I could explain the process to him.

The husband, though bright and courageous, exhibited a hardened cynicism toward both reflective exercise and the idea that health problems represent something more than chance interactions between a complex array of multiple factors. My suggestion that he might benefit from learning—which was Marybeth's reason for having him meet me—bounced off him like a marble thrown against an armored tank. His opinion of meditation was that it was a waste of time. It was far better to be working on behalf of a greater good.

Marybeth was disappointed in her husband's reaction, and later, as our sessions progressed, she confided her feelings about her situation. Some of those feelings had to do with giving up a promising career, but mostly she seemed resentful for the impositions her husband's disease had made on her life. Though clearly capable of shouldering the physical burdens of her husband's disease, Marybeth seemed especially put out with tangential concerns that only a person in her predicament would know. She resented the early years of her husband's disease, when she had to lie to everyone about why he was late or absent or walking with a cane. To keep their medical insurance from being canceled, she had to fend off company probes and plead with doctors to join in her effort to keep the matter from spinning out of control.

As Marybeth voiced these feelings, her commitment to reflective exercise seemed to increase. At the same time, her husband turned up the volume on his cynical comments to her about her efforts, and showed greater disrespect for the time she set aside to practice, interrupting her without hesitation over minor questions or problems that could have been dealt with later.

In addition to warning Marybeth to expect greater disruption and resentment from her husband, I invited her to take part in an exercise similar to the Parable of the Six Couples. Writing out the name of the six themes on six slips of paper, I asked her to arrange each slip in a vertical column, with her first choice at the top. Predictably, she rated health first, but the other top two were altruism and creativity, respectively. All were north island, refined themes. Empowerment was her fourth choice, and she later confessed that she wanted to rank it with her first three but felt that doing so showed insensitivity to others and self-absorption.

Marybeth's response told me a number of things. Her urge to represent empowerment demonstrated that her therapist had done a good job in helping her fight against the sense of powerlessness that haunts sexually abused children into adulthood. But her response also told me the psychotherapist hadn't gone far enough. The more basic themes of the "south island" lacked influence in Marybeth's life. We discussed the merits of looking out for one's self at the expense of others, a delicate issue for someone with a chronically sick husband. Still, I insisted that by taking care of herself, she could

*Practicing reflective exercise, working with psychotherapy, and seeing her various healers were all ways of balancing out a situation that was forcing her into an extraordinary emphasis on altruism, in other words, for caring for her sick husband to the point of damaging her own health.*

do more to help others over time. Practicing reflective exercise, working with psychotherapy, and seeing her various healers were all ways of balancing out a situation that was forcing her into an extraordinary emphasis on altruism, in other words, for caring for her sick husband to the point of damaging her own health.

My warnings that Marybeth's husband would become more of an interference proved accurate. But Marybeth persisted and actually got better. This encouraged me to continue working with her beyond the schedule I had originally laid out. We moved our practices to my office, and once removed from the controlled domain of her house, I began noticing that certain basic behaviors in Marybeth could have been causing or at least contributing to some of her symptoms. For instance, she lugged around an enormous satchel which pulled her musculoskeletal system down on one side. When I asked her to explain the need for such a tremendous burden, her answers were vague and unsatisfactory, especially in light of the fact that the satchel was hurting her. I suspected the satchel was a symptom of a stealth psychopathology.

Marybeth refused to give up her heavy load until I offered my interpretation of the satchel. I suggested that she may have laden herself with the appearance of having a "bundle" of things to take care of in order to justify leaving the house and her sick husband, effectively maiming herself at the same time, as though an unconscious element of guilt were at work. Well schooled from her years of therapy, she conceded the possibility and began carrying a lighter bag. In a short time, she felt better.

Despite these improvements, Marybeth continued to have shoulder pain, which put me in the unenviable position of suggesting that the massage therapist she had been seeing for a couple of years may have been partly at fault. I felt this to be the case for two reasons. First, the massage therapist, who had referred Marybeth to me in the first place, had such a bad case of eczema on his hands that his palms were as raw and red as if they had been skinned. This condition indicated to me that either he had contracted a virulent infection or he had distorted the equilibrium between his immune system and indigenous micro-colonies through the mechanisms of reflection, a diagnosis he rejected because he was offended and likely threatened by the idea that his work might be the source of his problem.

The second reason had to do with my growing conviction that Marybeth's psychosocial pathology had created a stealth thematic disparity. Her concept of health and healing was more other- than self-oriented. She laid too much stock in massage, a passive form of health recovery wherein someone else does the healing for the patient. According to the massage therapist, Marybeth simply needed to lie down and receive treatment, then spend another half hour verbally emoting, a good idea had it not been for the psychotherapist who was already employed and doing a pretty effective job. To turn her health into a sustainable resource, Marybeth needed to go in the opposite direction. Her will—a factor ruled by the theme of empowerment—had to be enlisted in the process of regaining and sustaining her health.

From the perspective of the six themes, the treatment given by the massage therapist pertained to the communications issue in the thematic continuum; it made Marybeth feel good immediately because she was already inclined in that direction. In the long run, however, the more she behaved according to altruistic and intellectual themes, the less she acted on behalf of the more self-oriented themes of empowerment and health.

My assessment of the situation required Marybeth to choose between the massage therapist and me. At first, she tried to talk to the massage therapist about my theory, but he became so distraught that she backed away for fear of offending him. For a while she tried to maintain a divided loyalty, but the massage therapist, who had been her friend and confidant much longer than I, won out. If Marybeth was "addicted" to altruistic and intellectual themes, then the massage therapist provided her favorite "drug."

On the day of our final session together, Marybeth made comments that suggested a mistrust of reflective exercise, reiterating some of the same cynical comments her husband had made about meditation being a waste of valuable time. Ignoring this, I encouraged her to continue to practice and to pursue health through self-oriented exercise.

A few years later I ran into Marybeth. Though still struggling with a few health problems (and maintaining her weekly appointments with the massage therapist), she reported that her health was good. When we discussed her husband, whose condition had continued to degenerate, she made it clear that the two of them had developed an understanding that her devotion to taking care of her health benefited both of them. It gave her the energy and personal happiness she needed in order to minister to his growing needs. He had stopped interfering in her efforts to take care of herself.

In an awkward way, I consider Marybeth a success because she eventually made self-care through exercise a high priority, a key element of Unified Fitness. Her technical failure with the Unified Fitness program illustrates the powerful role mental fitness plays in the quest for sustainable health. Left unaddressed, stealth psychosocial pathologies, especially those which create confusion among the six themes, keep the mind unbalanced and make lasting health an impossibility.

## How the Six Themes Helped Jack Come Back

In Phase 1, I described how former tennis champion Jack reclaimed his talent, health, and life direction. I didn't mention that Jack was one of my first students to use Exercises 5A and B to help him pull this off.

In less than six months of reflective training, the physical and immunological benefits Jack experienced had brightened his outlook, and he soon felt ready to take on a greater life challenge. Jack had made a lackluster academic showing in high school and college, which had filled him with a nagging sense of regret. He wanted to go back to school, but he was afraid he didn't have what it took to succeed there.

I asked Jack to respond to Exercise 5A, Mapping the Mind, and his answers revealed a primary triangulation between sexuality, empowerment, and health—all self-oriented themes. His daily routine outlined in Exercise 5B, Using the Map, accorded exactly with his first three thematic choices, showing an almost complete lack of intellectual, altruistic, or creative activity. As I got to know Jack on a more personal level, the reasons for this predilection became clearer.

Jack had grown up in a wild part of Montana. His father's people had been among the first to settle in the area, which was filled with grizzly bears, cougars, and people with pioneering spirits to match. More than most, Jack's father mirrored this rough land. A proverbial tough guy, he was a veteran of the Korean War, where he received a number of wounds, at least one of them serious. When he wasn't working for the U.S. Park Service or the local resort, he was a hard drinker and a brawler. Jack shared with me an early memory of seeing his father beat a member of his work crew who had done a poor job. The fight took place in Jack's home. Jack's father lifted the man off the ground like a rag doll and beat him senseless.

Given that his father embodied such physical force, imagine Jack's shock when at age ten he watched his father, only in his middle thirties, keel over dead from a heart attack while washing his car. When I asked Jack if he could remember what happened after that, he shook his head and gave a curt description of his mother hustling both his sister and him away from the scene to a friend's house where he waited for what seemed like hours. As evening began to fall, a strange man entered the house and told Jack that his father had died.

Jack ran to another room, wept a little, then buried his feelings. Neither he nor his sister attended their father's funeral. A few years later, his mother remarried, and Jack moved to New York where he experienced a different way of life, one that involved country clubs and highly civilized peers, a place far removed from the wilds of Montana.

Based on Jack's story and on his responses to Exercise 5A, Mapping the Mind, and 5B, Using the Map, it was clear to me that early exposure to his father's violence and harsh, premature death helped set up a mistrust of anything like tenderness and compassion. It effectively turned him away from the altruistic, communicative side of the thematic spectrum. As a result, he grew up seeking gratification from opposite themes, namely empowerment, and once he hit puberty, sexuality. Because of his advanced physical development, health was something Jack took for granted, until he lost it, which was what brought him to me.

My advice to Jack was to engage in as much communicative behavior as he could, such as enrolling in an MBA program, which would force him to articulate. To help him get started, Jack and I met for breakfast several times a week, during which time I asked him to explain his course materials to me. At first his answers were glib regurgitations of what he had heard in class, but I kept after him until he could explain in his own words, drawing on metaphors of his own invention.

Soon Jack developed friendships with the members of his class, and they spent a lot of time working together on joint projects and preparing for tests. In the end, Jack not only earned an MBA, but he allowed the formerly subordinate themes of intelligence, altruism, and creativity to blossom in his life.

Once he had mastered his fear of intellectual inferiority, Jack turned to facing his long-buried feelings over his biological father. Together we made a pilgrimage to Montana to visit his father's grave. I watched Jack kneel at the tombstone and bow his head. He stayed there for over a half hour. While I waited, I thought of my younger brother and realized I hadn't visited his grave in almost fifteen years. I promised myself that I would return to pay my respects.

Though a year later I made good on my promise, it would take several more years before I would be freed from the guilt and shame of assuming I had caused my brother's death. The same was true for Jack with his sorrow over his broken childhood and the loss of his father. What helped us achieve some degree of closure was a conscious effort to cultivate tenderheartedness, which allowed altruism to touch our lives. In doing so, awareness of the six themes and our respective triangular preferences proved highly useful.

# Chapter 10

## Days 33–34 Continued

### Exercise 6: Discovering the Spirit

Before you begin this exercise, gather old photographs and memorabilia of your childhood and put them around you. If you don't have such things available, call a parent, relative, or childhood friend and reminisce about old times. Venture back in memory as far as you can. If you have no one to talk to and the distance isn't too inconvenient, visit the place where you grew up and skulk around for a couple of hours. Then read and respond to one direction at a time from the following list in the order presented. Don't read all of the directions right away, because doing so could prejudice your answers. After responding to all the directions, read on to find out how to interpret your responses.

- Write out a brief explanation of your spirituality. Don't worry about precision or eloquence. Just get down your main ideas.

- Examine what you have written. Does the word *God* or the notion of a supreme entity appear? If so, write another brief explanation elaborating further on this notion. If not, write an explanation elaborating on your exclusion of such a notion.

- Study old photographs or memorabilia of your early childhood. If no photos or items are available, reflect on conversations about your childhood or the sight of the home where you spent your first few years. Write a brief explanation of how this makes you feel.

- Were you raised in a particular religion? If so, write the name of the religion and briefly explain your current attitude toward that religion. If you weren't raised in a religious tradition, write down what you most vividly remember your parents telling you about matters of spirituality. Briefly explain your current attitude toward that memory.

- Briefly explain your feelings about your parents and include some explanation of why you feel the way you do.

- Briefly explain your greatest fear and how long you've had it.

- Briefly explain your feelings about children and their purpose in the grand scheme of things.

## Interpretations for the Exercise

The previous exercise is designed to get at mental issues that lie on the border between mind and spirituality, a place modern psychotherapy and conventional medicine are loath to visit. Medicine and psychotherapy struggle to maintain an aloof but cordial party line toward spirituality, that it's a matter of personal choice for the patient but fairly irrelevant to healing. But recent studies showing that prayer can affect the degree of recovery in patients—even in those who aren't aware they are being prayed for—are forcing medicine to reconsider its commitment to such a bland position.

At present, however, spirit remains where it always has been: enshrouded in the murky boundaries of the faith of the believer. Exercise 6 helps you explore these boundaries, where our most tender feelings hide from the world.

Exercise Series 5 and the Parable of the Six Couples foreshadow the focus Exercise 6 uses to help begin the long process of discovering spirit, namely, early childhood (or the theme of empowerment). The association between infancy and spirituality is an old one. Lao Tsu, the father of Taoism, saw the human infant as an example of natural perfection and health. Christianity, one of the prime architects of Western culture, makes the link between Jesus and children a central theme. The British poet-philosophers William Blake and William Wordsworth, along with their American protégés Ralph Waldo Emerson and Walt Whitman, depicted small children as pure embodiments of spirit.

Even science-driven psychology concedes the specialness of early childhood which, by most accounts, is the very center of our emotions, most of which are hard-wired by the end of our second year. During those primal years or not long after, moral and mortal issues present themselves with unflagging insistence. Any exposure to spiritual or religious views must, given this inherent centrality of early childhood, make a profound and lasting impression, extending through time to help form our basic assumptions about the meaning of life and what lies ahead after death.

In light of the erosion of conventional religion's credibility during the Great Disruption, it seems likely that in the past forty years many people have found themselves spiritually confused, unable or unwilling to put their faith in any one doctrine or set of notions that attempt to delineate spirit and its life-and-death implications. A potential effect of such confusion is that early feelings, born in conditions of vulnerability and predictability, get covered by an adult veneer that, while it permits people to function, ultimately leaves them feeling hollow.

Exercise 6 can help clear up spiritual confusion by allowing you to separate adult, motive-enriched notions of spirituality from the motive-free notions of childhood. If the first three items in the previous exercise reveal little contradiction between your current and childhood spirituality, then your sense of spirit is likely to be strong, and you can draw on that strength in questing for sustainable health. Large differences between adult and early spirituality, however, indicate a weaker sense of spirit, which bodes poorly for achieving sustainable health.

Given the breadth and depth of the Great Disruption, many people will most likely register some disparity between their current and childhood views on spirituality. In general, a harsh, condescending attitude towards the personal past, the most tender and sensitive layer of being, suggests profound spiritual difficulties that are likely to wedge their way into life's picture sooner or later.

On the other hand, melancholy feelings provoked by this exercise show a strong potential spirit. Sad or forlorn feelings about childhood should be looked upon as a strong impetus to reconnect with early life. You can do this by visiting the place where you grew up, working to build closer ties to parents and relatives, and exploring the depths of your feelings, through journal writing, support groups, or counseling. Once you re-establish ties with your vulnerability, you may discover a renewed faith in ideas or traditions that once seemed completely unacceptable to you.

# *Randy and Me*

Of the five hundred or so people I have taught, the person who most dramatically demonstrated the powerful link between childhood and spirit was Randy. Standing five feet seven inches, Randy was not physically imposing, but he was one of the most skilled non-Chinese martial artists I have ever met.

Randy had learned from a number of adequately qualified teachers, but his skills came largely through rigorous self-discipline. He practiced every spare moment, from when he went to work cleaning the parking lot of a fast-food restaurant at three in the morning to the time he went to sleep. Oftentimes Randy got his practice in by having to defend himself from thugs who had heard of his prowess. Randy was not afraid to fight anyone. Once, when a local karate bully challenged him to a fight, Randy stared the bully in the eye and said, "Okay, spears to the death!" Assuming Randy had a couple of spears handy, the bully tucked his tail and ran.

While I never encouraged Randy to behave so recklessly, I understood why he was willing to do so. It was because *he* was actually a *she*. Randy was a full-fledged hermaphrodite.

Born with a uterus and an exaggerated clitoris, which passed for a penis until he got old enough to know better, Randy was raised as a boy, a colossally tragic mistake by his parents, who were apparently too simple to know any better. When Randy had to face the reality of his condition, the shock almost drove him mad. But doctors came to his rescue with medication for depression and hormones to keep up the ruse of maleness. If he stopped taking his medication, however, his body produced estrogen to the extent that he grew breasts.

Randy's family was working class, only a generation removed from the itinerant farmers who, in previous years, had lived as virtual indentured servants to the landed gentry of Virginia. In many respects, Randy and I were cut from the same cloth. Both my paternal and maternal grandparents were reared on Georgia farms. My childhood was filled with memories of visiting cousins and schoolmates with backgrounds similar to that of Randy. I had played in their homes, eaten food from their table, gone to church with them. Their hopes and dreams were like mine, their feelings just as easily hurt by slights and insults.

In that world, there isn't a lot of sympathy for someone like Randy. Working-class white Southerners generally scorn anything remotely divergent from heterosexuality. If you want to insult a man of that world, call him a "morphodite," a deliberately contemptuous corruption of "hermaphrodite."

As a result, Randy had to develop a tough hide, to the point that he was dangerous to himself and others. He got into fights on a regular basis and was constantly on the verge of wanting to beat someone to death; and the hormones and antidepressants he took were causing wild physiological fluctuations. Since I've known him, he has had to be rushed to the emergency room with a racing heart several times.

My strategy in helping Randy was, in terms of Exercise Series 5, to steer him toward the communication themes of those exercises. I encouraged him to continue working with those doctors who understood his emotional and physical dilemma. But Randy hated psychologists because of a bad experience years earlier.

When he was fourteen, Randy's parents took him out of school and put him in the care of a psychiatrist, whose bedside manner was cold and clinical. This doctor took a special interest in something Randy had told his parents: every night since he was a little boy a female spirit came into his room and sang him to sleep. To the psychiatrist, this could only mean that Randy was delusional. To Randy, the visitation was comforting, a sign that God was looking out for him.

As I got Randy to go into greater detail about this singing female spirit, the story got more complex. He revealed that from a very early age he had exhibited clairvoyance, especially in his family's charismatic church, which believed in speaking in tongues and faith healing. Randy claimed to have had waking and sleeping visions wherein he learned that various elderly members of the congregation were going to die and ascend into heaven. He didn't hesitate to tell the subjects of these visions, and when those he told passed away a week later, the members of the church became convinced that Randy had second sight. Randy's stature as a "holy" child grew within the church until people became aware of his sexual condition. At that point, the congregation shunned him, and he lost the sense of higher meaning that his role in the church had given him.

For Randy, the singing female spirit was a part of his visionary childhood that had made his life special, but the psychiatrist's insistence that the spirit was made up added insult to his injury. So, I was determined not to make the same mistake. When Randy began to respond to reflective exercise in a visionary way, I let him tell me all about it without any criticism or comment that would lead him to think I didn't believe him. As a result, Randy came to trust me more and became increasingly willing to accept my advice.

Though I was careful to keep a benign front with Randy, in reality I was jeeringly skeptical of his spiritual claims. I had spent many years educating myself out of my own fundamentalist, unrefined upbringing, and listening to Randy was a bit like being confronted with embarrassing photos my parents had taken while I was being toilet trained. To make matters worse, Randy voiced his strong opinions in a manner that violated the political correctness of my students, most of whom were unsympathetic to fundamentalist Christianity. He spoke unflinchingly to Jewish and agnostic students about the teachings of Jesus. He excoriated an openly gay student over what he considered a flagrant waste of the God-given privilege of being born with unambiguous gender.

Randy made conservative students squirm even more, especially when he decided to stop taking his hormones, promptly grew breasts, and began wearing bras and makeup to class. To a student's conservative parents, Randy introduced himself as a hermaphrodite, then offered to explain what a hermaphrodite was in case they didn't know. The parents politely declined the explanation, sat for a few uncomfortable minutes, then left quickly.

All my students felt sorry for Randy's predicament, yet incidents such as these helped make him a source of condescending gossip. Almost everyone was intolerant of Randy's spirituality and looked to me to do something. I took Randy aside and as tactfully as I could asked him to respect the different spiritual perspectives of the other students. Randy listened carefully, tilted his head to the side, then responded, "I don't want to upset your students."

Randy soon quit the school, and I was relieved. I not only felt that his problems exceeded my ability to help him, but watching him ruffle everyone's feathers made me feel sad and helpless. With Randy gone, these feelings vanished, and it would be years before I would be able to look back and understand my reactions. Randy eventually began the process of undergoing a sex change operation to become a full-fledged female, and credits reflective exercise for giving her the courage to face the truth about herself.

In my view, her courage was already abundantly present, but if reflective exercise helped her triumph over adversity, then she subtly aimed me in the direction of the precious power of innocent spirituality, glowing in the recesses of human darkness like a distant lighthouse. The story of how she used her belief in a loving God to hold onto her sanity proved an augury of a spiritual struggle I would one day face.

# A Painful Miracle

My wife and I had a rough go from the beginning. Ideologically, we were oil and water. Both of us held advanced degrees in English; mine was of a more classical type, and hers was steeped in the feminist perspective of the 1980s. As a result, our marriage recapitulated the discord that had been simmering in humanities departments for two decades. To my wife, my philosophical bent was nothing more than a tool of white male supremacy. To me, such anticlassical sentiments represented a high-sounding but petty grab for power, an intellectual fad whose currency would pass. Within a month of living together, bickering became our way of life.

The one thing we agreed on was that we wanted children, so we produced two sons in three years. This actually helped reduce the frequency of our daily quarreling. But in the long run, the pressures of raising children combined with daily arguing began to wear us both down.

In our arguments, we attacked each other's philosophies, provoking vehement reprisals that left no doubt as to the high value we placed on our ideas. We had good reason to do so. My wife and I used doctrines to cope with the emotional pain we had brought into the marriage. For her, it was a lifelong sadness over having been put up for adoption at birth. For me, it was culpability for my brother's death. Over the years we each had lost sight of how we used intellectualism to salve our vulnerabilities, which our argumentative strategies nonetheless inadvertently exposed.

Though the ideological strife was certainly a big reason for our unhappiness, a far more basic event caused the actual break up: a love affair I had with a young woman. Within a week, I confessed to my wife what I had done, and that basically ended our marriage. She asked me to move out, and I found a little cottage that suited me just fine. We tried marriage counseling, but it was too late.

With great hope that I had found at last a loving relationship, I turned to my new partner, but a pall of impropriety hung over us. There was our age difference and the fact that she had been my student. But the issue of my children, whom I feared would be harmed by divorce, also loomed ominously. At the same time, I had fought so constantly with their mother and with such anger that I felt a separation was in their best interest. The conflict left me feeling mentally bound from head to toe.

News of what I had done harmed my business. A number of my students quit in protest, but I shrugged off the damage and fell back on my new relationship by night and an old compulsion to overtrain by day. In a short time, I felt myself growing exhausted. Maintaining a six-day-a-week business that involved extreme physical movement, working long evening hours, and spending every night with my kids, playing, bathing, and putting them to sleep constituted an already crowded agenda; my new relationship required a great deal of attention and care as well. At the same time, the aches, pains, and strains of excessive exercise kept me on the brink of injury. Reflective exercise made recovery faster and easier than it would have otherwise been, but near the end of November something happened that threatened to bring my life down like a precarious stack of blocks.

Early signs of trouble included muscular tightness in my back and an odd pain that made it difficult to lift my right leg. One evening, after a long day of extreme exertion, I went over to my girlfriend's house to spend the night. Though uncomfortably sore, I passed out, waking around three in the morning to urinate. I moved stiffly to the bathroom, and after finishing, I walked into the bedroom where I felt something snap in my lower body.

The next thing I knew, I was on the floor, locked in the most excruciating pain I have ever experienced. Every muscle in my right leg locked into cast-iron spasm, a massive conglomerate of cramps that almost blacked me out. My screams woke my girlfriend, who stood by helplessly as I writhed on the ground, then rose up and tried to dress myself. Somehow I made it down the rickety stairs of her apartment building to my car, which I drove to the emergency room.

I got there in a matter of minutes. It would be over an hour before I saw a doctor, first a young one who looked like a high school kid. He said I had "sciatica." The next doctor, an older neurologist, disputed the younger one's diagnosis and advised me to lay off my exercise routine.

For the next month, I lived with leg, back, and hip pain I had no idea was possible. For the first time in a decade I was forced to see a doctor, who preferred a wait-and-see approach to getting an MRI. I worked with a physical therapist, exhaustively researched the Internet, and used my reflective skill to treat myself. It took two weeks to progress from the stooped position of a monkey to standing for brief periods—but after only a few minutes, sometimes less than thirty seconds, the pain in my hip and leg would overwhelm me. I slept an average of two to four hours a night, roused by the pain, which I would try to relieve with massage and reflective exercise. When the pain moved from the right side to the left, one day shortly after Christmas, I was forced to face the probability that I had damaged a lumbar disc, a condition Western medicine treats with surgery, which proved inept in the overwhelming majority of cases.

On the night of January 4, 1997, the twenty-fifth anniversary of my younger brother's death, I dropped my girlfriend at her apartment then drove over to my estranged wife's home to see my children. They were playing on the floor, and I struggled to hold back tears as I stroked their heads. Unable to control my sadness, I left quickly and began the long drive to my quarters in the Virginia countryside.

Sleep-deprived and on the verge of a nervous breakdown, I confronted the reality that I was about to have to undergo surgery that was likely to leave me impaired or crippled, destroying the credibility as an expert in self-healing I had spent almost a decade building. The doom I had been fleeing my whole life had apparently arrived, and there was no one but myself to blame.

I began to talk out loud to God, who had come to represent for me more of a founding principle of Western civilization than the omnipotent father of my Southern Baptist roots. Mindful of the remoteness of God, I began asking Christ why he had let this happen to me, the pain constantly stabbing into me, as though to say "wrong question." I hadn't felt so lost since my brother's death, and my tone changed to a softer plea. I intuitively used the word "Jesus" instead of the more formal "Christ."

Just saying "Jesus" released an odd, helpless feeling somewhere inside. It was a word Randy and his lot would have used, people I considered ignorant and gullible, but there I was using the word as I had as a child, when people like Randy and I weren't so far apart. I started to bargain. "Jesus," I said through both physical and psychological tears of pain. "If you'll give me a miracle, if you'll heal this wound in me, I swear I'll turn everything around. I'll give up my girlfriend and go back to my wife and get down on my knees. I'll do whatever it takes. Just please give me that miracle."

When I got home, I hobbled upstairs to my room. The pain was as bad as ever. I took pills that simply disembodied me from the agony so that I could sleep. I repeated my bargain, then passed out, exhausted, beaten, reconciled to the surgeon's knife.

At four A.M. I woke to urinate and could barely stand. I repeated the bargain. When I woke again at six A.M., the pain was gone.

It was like being suddenly released from a sadistic prison. Ecstatic, I went through my reflective exercise with ease, and during meditation I felt as though I had been lifted high so that I could look down on my life and see a pattern. All the resentment and hostility I had been carrying over disappointments and those I held responsible came into focus, and I realized that hostility and resentment had been beside me all along, like sad and angry ghosts, keeping my unhappiness alive. I could see that in virtually all cases my own choices had led to whatever unhappiness I had experienced and that others were rarely to blame, especially during my adult life. By the end of an hour's meditation, I felt wonderfully empty, drained of blame and rage.

> *"Jesus," I said through both physical and psychological tears of pain. "If you'll give me a miracle, if you'll heal this wound in me, I swear I'll turn everything around. I'll do whatever it takes. Just please give me that miracle."*

In the weeks that followed, the more difficult reality of fulfilling my end of the bargain began to bear down. My estranged wife, though initially touched by seeing me get on my knees and beg her forgiveness, remained skeptical about the miracle, seeing more potential for self-aggrandizement than salvation. Eventually, her reluctance to acknowledge such a powerful experience for me reignited old resentments, and I began to believe that some of my anger toward her had been justified.

In the meantime, my girlfriend, whom I had turned away in order to keep my word, contacted me repeatedly to express her continued love and support. This set off torrents of confusion, so I turned to a minister to help me evaluate what had happened. He assured me that

I had had an authentic experience, but I needed to join a congregation of fellow Christians as part of the full obligation of being a Christian.

I did so. I attended Sunday school, church, and special meetings where parishioners discussed their spiritual experiences. Nevertheless, the acrimony between my wife and me prevailed. We divorced, and I returned to my girlfriend.

A few months after my miraculous prayer restored my leg, the pain returned and stayed with me on and off for four years. During those four years, a number of my initial convictions shifted and circumstances took unexpected turns. I don't attend church as regularly as I did at first. In the first year following my recovery, I read the entire Bible, but rarely do so now. My ex-wife remarried, and my children, who visit me every other weekend, have not borne the scars I had feared they might. My girlfriend and I are engaged, though we haven't set a date. All four of us—my ex-wife, her husband, my fiancée, and I—continue to practice reflective exercise, which brought us all together in the first place.

Complicating my feelings further, I went to see an orthopedist/osteopath for the incessant pain in my left hip, and when he yanked on my leg, he produced the most satisfying pain I have ever felt. It was exactly what I had needed. When I described how the injury came about, he wouldn't rule out a bulging lumbar disc, but he was firm in his assessment that the pain I had been struggling with most of the time had been a sacroiliac joint displacement, the first he had ever seen in his forty years of practice. We briefly discussed the chance that my body's muscles had forced the displacement to prevent the bulging lumbar disc from rupturing, but he wasn't interested in carrying the discussion very far. If a lumbar disc had bulged four years ago, he said, it had obviously healed up by now or I would be suffering other neurological symptoms that hadn't shown up in the interview and diagnostic. I spared him the story of the miracle. He didn't seem like the receptive type.

I've decided to stop thinking analytically about what actually happened. Looking for causes of problems with physical, immunological, and mental fitness is helpful, but questions of causation in spiritual matters will likely lead nowhere. The most important things about my miracle lay on either side of it. When I meditated the following day and felt myself rise above the circumstances of my life to see how I had participated in every noteworthy outcome, good and bad, I achieved a vision that opened me to compassion and humility that otherwise might not have been possible. It brought a soft and lasting harmony to a turbulent situation. But the evening before, as I drove through the dark and prayed to the God of my childhood, I reconnected with a vital source that had slipped away so long ago it no longer seemed real.

In the throes of adversity, I discovered the precious ember of childhood spirituality, the final, elusive ingredient that unifies fitness and sustains health. When permanent night appears to be approaching, early childhood spirituality may be the last source of light, the part of the mind connected to a power that permeates history and individual lives. In the glare of day, we hardly see it, but in darkness, we move instinctively toward its soft glowing center, surprised when we touch instead something huge and powerful, which lifts us like a strong, concerned parent and carries us through the darkness. Once the darkness passes, the memory of that small glow and the feeling of being uplifted remains.

PHASE 4

# Troubleshooting Unified Fitness

# Chapter 11

## Day 35: Physical Fitness Fallacies

Phase 4 takes up the task of identifying problems in Unified Fitness, especially in Phases 1 and 2, though Phase 3 constantly enters this discussion. This final phase also summarizes the program, its supporting theory, and evidence, providing you with the rationale in condensed form that may help you stay with the program.

Three key fallacies bedevil physical fitness. The first involves confusion over conventional medical measurements of bodily phenomena. The second derives from a mechanical conception of exercise and its effect on the body. The third arises from unconscious cultural bias and thinly disguised sexual motivations. Acting separately or together, these physical fitness fallacies can stunt efforts to achieve sustainable health through Unified Fitness.

## The Risk Factor Fallacy

The first order of business for Phase 4 is to call into question fitness assumptions centered around current standards and methods used to determine predisposition for disease. Medical doctors largely employ three tests: blood pressure, blood lipids or fats (cholesterol), and blood sugar or glucose tolerance tests. Other "risk factors" considered in assessing health risks include age, family history, degree of activity, injuries, and disabilities. The assumption is that doctors, armed with these criteria, can make reasonably good medical or lifestyle recommendations appropriate for an individual's condition.

Though valuable, such assessments should never be mistaken for exact indications of health or illness. It is perfectly possible, for example, for a person to have excellent blood pressure and horrendous health problems at the same time. The only thing a medical expert can say about a blood pressure reading is that results over a certain number tend to be associated with certain diseases. Blood lipid or cholesterol measures are similarly limited. Though doctors may understand these limits and help their patients avoid confusing risk factors for signs of good or bad health, even the experts can make mistakes.

Experts have apparently made such a mistake in the case of obesity, a label determined by comparing a person's weight with his or her height. Glenn Gaessar's excellent book, *Big Fat Lies,* exposes the flawed assumptions that led to this mistake and suggests that being fit and fat (judged to be ten to twenty pounds overweight) is, at least in the long run, probably better than being thin or ostensibly in shape. Gaessar presents solid epidemiological evidence that a five-foot, four-inch tall woman who weighs between 160 and 180 pounds has a much better chance of living longer than a woman of equal height whose weight falls outside that spectrum (Gaessar 1996).

Though Gaessar's findings support the health risk associated with obesity (a person fifty pounds over a weight deemed appropriate for that person's height), they cast suspicion on the virtue of losing that "extra five to seven pounds" so often advocated by fitness experts trying to sell the public simplistic views of weight control and exercise.

Paul Ewald's theories about the link between infectious disease and lethal illness might account for the apparent disparity between Gaessar's statistics and the commonly held view of fat as the root of all health problems. In fact, much of what conventional medicine has now come to assume about the validity of risk factor measurements might be illusory: post-hoc fallacies that stem from failing to look deeply into infectious disease as the primary cause of chronic health problems.

Ewald points out in *Plague Time* that medicine's reliance on the term *risk* helps protect physicians from malpractice suits and the public from false hopes and the exaggerations of charlatans. But it also restricts causal analysis of chronic disease to genetics and chemical pollution, thus stacking the deck against arguments favoring infectious causes. This risk factor fallacy may originate from the Newtonian medical model, presented earlier, which sees individual efforts to control or affect health and disease as fruitless and deluded, thus steering attention away from the immunological possibilities of Unified Fitness.

## The Mechanistic Fallacy

A new addition to the family of fitness calipers is something referred to as VO2 Max or Maximum Oxygen Uptake. This is a coefficient that represents a combined assessment of physiological readings that indicate the efficiency with which the cardiovascular system uses oxygen in milliliters per kilogram per minute (ml/kg/min). According to the research so far, the average VO2 Max for a twenty-five-year-old male is 45 ml/kg/min, while for a twenty-five-year-old female, the average is 39 ml/kg/min. For top male athletes, the reading is in the 80s, for top females, the 70s.

VO2 Max demonstrates an increased technical sophistication in how the cardiovascular system is measured, but at its root is the unsophisticated notion that fitness is a matter of aerobic capacity, or endurance. This may be a primary concern for athletes, but it is not necessarily so for people trying to maintain their health. The untimely deaths of aerobically fit people such as Jim Fixx and Florence Griffith Joyner suggest that other factors beside aerobic condition determine sustainable health.

This assumption that leads medicine and fitness to ground fundamental definitions of fitness on the basis of athletic capacity is a deep-seated one. It began with the simplistic but persistent view of the cardiovascular system as a muscle-driven performance machine, much like the engine of a car. According to this model, putting the muscles of the trunk, arms, and legs into strain and motion forces the lungs and the heart to pump blood to those muscles, which are taxed and strengthened by the effort. As motion and strain increase, the heart has to work harder to pump blood through its arteries to get fresh, oxygenated blood to the muscles. Eventually the blood pathways to and from the heart and muscles expand in diameter, thus making the transfer of fuel-enriched and fuel-depleted blood more efficient. In this way, experts have come to believe aerobic exercise improves the operation of the cardiovascular system.

Though mechanically accurate, this concept of cardiovascular exercise has problems, not the least of which is that the musculoskeletal system, the basic engine of cardiovascular exercise, gets punished in the act, sustaining a number of unhealthy side effects. The experience of young athletes well illustrates the problem.

Encouraged to achieve greater performance-based results (that is, speed, strength, and endurance), they can develop injuries that dog them the rest of their lives. These injuries can happen in two ways. In the first way, a joint, tendon, ligament, or muscle group can be stressed beyond maximum capacity, resulting in a structural tear. Surgery is often the solution for such injuries. Once the young athlete appears to recover and resumes training at a pace equal to that prior to the injury, aggravating the damaged area becomes a way of life. The second sort of injury is more gradual, a slow destruction of the musculoskeletal system through repetitive motion. Because there is no obvious tear to treat with surgery, the young athlete falls back on superficial remedies, such as icing swollen, sore joints and muscle groups and taking anti-inflammatory drugs.

These conditions foreshadow consequences that can visit ordinary exercisers in their middle thirties, when the once good results of standard fitness regimens tend to reverse themselves, especially if the exerciser has been pushing hard for a number of years. Lacking the strength and resilience of former years, muscles, tendons, ligaments, and joints are more susceptible to damage. Even if the exercise routine is relatively modest, the same repetitive motion that causes injury in young competitive athletes may begin to take its toll.

These sorts of injuries are especially difficult to anticipate and to deal with because relatively little outward aging occurs between the twenties and thirties. Thirty-somethings with gradually forming injuries sometimes refuse to heed their own bodies' warning signals. For a period of time, they may fight to maintain their exercise level, hampered by pain and restriction, until a final big injury forces them to stop. The diminishing return on constant mechanistic exercise gets worse in older age brackets.

No matter what your age, whether or not the destructive potential of mechanistic exercise manifests is a question of time. Repeated exertion tightens muscles and decreases range of motion. Decreased range of motion leads to loss of circulation, because movement is the primary way the cardiovascular system is stimulated, especially on a micro level. Loss of circulation leads to tissue degradation, thus increasing the likelihood of injury. Injury leads to disruption of motion, which further degrades the cardiovascular system. In order to counter this, more time is required for stretching and cooling down, adding a time cost to the deleterious effects produced by exercise itself.

In spite of these consequences and recent cautions by fitness and medical research to exercise moderately, fitness industry figures such as Billy Blanks of Taebo fame carry on the logic of Jane Fonda and other exercise mavens of the 1970s and 1980s, who encouraged people to push beyond their range of comfort. As a result, the issues of well-being and longevity get lost in the pursuit of performance and dubious results such as weight loss. Even if someone manages to keep his or her exercise routine modest, there still exists the possibility of creating an unhealthy cycle through exercise. The mechanistic fallacy, which frames the definition of fitness in simplistic physical terms, is the chief reason people continue to fall into this cycle. Their narrow understanding of fitness blocks them from giving adequate consideration to the immune system and the mind. To them, a program such as Unified Fitness is either inconceivable or superfluous.

## The Herculean Fallacy

Several years back, I had an ongoing encounter that illustrated another bit of flawed physical fitness thinking usually associated with the mechanistic fallacy. It happened at a university fitness facility where I practice Unified Fitness: a twenty-minute swim, followed by subtle movement and Reflective Meditation. On many occasions, both before and after my routine, a retired history professor in his mid-seventies, who prided himself on swimming a languid breaststroke everyday, went out of his way to question me about the Chinese portion of my workouts. He knew from prior conversations that I had studied classical languages and culture as an undergraduate, and he couldn't understand why I wanted to venture beyond what was for him self-evident superiority. That I would think the classical Greeks hadn't figured it all out and that I would need to look beyond their culture baffled and even irritated him.

I am partly sympathetic to the professor's conviction that Western civilization, including notions of fitness, rests on the shoulders of classical Greece. But the force of that conviction had at least two submerged sources that are ultimately as flawed as both the risk factor and mechanistic fallacies. The first had emerged briefly the first few times we spoke. The professor made, and I rebuffed, several thinly veiled sexual passes. The second never came into the open, but loomed in the background like a giant shadow. It was his lack of genuine curiosity toward the reflective exercise portion of my routine, suggesting a seemingly willful disregard for ancient Chinese culture. His former employer mirrored this lack of regard. A major state-run university, its highly respected art department offered only a single elective Chinese course, and its physical education department had no traditional Chinese fitness in its curriculum.

The professor's intense allegiance to classical Greek ideals, sexual preoccupations, and willful ignorance of traditional Chinese fitness form the core of what I call the "Herculean fallacy," so named because the mythical strongman Hercules, helps delineate the crucial distortions this fallacy thrusts upon contemporary views of fitness. The Herculean fallacy consists of confusing physical strength, sinewy musculature, and sexuality with fitness. This confusion impedes the Unified Fitness goals of basic flexibility, endurance, and strength (physical fitness), reflective skill (immunological fitness), and thematic balance (mental fitness).

The tyranny of classical Greek culture over the West isn't the only reason Hercules still stands as the shining symbol of Western fitness. Historically, physical strength played a critical role in survival and warfare, and only in relatively recent times in developed countries has its staying power diminished. Even so, the sports, fitness, and entertainment industries—which together constitute an "unholy trinity"—continue to invigorate, sensationalize, and sexualize Herculean virtues, such as big, highly defined muscles, demonstrations of physical superiority, and a militant distaste for body fat. The unholy trinity has persuaded millions of people to invest lots of attention in the lives of large, physically powerful people (usually men, though women are gaining rapid representation) and to believe such people embody true fitness.

*The sports, fitness, and entertainment industries—which together constitute an "unholy trinity"—continue to invigorate, sensationalize, and sexualize Herculean virtues, such as big, highly defined muscles, demonstrations of physical superiority, and a militant distaste for body fat.*

I was just a kid when the sports-fitness-entertainment trinity began to promote this Herculean definition of fitness in the United States. It started with middle and high school team sports for boys of the 1950s and 60s. These sports consisted of sprinting, jumping, blocking, tackling, pushing, grappling, and so on, the same physical skills involved in team sports at collegiate or professional levels. In the 1960s, college and professional sports grew rapidly into forms of lucrative entertainment that kept millions of young people (including myself) fully in the Herculean loop long after dropping out of actual competition in high school.

Unlike most kids my age, however, I fell even more deeply under the spell of the Herculean fallacy before I dropped out of competitive sports. A desire to be admired by both women and men initially inspired my lifelong devotion to fitness. I deliberately set out to cultivate a look inspired by comic book superheroes, Charles Atlas, Tarzan, sports figures, and various musclemen featured in bad "sword and sandal" movies of the 1950s and 60s. At twelve, I took up body building, and by the time I was fourteen I had only about 4 percent body fat, which is dangerous by medical standards.

Though I went through a period of debauchery and fitness oblivion in my late teens, my reflex to maintain a svelte physique reemerged with a vengeance by the time I turned twenty-one, and by age twenty-three I was in the height of a renewed Herculean mania. I also had a new role model—Bruce Lee—sold to me, once again, by the unholy trinity. Apparently it had also sold Lee on Herculean physicality. Some believe his effort to develop a fat-free, muscular body led to his untimely death. My efforts to model myself after him suggest this belief has merit.

One day, while I paraded bare-chested around the perimeter of the pool I lifeguarded, a bearded, academic-looking man who had been swimming laps approached and asked if he could conduct some tests on me. I took this to mean that he was so impressed with my muscular development that he wanted to investigate it further. After immersing me in water—he was using Archimedes' principle to measure my muscle/fat ratio—and giving me a breatholator test to check my metabolism, he informed me that I had less than four percent body fat and that if I didn't increase my fat stores my body would be forced to metabolize other fat sources, such as my kidneys, brain, and muscle. He predicted that my general health would decline, beginning with weakness and fainting spells. In fact, just two days earlier, I had blacked out while getting a drink of water at my martial arts class.

My condition back in those days wasn't just some naive, uninformed phenomenon of the times. In January 2000, while dressing in the locker room of a local fitness center, I overheard two buff men in their thirties discussing how adamantly they were striving for twenty-nine inch waistlines. One man was a little over six feet tall; the other was much shorter and built like a fire hydrant. "What's your body fat percentage?" the shorter man asked the taller. "Four percent," he answered. When the shorter man expressed surprise that the taller man wanted to continue to lose weight, the taller man replied that he wished he could go down to two percent body fat, even though, he confessed, his extremities went numb when he went outside into the winter cold.

A few weeks later, at the facility where the retired professor swam his breaststroke every day, I overheard five working professors, from their mid-thirties to mid-sixties, discussing how much discomfort their workouts caused them. After a minute of good-natured laughter at themselves, one of them stopped smiling and said sadly, "If we don't die, we might actually get in shape one day."

Given the current state of medical and fitness knowledge, how does such thinking continue to dominate our ideas of physical fitness? One explanation is that men such as I have described lived through the period during which definitions of fitness came under the influence of the unholy trinity. The power of this influence becomes apparent when you consider that during this same period, physical education—the rational basis for the fitness industry—developed into a respected science that includes physics, human biology, biochemistry, and even basic medicine in its scope.

Today, advanced degree programs in physical education contain medical school level curricula. People holding these degrees, many of them highly trained professionals with a core knowledge based in the latest research, currently staff upscale fitness centers. Yet in spite of this growing sophistication, many fitness centers and health clubs seem haunted by the ghost of some high school gym teacher of the 1950s. Whenever I hear a young aerobics or cardio kick boxing teacher encouraging her class to "feel the burn," I see, so to speak, behind her a sunburned man with a crew cut, muscular legs protruding from red gym shorts, his voice pitched loud, exhorting boys to hurl their bodies forward with maximum effort.

Without realizing it, these fitness professionals are helping to sustain the Herculean mentality of team sports, especially those that became forms of money-producing entertainment, such as football, basketball, and track and field. Many fitness facility professionals over-value qualities expected in collegiate and professional athletics, where the basic skills needed are speed, strength, and durability. We rarely hear about the post-career lives of competitive athletes, which are more often than not stories of pain and debilitation. If we knew more about these outcomes, we might think twice about subscribing wholeheartedly to the Herculean model of fitness. We might give physical fitness its just due and investigate the virtue of the Unified model of fitness, which encompasses the immune system and the mind.

## Samson among the Philistines

From the peewee leagues to the professionals, the life of an athlete is completely circumscribed by the Herculean fallacy, but a more apt metaphor might be that of the biblical figure Samson, who was weakened by the scheming Delilah, then blinded and enslaved by the Philistines. If you consider the level of endurance, strength, and speed enjoyed by collegiate and professional athletes at the outset of their careers, the condition in which many find themselves when they retire at the "ripe old" age of forty-something (if they're lucky) resembles that of the defeated Samson. The cases of such athletic greats as Jim Thorpe, Babe Ruth, Joe Lewis, and Sonny Liston illustrate the accuracy of the Samson comparison.

The problem isn't limited to the great athletes alone. The amount of training required of college and professional athletes is anything but healthy, and the situation for high school sports, especially for participants who show promise, is a kind of preparation for advanced conditions waiting for them in college.

When I was an undergraduate, I had the pleasure of meeting Jonti Skinner, who at that time was the world's fastest freestyle sprint swimmer. As awestruck as anyone might be by chatting with an athlete of Jonti's magnitude, I was surprised when he dolefully commented to me that his dreams consisted mostly of swimming laps. This was understandable for someone who spent six hours every day in a pool. But I also knew that in spite of Jonti's swimming proficiency, his workouts were grueling and painful. It seemed sad that even his dreams provided him no refuge from the ardors of his relentless athletic training.

The sports-entertainment-fitness trinity makes little mention of this aspect of the star athlete's life, and if it does, triumphant theme music plays over a montage of images suggesting success and defeat, watering down comprehension of the constant physical and mental stress that eventually ruins most athletes. Those who fail too many times or get seriously injured are soon forgotten. Sometimes they raise a ruckus in their descent. They might commit a crime or fall prey to drugs and alcohol. High salaries and limited intelligence usually gets the blame, which may be true. But painful, debilitating training schedules that treat human beings like racehorses are also at fault.

The stress of pushing the musculoskeletal system beyond reasonable endurance eventually mounts, and athletes either lash out or do whatever it takes to feel good. Like the blinded Samson laboring under the oppressive Philistines, harried athletes may pull down the pillars of their lives, crashing the roof down on their heads. When this happens, as it did in the case of Mike Tyson, spokespeople for the sports-fitness-entertainment industry frown and scold while the public watches with detachment. Given the conditions of competitive athleticism, it's probably safe to assume that Mike Tyson won't be the last athlete to self-destruct.

Unified Fitness offers a pertinent solution to the Samsons of modern athletics. If competitive sports cripples and maddens athletes, then reflective exercise techniques such as subtle movement and meditation provide a way to heal and soothe without the destructive effects of mood-altering substances. Though I haven't taught any athletes on the level of Michael Jordan or Pete Sampras, those I have taught have been able to recover from the damage done by their conventional training and competitive events. Their performances improved, and they stayed well longer than they did prior to learning subtle movement and meditation.

## Sex and the Herculean Fallacy

The sexual aspect of the retired professor's Herculean bias was as easy to spot as it is in contemporary physical fitness culture. Training facilities, best-selling books and videos, and magazines for both men and women blatantly work "sexy" into the "muscle equals fitness" equation.

Sex may always be the ally of the cult of Hercules, partly because natural selection rewarded physical strength in the reproductive cycle, a pattern repeated across mammalian species. Only in the past few thousand years—a very short time in the grand scope of human evolution—has natural selection been so kind to nonphysical skills. But in recent times the sports-fitness-entertainment trinity have so exaggerated the link between sexuality and Herculean fitness that a singles' bar mentality has come to pervade many health clubs and wellness centers. Herculean fitness instructors help reinforce the lust-fitness relationship.

Over the years, I've known quite a number of men who enroll in classes simply to meet women or ogle the shapely, spandex-bound instructor. Likewise, I've witnessed hordes of sweaty women, perched on stationary bikes, straining to keep up the sadistic pace of hunky alpha males, shouting what sound like war whoops over the constant wail of heavy metal guitar music. Minus the exercising, such scenes could easily take place in a swinging disco.

The assumption here is that most people wrongly hate physical exercise and therefore must be seduced into it. If the outcome of exercise is sustainable health, this assumption has two main problems. First, as the mechanistic and Herculean fallacies demonstrate, there is some credible basis for disliking constant physical exercise. Second, exercising to loud noises and being surrounded by sexually provocative images makes any sort of mind-body benefit impossible to achieve.

Conventional fitness facilities often hear of my fitness approach and invite me to teach for them. Such invitations always call for some consideration of the role sex and the Herculean fallacy play at the facility in question. I have come to see such facilities as tree houses built on the branches of a Herculean tree with thorns that poke through their floors. A large number of those thorns are sexual. In an era of political correctness, everyone avoids speaking about the thorns, but walks carefully around them or gestures to indicate awareness of their presence.

Life in these Herculean tree houses seems orderly enough, until I ask for a quiet room that doesn't have the air conditioning turned to freezing temperatures. Then eyes blink in confusion or narrow like those of a priest hearing a blasphemy. These are very non-Herculean requests, and they are definitely not sexy, especially the quiet part. At this point, I have pressed us very close to the thorns, but not enough to stop the negotiation, so I push on until the facility finds a room that isn't filled with weights, exercise machines, or aerobic dancers.

Forcing a dance class to reschedule brings the thorns perilously close, though not enough to prick the skin. With the situation tightening, I then proceed to the issue of regulating the room's temperature, another problem because most facilities have a central unit that affects the entire building, which must be kept cool for Herculean physical exercisers.

Insisting that the air conditioning be turned down from the central unit is often all it takes to thrust the facility managers into the thorns, destroying my efforts before they can begin, so I usually accept the unhealthy cold and advise my program participants to dress warmly. If the room has independent temperature controls, Herculean fitness instructors using the room before and after my program may object. They may be disdainful of an exercise that appears to use so little exertion. They may not understand why anyone would want to exercise without air conditioning. Either of these reactions indicates that the thorns have broken somebody's skin, but the program usually survives a bit longer. Pressing for quiet usually kills things. To do so thrusts the facility against the sharpest sexual thorns of the Herculean tree: the discothèque music, the TV screens, and the perpetual strutting in front of mirrors.

These ill-considered, sexually driven conditions that dominate most Herculean fitness facilities—the showbiz-like distractions, skimpy outfits, and obsession with improving appearances—bolster their already lopsided conviction that building big muscles, trimming waistlines, and sweating profusely are the keys to fitness. Thus the Herculean fallacy promotes a confusing association between health and sexual attractiveness, making appreciation for reflective exercise, much less teaching or practicing it, even more difficult.

Consequently, the benefits you're likely to gain from training at a conventional fitness facility remain limited, no better or worse than what you would have gotten at a YMCA during the 1960s. You might grow stronger, faster, and sexier, but not necessarily healthier. For sustained health, you must add reflective exercise to your physical fitness routine and work for thematic balance of the mind.

*Consequently, the benefits you're likely to gain from training at a conventional fitness facility remain limited. You might grow stronger, faster, and sexier, but not necessarily healthier. For sustained health, you must add reflective exercise to your physical fitness routine and work for thematic balance of the mind.*

## Arnold Conquers Hercules

Arnold and I used to get unending pleasure from imitating his namesake Arnold Schwarzenegger in the manner of the *Saturday Night Live* characters Hans and Franz, but in reality it was no joke. Arnold's body was solid muscle; an accomplished athlete on all levels, he was a true "Iron Man." He was the most Herculean sports specimen I ever introduced to Unified Fitness.

Just before he started training with me, he had dropped out of college football to pursue academics, but he had remained so devoted to competitive-level workouts that, when I met him, I knew the Herculean fallacy was driving him. His routines invariably produced exhaustion, which opened him up to upper respiratory disease. Once he learned how to counter the problem with reflective exercise, I had his full attention, and he was willing to take a step back and reevaluate his understanding of the term fitness.

Arnold admitted that if he didn't work out every day and perform at the same high levels, he felt despondent. As time went by in his reflective exercise training, Arnold became aware of a tremendous amount of fear and anger percolating beneath the surface of his life; largely it had to do with a conflict in him to excel both in the classroom and on the playing field. He found he couldn't maintain this dichotomy.

Probing further, I learned that Arnold was locked in sibling rivalry with an older brother, who had been a successful college athlete and student. This suggested to me the pattern had to have come from Arnold's parents. They showed all the signs of depressed people (see chapter 8); the father in particular drove himself relentlessly to succeed in both business and competitive sports. As it turned out, regular phone calls Arnold made to his father turned into locker-room pep talks, laced with jock-style pejoratives such as "quitter" and "wimp." Arnold's decision to quit football was something for which his father made him pay dearly, and anything less than straight A's was interpreted as a mark of inferiority.

Though reflective exercise had a big impact on Arnold, I knew that in the face of psychological pressure from his family and from deeply ingrained Herculean habits, he would lapse into self-abuse. As a further measure, I suggested he get counseling. Through this, he was able to comprehend the lessons reflective exercise had begun to teach him.

Shortly before graduating, Arnold confronted his father and managed to carve out his own set of rules for conduct. Rather than a life of self-punishment inspired by a blind and intrinsic devotion to Herculean fitness, Arnold now enjoys the fuller meaning of fitness through the Unified Fitness approach.

## Laura Learns to Separate "Lean" and "Love"

Laura began training with me because she wanted to learn Long Fist, a form of Chinese martial art that features high kicks, big jumps, and floor gymnastics. Thin and muscular, she was a medical student who had grown up on a farm. At first glance, I estimated her body lacked the fat needed to manufacture the hormones governing her menstrual cycle, a phenomenon often seen in anorexic women. When I asked about health problems, I learned that in addition to irregular menses, she had insomnia, suffered from chronic neck pain and headaches, and was susceptible to upper respiratory infection. Laura bore all the signs of the female victim of the Herculean fallacy.

It took about a year to wean Laura from her need to exercise vigorously. During that time she became one of my best Long Fist students. She enjoyed reflective exercise, though for slightly inappropriate reasons. She told me it helped her recover from strenuous workouts so that she could keep exercising at a furious pace.

Eventually, reflective exercise won her over to a different kind of living. She discovered and began to enjoy the more gentle, vulnerable side of her nature, to which she gave more attention. In time, her need for repose and rest balanced out her love of exertion, and she enjoyed greater health than she had since she was a child.

Armed with the peace of mind that comes with Unified Fitness, Laura courageously began to examine the causes of how she had become so Herculean. She read a few psychotherapeutic books I recommended, then went into counseling. Her search took her to the psychological examination of her family, in particular, her mother. She was a compulsive woman who drove Laura and her siblings to believe that they were only lovable if they were laboring as hard as they could. Once Laura uncovered this stealth psychosocial pathology, she was better able to grasp the impetus behind her compulsion to exercise, which reasserted itself in times of stress.

In a short time, Laura came to terms with these feelings and achieved a degree of closure with her family that she feels comfortable with to this day. She completed her medical degree and married another doctor. Shortly thereafter, she gave birth to a healthy child. She continues to practice Unified Fitness, which turns her exercise routine into a source of health and keeps her free from the Herculean compulsions that once robbed her vitality and kept her trapped in a cycle of needless suffering.

# Chapter 12

## Day 35 Continued:
## Troubleshooting Reflective Exercise

While physical fitness may be fraught with difficulty, gaining immunological fitness is no easier. Many obstacles stand or appear to stand in the way. My purpose in this chapter is to alert you to three of the biggest and most common. I will use sixteen case studies to illustrate these obstacles. My hope is that these cases will provide both inspiration and insight into any problem you bring to learning Unified Fitness.

The three main difficulties that can stem progress with reflective exercise are shifting immunological reactions, the time it takes to develop reflective skill, and the myriad forms of pleasure. These difficulties show up right away and can persist or disappear, depending on what strengths and weaknesses you carry into the practice.

A reflective exerciser with a chronic health condition, for example, is likely to have persistent shifting immunological reactions that might undermine confidence and commitment to regular practice. Refusing to budget time to develop reflective skill can also doom reflective progress, as can stubborn devotion to pleasurable habits that interfere with acquiring sustainable health. These three sorts of problems are likely to arise, so be prepared. Discipline and the knowledge that unified, sustainable health would be impossible otherwise can get you past these and other problems that reflective exercise may reveal.

# Shifting Immunological Reactions

When a reflective exerciser suffers from health problems, ranging from low-grade to acute, seemingly unrelated symptoms may appear, shifting abruptly or remaining constant for periods of time. Traditional Chinese medicine would say these reactions indicate that an imbalance is progressing toward balance or that stagnant or "sick" Qi is working its way out of your body. Conventional medicine would most likely see the symptom as unrelated. Evolutionary-based reflective medical theory would indict infectious agents forced into conflict with a neurologically charged immune system.

The following is a list of common fluctuating symptoms that such a neurologically charged immune system might unearth, even if the reflective exerciser has no overt health problems. The list is only a partial one, and symptoms can appear in combination or isolation, depending on the evolutionary fitness of the infectious microorganism.

- Phantom sensations on the skin, such as tickles or itches, as though provoked by insects; or involuntary flickers, as though the insects have made their way beneath the skin's surface
- Excessive tiredness
- Excessive energy
- Increased body heat
- Decreased body heat
- Mood swings
- Low-grade phantom pain, burning, or cold sensations in gums and/or teeth
- Itchy or painful rashes, eczema, blisters, pimples, or sores on the skin, especially in lymphatic regions such as the armpits but also on the scalp, back of neck, ears, and nostrils
- Cessation of chronic symptoms, such as the pain of a frozen shoulder, followed by similar symptoms appearing in a new area or by the appearance of a seemingly unrelated symptom, such as a clogged sinus
- Ulcers inside the mouth and/or on the tongue
- Increased urination

- Abdominal cramping
- Diarrhea

These shifting symptoms can vary in intensity, depending on the health of the practitioner and the evolutionary fitness of the offending germ. A person with severe chronic fatigue symptoms, for example, is likely to have intense, multiple shifting reactions. This is probably the work, at least in part, of the Epstein-Barr virus, whose role in chronic fatigue continues to baffle medical science. A member of the herpes family of viruses, this resilient, wily microorganism is not apt to give ground without a fight that may last a couple of years. On the other hand, someone fighting off a cold virus, a clever but lightweight microbe, may feel nothing more than the phantom skin sensations or a mild rash for a few minutes or a couple of days.

In any case, shifting immunological reactions such as the ones listed above indicate that reflective exercise is forcing the offending infection to make fitness choices that eventually may nudge its evolution away from virulence, toward benignity.

# Time and Reflective Skill

The most common complaint about reflective exercise is that it is too time-consuming. Such a complaint says more about the general naiveté toward health than it does about reflective exercise being time-consuming. Once a person develops reflective skill—the ability to affect internal immunological activity by manipulating reflections—complaints about time tend to fade. The difference between having and not having reflective skill is analogous to the difference between having and not having the ability to perceive three dimensions. A person with three-dimensional perception can see a sphere, but the person with only two-dimensional perception can see only a circle. Until the two-dimensional person develops three-dimensional capacity, a sphere is impossible to conceive.

Fortunately, the potential for reflective skill lies within almost everyone's reach, and it takes very little time to experience the outer fringes of that potential. But opening the ventral neurovascular pathway pushes the time envelop to the limit. Relatively few people have ever sat still for twenty minutes and practiced Reverse Breathing. Therefore, having a solid rationale for doing so is an important first step. The promise of immunological fitness isn't usually sufficient because, like the sphere for the two-dimensional person, it is beyond comprehension.

An effective rationale for spending time developing reflective skill is to think of it the same way you think about developing the skills necessary to earn a college degree. These days, few would argue against the sagacity of devoting time to college education. A hundred years ago, most would. Like learning at the college level in the late nineteenth and early twentieth centuries, the ability to self-heal through reflective exercise is just beginning to dawn in the public mind. Once the importance becomes as recognizable as that of higher education, an increasing number of people will find the time. When that happens, the same disciplinary lessons imparted by college-level learning—that attending class, doing the assignments, and engaging the material in a thoughtful manner ensure success—can be applied to the practice of reflective exercise.

How much time does the practice take? The answer depends on what you want to get out of it. If you only want to learn slow movement, which can build lower body strength, increase balance, lower blood pressure, and relieve stress, then you simply have to put in fifteen or so minutes every day for a couple of months. To begin sensing, then controlling, the ventral neurovascular pathway, you will have to invest more time and effort. However, to get the Unified Fitness results in thirty-five days, you should practice twice a day for forty-five minutes each session. This may seem like an impossible task, given the demands placed on the average person's time. But when looked upon as a skill analogous to that of making high marks in college, the time spent seems more reasonable. When the fitness ramifications are factored in, the thirty-five-day proposition starts seeming like a bargain.

The assumption about earning a college degree is that it will lead you to a higher quality of life. The same is true of reflective exercise. Once you open the ventral neurovascular pathway, you have an unprecedented degree of control over what may be the lynchpin in long-term health: susceptibility to infectious disease, especially upper respiratory infection.

In essence, as a practitioner, you use the ventral neurovascular pathway to either chase infections out of your body or to put pressure on them to evolve toward benignity. This ability represents a huge fitness advantage, in the evolutionary sense. An organism (you, not the microorganism) with that kind of control is more likely to survive longer and better than an organism that doesn't have it.

Once it is established, you can drive, sit at your desk, take breaks at work, or relax on the sofa and maintain the ventral neurovascular pathway with movement, breathing, and meditation routines. What's more, you can combine a short reflective exercise routine with a longer conventional cardiovascular workout and reap even greater rewards.

## Pleasure and Reflective Exercise

It's worth noting that touch—the primary mechanism of reflective exercise—is perhaps the most erotic of the five senses and that the locus of sex drive is deep in the middle of the hypothalamus, the brain's pleasure center. Thus, anatomy places pleasure smack in the middle of the subtle neurological link reflective exercise builds between the vagus nerve and the thalamic and parietal tactile centers. Any tactile sensation must pass through this erogenous pleasure zone before reaching either the thalamic or parietal center. Moreover, it sits between the thalamic tactile center and the vagus nerve, the key to developing reflective skill.

These anatomical complications are probably the reason traditional Chinese fitness takes a cautious, near puritanical approach to most mainstream forms of pleasure, such as alcohol, drugs, rich foods, and sex. Indulging in these substances and behaviors activates the hypothalamus and could easily short-circuit a subtle connection to the vagus nerve. In addition, pleasure-arousing substances combine with hypothalamic perturbations to set off adrenal and liver secretions, vastly altering the biochemistry of the blood, and perhaps further interfering with the vagus nerve activity in the lower abdomen.

Perhaps experience taught the first advocates of Chinese fitness to be especially concerned with sexuality, reproduction, and orgasm in particular, which they believed diverted energy from the crucial struggle against aging and disease. According to this view, men suffer most when they ejaculate, women when they menstruate or bear children. These deficits get worse with age. Though the tradition recognizes that sexual impulses can't be eliminated, it prescribes detailed methods to counter their deleterious effects.

Like most Westerners, I bridled when the idea of limiting pleasure, especially sex, entered my reflective training. But the efficacy of reflective exercise persuaded me to take the traditional Chinese viewpoint seriously. By experimentation, I learned there was substance to it, and by digging into medical science, I found plausible explanations. Gaining this knowledge forced me to change the way I experience pleasure. From the reflective exercise perspective, pleasure becomes a trade-off, a short-term high in exchange for a subtle but perceptible degradation in vitality. Such a perspective provides insight into the motives that led many ancient Chinese Buddhists and Daoists into lives of celibacy and asceticism.

But celibacy and asceticism are extreme reactions. So long as indulgence in pleasure remains moderate, reflective skill grows with regular practice. Regarding the enervations of sex, Reverse Breathing provides a happy solution, enabling a man to withhold ejaculation during sex. This allows him to remain erect longer, permitting greater satisfaction for the woman, who loses relatively little through orgasm, compared to the losses of menstruation and pregnancy. By halting ejaculation the man helps reduce the risk of impregnating the woman, a risk that can be reduced even more with the use of condoms. But condoms might pose a different problem, encouraging the man to ejaculate by removing the threat of pregnancy. On the whole, the burden of making this work falls mostly on the male.

I have ample evidence that unbridled hedonism and sexual pleasure degrade the neurovascular pathway, and that periodically withholding ejaculation and being moderate with alcohol and rich foods serves everyone's health needs. In time, reflective practitioners gain more pleasure from controlling and sustaining their health than they do from substance-

or sex-induced euphoria. Men who practice both reflective exercise and non-ejaculatory sex have the biggest burden and the most to gain.

The first step is learning to use Reverse Breathing to withhold ejaculation. That may involve a good bit of trial and error. Assuming strenuous positions, such as standing and lifting the partner during intercourse, can help as well. If strenuous positions aren't possible, then pressing the feet against the wall or the foot- or headboard of the bed may stave off ejaculation. After sex, males should immediately do Exercise 2B, Six Subtle Movements; 4B, Gentle Chaosercise of the Three Centers; and 3D, Seated Reflective Meditation, for five to ten minutes total.

For females these exercises are optional, but reclining in any comfortable position and moving the pulse along the neurovascular pathway are musts. Such postcoital reflective exercise helps distribute sex-induced endocrine and neurological secretions throughout the body, just as it does with the stress-induced secretions of Exercise 1B, Cardiovascular Exercise, and Optional Exercise 4D, Rigorous Chaosercise. In this way, reflective exercise turns sex into a form of Unified Fitness.

In the main, providing greater satisfaction for female companions isn't enough to compensate men who treasure ejaculating. But with enough practice, they may begin to experience a different set of feelings when they do ejaculate. They may sense an immediate loss of vitality or they may feel an odd discomfort. At this point, they have arrived at an understanding that can help them reform their ejaculatory reflexes. Now they know what the architects of traditional Chinese fitness were talking about.

# Difficulties and Triumphs: Sixteen Case Studies
## Darren Loses a Cold and Gains a Rash

Darren was a practicing physician in his early fifties, with a flair for risk and adventure. In addition to white-water kayaking and bungee jumping, Darren had also visited China to see for himself what sorts of healing powers traditional medicine could boast. The visit impressed him enough to give my instruction a try, and in keeping with his full-bore nature, Darren went as deeply and as quickly into reflective exercise as I could take him. A seasoned runner on top of everything else, Darren confided to me when I mentioned the disease-fighting potential of the practice that he rarely got sick. In my experience, as soon as anyone proclaims they "never get sick," they come down with something inside of a week.

Sure enough, Darren caught a cold shortly following his boast, and after trying all of his usual tricks—such as dosing with vitamin C and gargling with salt water—he decided to do a full-scale reflective work-out, including Rigorous Chaosercise. After completing a forty-minute routine, the cold symptoms seemed to vanish, but when he looked in the bathroom mirror, he was alarmed to see that his face, neck, and torso had broken out in red welts, a "histamine response," he later told me. Darren also confessed that, in panic, he called a colleague who drove over and debated the pros and cons of taking medication to deal with the rash. He decided against medicating, and in a day or so, the welts vanished. The cold was gone as well.

From my perspective, Darren's histamine response was merely an effect of his exerting an influence on the course of the germ's evolution. Because he was able to bring a greater quantity of "smart" lymphocytes to bear on the site of the infection, the virus had to move to other tissues to continue its colonization. In forcing the virus to move, Darren inflicted a hit on the evolutionary choices the germ had. In the skin, the virus was forced to contend with conditions to which it was poorly adapted. There it took its last stand and perished.

## Mary Beats Lupus

Mary hobbled into her first Taiji class with a smile. Middle-aged and draped in Native American jewelry, Mary was so cheerful that I was surprised to learn later that she suffered terrible pain as a result of multiple problems her doctors had diagnosed as lupus, fibromyalgia, chronic fatigue syndrome, and arthritic knees. Lupus is an autoimmune disease that creates inflammation which concentrates primarily in the joints, but can spread throughout the entire body and consequently can cause symptoms similar to those of fibromyalgia, chronic fatigue, and arthritis. An avid hiker and outdoorsperson who associated with some seasoned and tough hunters, Mary was tormented by her condition.

Mary spent a year learning Taiji, and it seemed to spur considerable improvement in her strength and stamina. The improvements gave her the false impression of recovery, which led to a number of overextended hikes in the woods, which in turn caused her condition to worsen. Her pain grew to the point where she had to sit out a few classes. I encouraged Mary to proceed further with a reflective exercise class that was forming within her Taiji class. Though reaching the end of her rope, Mary agreed to give it a try.

After a month of training, she experienced the lower abdominal pulse, which she thought was "nice" but not as effective as what Taiji gave her. But two months later, a remarkable improvement occurred with regard to her constant pain. I warned her about getting cocky, but Mary's exuberance over finally feeling relatively pain-free was exceeded only by her stubborn need to stay active. She immediately resumed her habit of hiking vigorously in the mountains and went bow hunting in deer season. One night she slept in a tree stand and sometime before dawn fell ten feet to the ground and landed on her shoulder. Fortunately nothing was broken, but the event produced a flare-up in her condition.

The pain was excruciating, she said. It had spread from its usual location in her back to her arms and legs. After rest and a regimen of reflective exercise, the pain returned to its normal locations in her upper back and neck. It stayed there for several months, until Mary began a class to help her open the neurovascular pathway up her back. Then the pain rushed out to her extremities again, and this sent her into a panic. I asked her how the pain in her back felt. After moving her shoulders and head around for a few seconds she admitted that it was hardly there. I told her she could expect more of the same if she stuck with the program.

After three years with reflective exercise at the center of her life, Mary's symptoms subsided to manageable levels, sometimes vanishing, returning only when she overextended herself. It had taken a while, but her persistence in the face of shifting immunological reactions to reflective exercise paid off. Reflective exercise also helped reveal a stealth psychosocial pathology to drive herself beyond reasonable limits, which may have weakened her immunity so that the lupus-causing microbe was able to colonize her body. Thanks to reflective exercise, her obsessive and punishing exertions in the woods became healthy cardiovascular exercise, the first step in a sequence that always ended with reflective exercise. She learned to live by Unified Fitness.

*After three years with reflective exercise at the center of her life, Mary's symptoms subsided to manageable levels, sometimes vanishing, returning only when she overextended herself. It had taken a while, but her persistence in the face of shifting immunological reactions to reflective exercise paid off.*

## Constance Subdues Graves' Disease

Constance was a thin woman in her early forties who had already spent a number of years learning Taiji from an Asian teacher. She was very satisfied with his Taiji instruction, but she needed something more. For six years, she had been struggling with Graves' disease, made famous when former President Bush's wife, Barbara, admitted she suffered from the thyroid gland disorder. Some medical experts believe an infectious agent, probably a virus, causes the thyroid to become hyperactive, promoting the development of a goiter, which makes the neck and eyes bulge. Heat intolerance, rapid pulse, and hand tremors are also symptoms of this problem and can interfere with daily life. Because the thyroid secretes hormones crucial to overall health, especially for women, its dysfunction bodes ominously and may signal bigger problems ahead.

Constance was on medication, but she wanted to reverse the disease using natural means. Her experience in Taiji had made her a believer in traditional Chinese medicine, especially Qigong. I gladly accepted her into a reflective exercise program.

Constance's response to reflective exercise was strong, and her symptoms abated swiftly, in particular her heat intolerance and rapid heart rate. Within a few weeks, however, the potency of the practice fell off. The pulsing sensation in her lower abdomen weakened, sometimes fading altogether. The initial euphoria of believing she could immediately turn her condition around subsided. She began to lose faith. I warned her not to give up, that fluctuating responses were common, especially for someone suffering from a chronic illness. Constance nodded agreeably, though the disappointment in her eyes was obvious.

Somewhere in the midst of her reflective training, she got laid off from her job. This was a jolt that might have destroyed another person's resolve to continue practicing, but Constance's persistence, plus the discipline she had acquired in learning complex Taiji forms, enabled her to complete the training. It took her about two months, but she finally obtained a working sense of the ventral neurovascular pathway. When we parted, I said I hoped she would stay in touch, and she promised she would.

A month later, I received a card from Constance informing me that she felt so much better that she had decided to start her career moving in a new direction. She was going to open a Taiji school, which would put her in competition with my business. The card concluded with a hearty thanks and an expression of hope that there would be no hard feelings.

For the first year, Constance struggled for credibility and attention. She attended Taiji and Qigong retreats and increased her knowledge base, which seemed to bolster her confidence. I began seeing her flyers posted all over town, listing impressive credentials and teaching lineage. Finally, her business got its legs, and she continues to make a go of things.

Without reflective exercise, Constance's Graves' disease would most likely have reasserted itself under such stressful conditions—first losing her job then diving headlong into a business with very poor prospects. She didn't let small disappointments undermine her belief in her own capacity to recover her health. Her reward is a life centered on Chinese self-healing exercise.

# Andrea Unmasks the Emotions behind Her Crohn's Disease

Andrea, a middle school teacher, was married with two children when I first met her. She suffered from a chronic gastrointestinal disorder called Crohn's disease, a mysterious inflammation of the digestive tract whose symptoms include pain throughout the digestive system and uncontrollable diarrhea. The condition had plagued her since high school.

After the first few weeks of reflective exercise training, it became clear to me that Andrea was unhappy for reasons that exceeded her health problem. She constantly dropped hints about marital difficulties, which from her perspective centered around her husband's emotional distance. He also had an alcohol problem, which made her withdraw as well. Even so, Andrea did well with reflective exercise and in due course was able to influence her gastrointestinal disorder, at least until our lessons came to an end. Then the trouble returned, and she insisted on continuing with private instruction. I agreed, but asked her questions about her past.

I began by asking about her relationship with her husband. It began in college, where her husband had been an athletic and academic standout. Since her health problem began shortly before that time, I asked her what sorts of relationships she had enjoyed in high school. Though evasive at first, she began to play out a long story about a romance with a boy named Pete, who, like the man she married, was a local athletic star. But unlike her husband, who conformed to the rules, Pete was a rebel with superior intelligence which he used to manipulate people in the small community in which he and Andrea grew up. In fact, it was Pete's flouting of authority that ended up driving a wedge between him and Andrea.

After Pete repeatedly got in trouble with school and law enforcement officials, Andrea's parents pressured her to break it off with him. Her senior year of high school was a struggle between her feelings for Pete, whom she had come almost to worship, and her fear that her parents' contention that Pete was destined for a life of turmoil and poverty was accurate. Finally her parents won, and she broke up with Pete.

While certainly a traumatic moment, I doubted that the breakup was the end of the story, and I persisted in asking what had happened to Pete. Andrea grew morbidly quiet and reported that he had died.

I didn't feel comfortable pressing any further and decided to leave the story alone, but I had started something that I couldn't turn off. Andrea seemed to attach herself to our lessons more firmly than ever, and she insisted on talking a great deal about the first year of her relationship with her husband, which started two years after breaking up with Pete. She described how happy she had been, and how during that time she had no symptoms of the gastrointestinal disorder she had suffered shortly after breaking up with Pete.

Then one day she darkened like a stormy sky and remarked that she had gotten involved with her husband to help her get over Pete, with whom, she admitted, she was still in love. I responded by taking the tack that she had made the right choice in breaking up with Pete, whose premature death would surely have hurt her a great deal. Andrea answered this by recounting the moment she ended the relationship with Pete over the phone. He reacted to the news with rage and sadness. After accusing Andrea of abandoning him, Pete hung up the phone, took out his father's revolver, and shot himself in the head.

When Andrea said this, she exploded into weeping, and I did my best to commiserate. I asked her if she had told anyone else about the phone conversation; she said she hadn't. Just as I had accepted the blame for my brother's death, so had Andrea internalized fault for Pete's suicide. To my thinking, this internalization had to be at least partly responsible for her Crohn's disease.

Andrea's confession not only helped remedy her health problem, but it was a good reason for her to enter into psychotherapy, in which she could work out her emotional problems. In spite of the clear benefit of counseling, she couldn't rid herself of her symptoms without continuing with reflective exercise, suggesting to me that there may have been an infectious component to her condition enhanced by her unresolved emotional state. But even with these improvements, her relationship with her husband went from bad to worse, and finally they separated in a bitter and contentious manner. She moved to another town and started her life over again.

Because I could no longer work privately with Andrea, I lost touch with her. But the progress she made in facing her troubled emotions and her improved immunological fitness through reflective exercise helped free her from a chronic disorder that had severely limited her happiness.

## Sydney Controls Her Migraines and Sciatica

Sydney was in her middle thirties with two small children when she signed up for a Taiji class sponsored by a local hospital wellness center. She had suffered from sciatic pain since the birth of her second child; the sciatica had been brought on by a misaligned pelvis, her physical therapist said. Sydney had been treated with acupuncture, which gave her noticeable but transient results. It was, however, enough to encourage her to experiment with Taiji. When Sydney confessed that she also endured massive migraine headaches during menstruation, I suspected that more was involved than a musculoskeletal problem.

After Sydney completed the Taiji course, I invited her to join a reflective exercise class. Sydney's sciatic pain had lessened to such an extent that the prospect of getting even better results with Reflective Meditation convinced her to try it. At first she was disappointed. Though able to sense and vaguely control the lower abdominal pulse, Sydney had limited success in reducing her symptoms, especially her migraines, which came with her menses. Rigorous Chaosercise would probably have sped things along, but her sciatic pain limited her ability to move vigorously. Still, the limited amount of Rigorous Chaosercise she was able to do had a noticeable effect on her sciatica and migraines, and Sydney was persuaded that she was on to something good for her health.

Over the course of a year, I watched Sydney battle her condition with reflective exercise, observing a metamorphosis, whose most intriguing aspect was a severe outbreak of contact dermatitis on her foot, on the same side of her body where her sciatica manifested. With the appearance of the rash, both her sciatic and migraine symptoms faded. Once the rash cleared up, the sciatica and headaches returned, though less intensely than before. Each time she concentrated on opening a neurovascular pathway to her hip, leg, and head pain, the rash came back. After a month or so of these shifting immunological symptoms, she began to feel a sense of control over her condition, and the pain grew increasingly dim.

Just when Sydney thought she had overcome the problem, it rose up again. She fired questions at me one day that suggested she felt betrayed over what seemed like false goods. After reminding her of her previous victories, I asked her a few questions, which disclosed the obvious reason for her relapse: stress. Sydney's life was loaded with stress, from the two small children she had to care for to her hardworking husband who had little time or energy left for her or their children when he got home in the evening. I also learned that Sydney suffered from low self-esteem, which she masked with perfectionism and constant activity.

Our discussion spread out over several months, but eventually Sydney recognized that if she wanted to overcome her problems, she had not only to practice reflective exercise devoutly, but also to learn to recognize how she invited stress into her life. In time, Sydney was able to take a step back from her situation and rethink who she was and where she had come from. This led her to explore her relationship with her parents, who were themselves troubled people. The more she put into this effort, the easier it became for her to control her own stress-induced reflexes, and reflective exercise became a tool that helped her to clarify her emotional response to stress and to reduce her sciatic and migraine symptoms.

# Will Prevails over Prostatitis and a Ruptured Lumbar Disc

Will was born in Germany where he lived with his family until he was twelve. He looked and acted like all the other nineteen-year-olds enrolled at the university and had no trace of an accent; it seemed as though he had worked hard to fit in. But Will couldn't help but stand out. He was brighter than most, and he suffered from a chronic lower back pain that usually visits people later in life.

Will began an exercise program with me to relieve the relentless back and sciatic pain that had been troubling him. He traced the problem back to a skiing accident, in which he had fallen and taken the impact on his lower spine. After several months of stretching and lower muscle strength training, it became clear that Will's problem required medical attention. He saw a back specialist who took an MRI that showed that Will's fifth lumbar disc had been ruptured. The doctor recommended surgery. I recommended reflective exercise.

Within two weeks, Will had attained the lower abdominal pulse and was able to work the ventral pathway, but he was not effective at self-treating his back. Primarily this was because he hadn't been practicing long enough to open up the more difficult dorsal route. Because I had never experienced such pain myself and because of Will's youth, I continued to oppose the idea of his undergoing surgery, my self-healing experience with my hand being my only argument. I backed down finally when Will came in to see me in tears, his agony so apparent it practically wafted off of him like heat. He had the surgery, spent a month in rehabilitation, then began training with me again.

Not long after his operation, Will developed another problem: chronic prostatitis, an inflammatory swelling of the prostrate gland causing pain during urination and ejaculation. Prostatitis isn't a health problem one would expect to find in someone so young, but several physicians agreed on the diagnosis. They prescribed a dozen or so antibiotics, including the heavyweight Cypro, none of which had much effect, except to worsen the constipation Will had suffered from since childhood.

Regarding the constipation, I suspected an emotional psychosocial pathology was at work, so I recommended that Will see a psychotherapist. He followed my advice, and in a short time discovered that his German parents were the source of a great deal of his unresolved confusion. His mother, a concerned and protective woman, inadvertently contributed to his confusion.

Though helpful, this insight didn't make Will's prostatitis or constipation go away, so I began to agree with Will's doctors that some sort of antibiotic-resistant microbe was causing the problems. It had been about a year since his back operation, and according to his flexibility and lower-body strength he seemed capable of starting Rigorous Chaosercise, which he hadn't been able to do before his surgery. I instructed him on how he could use vigorous gyrating movements to break up the infection in his pelvis. After completing the Rigorous Chaosercise routine in full, he followed with Exercise 3D, Seated Reflective Meditation, for no less than twenty minutes, twice a day. The routine was painful for Will, but he noticed after a few sessions that he was able to dissipate the pain. This encouraged him to persist and to follow the routine to the letter.

Two weeks later, Will strolled into my office with a big smile. His prostatitis was gone, and his constipation had let up. His doctors were scratching their heads, but were relieved that the year-long problem had resolved itself. Will recounted how he had tried to explain to his doctors that reflective exercise had done the trick, but the looks on their faces silenced him. "Get used to it," I advised, congratulating him on his victory.

Will's case demonstrates the efficacy of Rigorous Chaosercise in turning the tide on stubborn infections immune to antibiotic treatment. The infection's location—the extreme lower abdomen—showed that Will's lower body immunity lacked sufficient power to defend the area. The disappearance of disease symptoms suggests that the entire reflective routine imparted the necessary power. It may have done so by first increasing circulation in the prostrate/colon vicinity, creating more opportunity for lymphocytes and phagocytes to get to the infection. Gentle Chaosercise and Reflective Meditation probably encouraged the vagus nerve and the "brain in the gut" to secrete neurotransmitters that further enlivened the immunological activity around the infection.

Once the infection was tamed, inflammation and swelling went down. The prostate gland and the colon were free to function normally. The resolution of the infection allowed him to stop taking the antibiotics that seemed to be making his constipation worse. Not long after finishing his last round of pills, the constipation vanished.

With this immediate health threat out of the way, Will spent the next few years managing the occasional pain in his lower back with Exercises 1D, Optional Advanced Stretching and Strengthening; 1C, Cardiovascular Exercise, (brisk walking); and 3-4 reflective exercises. In addition, the work he began in psychotherapy continued to improve his mental fitness, allowing him to reconnect with his former life in Germany and to establish healthy boundaries between his parents and him.

## Jerry Controls His Allergies

Jerry came to me to study reflective exercise in the first few years that he was an assistant professor in East Asian studies at the local university. Having spent extensive time in India, Tibet, and China, Jerry was familiar with a number of high-level yogic practices and with an array of gurus, masters, monks, and priests.

In spite of this background in Eastern spiritual traditions, he suffered relentlessly from allergies, and they made his life difficult. Under the stress of getting tenure, his health situation was going from bad to worse. With a graduate student in Hindu studies who also suffered from a health problem (a bad lower back), Jerry began studying Taiji and Chinese martial arts with me, then took up reflective exercise after I persuaded them to try it.

It was a tough sell. Both young men had a lot invested in meditation practices that consumed whatever remaining time they had, but I challenged them to substitute reflective exercise for their usual practices for a couple of months. At the end of that time, they would either have greater health or the satisfaction of discrediting my theory.

In the short run, both of them experienced improvements, but the graduate student's health problem was much worse than Jerry's, so his change was minimal. Though the severity of his ailment influenced the speed of his progress, the graduate student was also hampered by skepticism from the outset. Jerry, on the other hand, had much better results, largely because reflective exercise delivered the right remedy to the area of his body most in need: increased blood and lymphocyte flow to the nasal sinuses.

But Jerry had also seemed less threatened by the prospect that what he was learning from me exceeded the immediate value of the practices he had already learned in the East. In time, Jerry's allergies came increasingly under the control of his neurovascular ability, though publishing deadlines, hectic grading periods, and tenure committee meetings took their toll. Once he made tenure and his life settled down, he was able to manage his condition better than ever, even during the spring, which was usually the worst time for his sinuses.

*Jerry's case is as a model for how an advocate of a particular idea, faith, or tradition can maintain interest and commitment in his beliefs, while focusing on the core fitness benefits of reflective exercise.*

The graduate student, who left town and finished his degree at another university, continued working with his neurovascular ability, combining it with various yogas and meditation techniques that gave him a greater sense of ownership or participation. Eventually he was able to dissipate his lower back pain by sending the lower abdominal pulse to his back.

Jerry's case is a model for how an advocate of a particular idea, faith, or tradition can maintain interest and commitment in his beliefs, while focusing on the core fitness benefits of reflective exercise. Both Jerry and the graduate student found in reflective exercise a wealth of experiences and insights that illuminated their other studies. People such as Jerry may become the voices of a new generation of East-West culture, able to discern the threads of truth that weave in and out of the major Eastern traditions, leading us into greater understanding of what ancient Eastern texts have to teach us about body and spirit, and the relationship between the two.

## Connie Conquers PMS

Connie was a graduate teaching assistant in computer science who began studying Taiji and reflective exercise with me at the age of twenty-six. Though gentle and very sensitive by nature, Connie had been an overachiever since childhood and had developed an intellectual aggressiveness to distinguish herself in what was at the time a male-dominated field.

Connie seemed healthy, but she had one problem that bode poorly for her: intense PMS. It gave her such severe cramps that she took as many as twenty-eight ibuprofen pills a day to function. At this time, Paul Ewald had not yet published *Evolution of Infectious Disease,* so my perspective on Connie's condition was strongly influenced by traditional Chinese medicine, which places menstrual cramps on a pathological continuum, with mild endometriosis at one end and uterine cancer at the other. After explaining the potential danger of her condition, I outlined how reflective exercise in general, and Rigorous Chaosercise in particular, could help head off possible disaster. Connie seemed skeptical, having lived with her condition since she was fourteen, but she was disciplined and willing to try anything to avoid developing a greater health problem. Added incentive came from Connie's roommate. She was a young woman in her mid-twenties who suffered continuously with uterine bleeding and pain.

When Connie first began Rigorous Chaosercise, she felt a cramp in her liver (which traditional Chinese medicine identifies as the organ that controls the menstrual cycle). I encouraged her to keep moving until the cramp became unbearable, which it did in a short time, dropping her to the floor. When the cramp diminished, Connie got back up and provoked it again with rigorous movement (the Elvis proved especially effective here).

Within a week, she found that she could move longer without developing the liver cramp, and a couple of weeks later, when her menstrual cycle began, she menstruated with a minimum of cramping, resorting to one or two ibuprofen on the worst day. This encouraged her to keep working with Rigorous Chaosercise, and the next menstrual cycle was a shade milder. Within three months of beginning her reflective exercise training, Connie's menstruation was asymptomatic, and she no longer took medication for the discomfort.

Over the course of a year of committed practice, she not only eliminated her cramps, but took up a daily regimen of Unified Fitness. As she gained greater control over her health, she discovered that much of the personality she had evolved in the process of trying to distinguish herself intellectually was adding to the problem. She learned to recognize and avoid aggressive behavior that brought into play the sympathetic nervous system, which she could feel subtly eroding her reflective skill. Eventually she went into therapy to access the more gentle and sensitive side of her character, which led to greater insights and more healing.

Connie went on to marry and bear two children. Though unable to use reflective exercise to affect her first birth—it was an unfamiliar and uncontrollable experience for her—she was more confident with the second birth and used her power to manage her contractions. By Connie's account, the midwives and nurses marveled whenever she got off the bed during a contraction, passed her hands through the air a few inches over her swollen abdomen, and calmly reported that the contraction was over.

# Deborah Defeats Lyme Disease

Deborah was in her early fifties when she started taking Taiji lessons from me. A lithe, humorous woman who dyed her hair purple, Deborah owned a boutique that specialized in outlandish clothes, jewelry, and greeting cards. A month after moving from Taiji to reflective exercise, she woke one morning after a day of puttering in her garden to find on her skin the bull's-eye mark of a deer tick bite, a sure sign of the infection that leads to Lyme disease. Though she sought treatment immediately, the flu-like symptoms were on her within a week, leaving her constantly exhausted and her joints sore.

One night, after practicing reflective exercise for a couple of weeks, Deborah went through her reflective routine, which consisted at this point of subtle movement, Gentle Chaosercise, and Reflective Meditation. When she finished, she reported that during Gentle Chaosercise, she felt an odd heat fill up her body and suffuse from her skin into the air, as though some inner contaminant had been driven out of her, creating the sense of a burden lifting off her. While seated in meditation, she also felt the lower abdominal pulse, which climbed the ventral pathway to her sinuses, then dropped back down to the pelvis in time with her breath.

*The stealth strategy of the Lyme bacterium is part of the secret to its success in parasitizing humans. . . . Deborah's heightened immunity through reflective exercise probably struck a fatal blow to the germ when it was most vulnerable to attack.*

In the days that followed, Deborah showed up for Taiji class with the happy news that her Lyme disease symptoms had vanished. Her joints no longer hurt, and the feverish weakness that plagued her throughout the day had relented. She was as pleased as I was astounded. Based on what I knew about Lyme disease, I was expecting more resistance. I suspect that early intervention had a lot to do with the ease with which Deborah had dispatched the infection. To this day, her health remains good and the Lyme disease hasn't recurred.

The stealth strategy of the Lyme bacterium is part of the secret to its success in parasitizing humans. Like syphilis, the microbe works slowly, spreading throughout the body to infest not just muscles and joints, but also the brain, lungs, and even the heart. Deborah's heightened immunity through reflective exercise probably struck a fatal blow to the germ when it was most vulnerable to attack. Dealing with the effects of the bacterium at later stages would have been tougher. Her immune system might have killed off the germ, but the damage done to nerves and tissues might have been irreparable.

## Cara Overcomes Chronic Sinusitis

Cara was a hardy, vigorous woman in her late forties who had helped start and preside over a leading hospital's emergency room. With little outside help, she had planned and built her own house. She had single-handedly raised a daughter who won an academic scholarship to a prestigious university. Cara also ran her own landscaping/

horticultural business. I recognized that such exertions had surely exacted a price in terms of Cara's health. For twenty years, Cara's sinuses had been so clogged that she could neither smell nor taste.

A number of factors might have been responsible for Cara's blocked sinuses. Of course, she had allergies, and working among plants certainly didn't help this. Then there were the twenty years that she had been a chain-smoker. She also kept a large number of animals, which, with a career that literally kept her beating the bushes, led me to suspect she had been chronically infected by deer tick bites. When I questioned her about deer ticks, she laughed and said she plucked them off her skin almost every day. If Lyme disease were part of her problem, then the advanced stage of the disease made her prospects for recovery quite different from those of Deborah.

In any case, I was confident Cara could relieve her sinuses if she could develop and sustain the lower abdominal pulse. But first Cara wanted to learn Taiji, something that required less practice time and which she could easily drop if she didn't like it. I agreed to the arrangement, but at least once a week I demonstrated or talked about the virtues of reflective exercise, especially regarding its ability to clear the nasal sinuses. With each of these hints, Cara's interest grew stronger, and after about four months of Taiji, she was ready to try reflective exercise.

The reflective exercise group that Cara joined met only once a week, so things went slowly. But after six weeks, Cara began to feel the lower abdominal pulse; it registered in her head as a nonlocalized throb, but it failed to unblock her sinuses. A few weeks later when the class took up Rigorous Chaosercise, Cara began to get results.

At first Rigorous Chaosercise made her head hurt. I encouraged her to regard this pain as the source of the block and advised her to shake her head, no matter how painful. Eventually, the pain would either subside or migrate. It did both, finally retreating to the back of her head. At that point, the pulse rose into her sinuses and opened them. In disbelief, Cara tested each nostril. They were open.

The next time I saw Cara, she brought me a chocolate cake she had made. It was one of the best I have ever eaten. When I complimented Cara on her baking skills, she confessed that cooking was something in which she had always excelled. "Now after twenty years, I can finally taste my work," she said.

I wish I could say that Cara's recovery was that easy, but like most people with chronic, infection-based illness, her battle had only just begun. The swelling that robbed her of taste and smell returned repeatedly, but each time, Cara used reflective exercise and Rigorous Chaosercise to fight back. So long as she maintained a twice-daily routine, she could keep the problem under control.

After a year of fighting the problem by using the ventral neurovascular pathway, Cara was able to open the dorsal pathway so that she could put pressure on the cerebellum, the place the pain preferred (at the back of her head), whenever she cleared her sinuses. Eventually, she manifested a number of shifting immunological reactions, especially on her skin, indicating that she was pressuring some infectious agent—perhaps the Lyme bacterium—to migrate again, forcing it to adapt to another environment. With each symptomatic change, Cara's nasal difficulties lessened, though she still remained dependent on maintaining her routine.

By taking a series of blood tests, Cara could determine whether or not the Lyme bacterium was part of her problem. But her success with reflective exercise makes the effort unnecessary. Whatever the infectious cause, Cara's case illustrates that reflective exercise can greatly reduce a chronic condition by forcing the responsible entity to move and adapt to terrain that hinders its ability to harm its host.

## Grover Grapples with Salmonella *Poisoning and Wins*

At twenty-six, Grover was working on an advanced literary degree at a nearby university, but he looked more like a young potato farmer from *The Grapes of Wrath*, whose large hands seemed better suited for digging with a hoe than clutching a pencil, pecking the keys of a word processor, correcting freshman English essays, or writing critical papers on modern American poetry. But it was Grover's love of

American romantic poetry, which had sent him on a search for greater insight through meditation, that led him to reflective exercise.

Grover achieved the abdominal pulse quickly and was able to move it up and down the ventral pathway fairly easily. He dissipated a couple of head colds before they could set in, which pleased and impressed him. But Grover was a private man, uneasy in groups, so when he completed the program, he set off on his own.

Six months later, he showed up to participate in a program to help open the dorsal neurovascular pathway. This was a relatively brief course that took two weeks. Afterwards, Grover vanished as he had before, and I would have lost track of him entirely if a friend of his who trained with me hadn't kept me informed. Far from letting his practice languish under the pressures of graduate school, Grover made his reflective routine central, developing a ritual that included burning incense and poetic touches such as lighted candles, pictures of his favorite authors, and old Celtic symbols.

Then one day Grover showed up on my doorstep, looking pale and thin. He had been ill the past couple of days from an infection that had almost overwhelmed him. Using only reflective exercise, Grover had fought off the disease, but was so daunted by the severity of the symptoms that he went to a doctor afterward to find out what had made him so sick. After hearing Grover's story, the doctor concluded that he had most likely been poisoned by *Salmonella* bacteria.

Grover's troubles started when he ate chicken fricassee at a local restaurant that had a reputation for making people sick. Fricasseeing a chicken involves cooking the bird at a low temperature, which allows a bacterium like *Salmonella* to live. Within hours of eating the chicken, Grover was beset with abdominal cramps and a high fever. He felt exhausted but was too uncomfortable to sleep, so he practiced reflective exercise and Rigorous Chaosercise, which caused some of the cramping in his viscera to migrate to his muscles and extremities. But the majority of the pain localized along his right side, around the liver, and refused to budge. After completing the moving portion of the routine, he meditated for half an hour and felt better, though the pain, fever, and weakness persisted.

Grover rested for an hour, then did another reflective session. During Rigorous Chaosercise, the abdominal cramps moved across his viscera to his left flank, around the stomach and pancreas area, and from there the cramps shot into the muscles of his chest, shoulders, and back. The fever and weakness subsided.

Meditation dissipated the pain even more thoroughly, and he was left with only an odd sensation on the lower end of his left latissimus dorsal muscle, which began to jump and twitch as though an angry bee were trapped beneath the skin. For hours afterwards, Grover lay on his right side and watched the muscle leap and spasm. Eventually the spasms stopped. A day later, a patch of purulent boils formed on his left forearm. These boils were most likely the vague remnants of the *Salmonella* infection that had almost sent him to the emergency room two days before.

Grover's experience illustrates that reflective exercise and Rigorous Chaosercise can effectively stem acute infections. It also shows a progression in how the exercises can help the immune system do its job. First, reflective exercise excites the immune system, then Rigorous Chaosercise amplifies that excitation and provokes pain to help locate deep concentrations of the infectious agent. The vigorous movements seem to encourage these deep concentrations to migrate to superficial layers of the body until they are trapped and dispatched in the skin. This progression is natural, but reflective exercise and Rigorous Chaosercise appear to speed the process.

## Sylvia Reverses Her Chronic Bladder Infection

Sylvia and her husband, Dirk, were an affluent couple in their late thirties who led busy, interesting lives. Though both were physically active—Sylvia rode show horses and her husband rock-climbed—their bodies were starting to register the punishment their chosen diversions put them through over the years. With all the publicity stirred up by Taiji and yoga, they were curious to see what all the attention was about. Their massage therapist referred them to me.

Bright and savvy, Sylvia and Dirk learned reflective exercise quickly and integrated it into their lives. It helped counter some of the damage their horse-riding and rock-climbing inflicted, and showed them how the Herculean fallacy was undermining their health. Of the two, Sylvia experienced the most profound healing, because she suffered a chronic problem: bladder infection, or cystitis.

Doctors generally treat chronic cystitis in women with a regimen of antibiotics, cranberry juice, and sexual abstinence, because intercourse can irritate the bladder and urethra. In fact, sexual activity often can provoke an infection—but so can stress. According to Sylvia, her bouts of cystitis had come on several years earlier, and flared up between five and seven times annually, each lasting a week to ten days. Aside from the annoyance of the infection itself, the antibiotics created side effects such as slight abdominal cramps and nausea.

During her initial training in reflective exercise, Sylvia's bladder was asymptomatic, but a few months later it began to show signs of infection. Her symptoms began as a cold (tiredness, stuffy sinuses, swelling and irritation in the throat), but then rapidly changed into those of a bladder infection. Rather than run to the doctor and refill a prescription, she decided to use reflective exercise.

Though Rigorous Chaosercise seemed to help reduce symptoms such as the constant urge to urinate, she got the best results with meditation. During that time, she directed the lower abdominal pulse up to her head, then down to the bladder, where she felt immunological reactions such as tingling, twitches, and pinpricks on the skin. When she finished, she went to the bathroom and urinated a thick, bloody discharge. After that, all symptoms of her bladder infection vanished. Since then—it's been three years—Sylvia has suffered no relapses.

Sylvia's reversal of her cystitis shows patterns seen in previous cases. Reflective exercise caused her immunological reactions to shift and to speed the natural progression by which the body rids itself of infection. The bloody discharge was probably the result of increased vascular and inflammatory activity focused on the site of infection through Reflective Meditation. She was able to express the consequences of that activity through her urethra, rather than through her skin, as Grover did in overcoming his *Salmonella* infection.

The unusual thing about Sylvia's case is the way her cold symptoms appeared to transform into cystitis. This suggests that different infectious agents may work in concert to degrade health, a phenomenon now well documented in HIV research. Synergy between germs could be what makes the symptoms of chronic diseases flare. If so, then the added boost to immunity that reflective exercise produces may prove a cheap and effective way to manage the problem.

## Daphne Crushes Kidney Stones with Lithotripsy and Reflective Exercise

Daphne was a professional counselor who observed many positive changes in a client after he learned reflective exercise from me. This piqued her interest, as she had a bad back that continued to trouble her in spite of years of yoga. In fact, at one time she had been one of the top students of a famous guru, and though she had grown disillusioned with the guru and the culture he had created around him, she still practiced many of his stretches and postures.

In her early forties when she first sought my help, Daphne willingly shared many stories and lessons that illuminated mental health issues pertinent to me and my students. Her childhood had been troubled, which had led her into a number of unhealthy relationships, including a marriage that ended in divorce. Psychotherapy had helped her reconcile hurt feelings over these bad experiences and identify the aspects of her personality that had set her up in the first place. But there was a layer of unresolved sadness slightly noticeable in her voice and manner, and I felt certain that Daphne's ability to unearth this remnant of grief would determine her success with reflective exercise.

As I predicted, Daphne's progress went slowly. She took double the normal time to achieve the lower abdominal pulse, and when she got it, her sense of it was fleeting and insubstantial. Her disappointment only made things worse, so I decided it was probably best if I began pushing her a little to confront her unresolved feelings—ironically, a difficult thing for a professional psychotherapist to do.

I felt Daphne was up to the challenge, and she didn't disappoint me. During her meditations, she went into a pool of fears and anxiety and surprised herself by sobbing several times. Once she had cleared that hurdle, the abdominal pulse became more consistent, and she was eventually able to move it up and down the ventral pathway. Combined with Rigorous Chaosercise, her reflective routine began to have an impact on her aching back.

As time passed, Daphne employed reflective exercise to successfully handle the stress of her job and the constant onslaught of infection. (In my experience, psychotherapists tend to suffer a great deal of low-level infection.) These successes encouraged her to take up Taiji and the stretching and strengthening program presented in the opening chapters of this book.

Things appeared to be going well for Daphne, but then she caught a serious upper respiratory infection from a client. Reflective exercise merely held the germ at bay, and so she turned to medication to reduce the symptoms.

A month later, she awoke in the middle of the night to urinate and experienced excruciating pain in the process. The pain was severe enough to send her to the doctor, who sent her on to the hospital for a battery of tests, including ultrasound. This showed the presence of a large kidney stone, eight millimeters in diameter. The doctor laid out the possible strategies, the most effective being lithotripsy, which entailed immersing Daphne in water, then using a powerful ultrasonic pulse to shatter the stone. The downside was that the doctor would have to insert a metal rod through Daphne's urethra to move the stone, which was blocking the opening. The rod would undoubtedly irritate and hurt the urethra, ensuring even greater pain when she passed the fragments of the stone. When Daphne called me for advice, I told her to listen to her doctor, but emphasized that she should use reflective exercise to recover.

The lithotripsy broke up the stone, but the pieces were larger than expected—one of them about three millimeters—certain to cause urethral pain when it passed with her urine. The doctor gave Daphne a sedative and warned her to expect severe pain.

He gave her more sedatives for home use, but Daphne's tolerance for such drugs was limited. Rather than resort to medication, she spent the next day resting and practicing Reflective Meditation, barely able to feel the pulse in her lower abdomen. Several times she got up to urinate, cringing in anticipation of the pain, but the pain never came. When she called her doctor and told him that she hadn't felt any pain, he immediately assumed the medication had vanquished the problem. She didn't tell him that she hadn't taken the drugs.

*Given the evidence of the immunological function of reflective exercise, it is equally possible that Daphne increased blood flow and phagocytic activity in the pelvis, and in so doing eroded the kidney stones so they could be passed without discomfort.*

A month later in her follow-up visit with the doctor, the three-millimeter stone had not passed, and the doctor again warned Daphne to expect pain when it did. Daphne continued to use reflective exercise to focus on her bladder. The pain never came, and six months later another examination revealed that the stone was no longer inside her. Scratching his head, the doctor gave her the good news that somehow she had managed to pass the large fragment without pain.

At first blush, Daphne appeared to have used reflective exercise to self-treat for pain, suggesting a purely neurological or even psychological result. But given the evidence of the immunological function of reflective exercise, it is equally possible that Daphne increased blood flow and phagocytic activity in the pelvis, and in so doing eroded the stones so they could be passed without discomfort.

## Tom Controls His Meningitis

Tom, a tall man in his early forties, began studying reflective exercise with me when he was in the throes of divorce, but he had bigger problems. For a number of years, he had suffered from osteoarthritis, formerly considered a disease with genetic and unknown causes.

Currently, evidence suggests that infection may play a role. Tom's case indicates that role may be quite large.

Tom's arthritis was in his knees and hips, but it was especially concentrated in his right shoulder, where in childhood he had undergone corrective surgery. Tom experienced such pain that he could barely do subtle movement. An additional problem that appeared to be related to his arthritis was an occasional flare-up of meningitis, an inflammation of brain tissue that can result in death in some cases. Because of the sporadic nature of this aspect of his health problem, Tom failed to mention it to me, so I was unable to offer Tom any warnings other than my standard caution that reflective exercise can awaken old symptoms or create new ones.

To make a complex situation even more so, Tom was a very ambitious fellow. As it turned out, he had been experimenting with various forms of Qigong. He knew just enough about Qigong to get himself in trouble. Despite my admonition to stick with the ventral neurovascular pathway—ideally the one and only initial goal of reflective exercise—Tom decided he was the exception to the rule and began experimenting with the dorsal pathway far ahead of schedule.

The first thing that happened was Rigorous Chaosercise appeared to make the pain in Tom's right shoulder move to his left shoulder, leaving his right shoulder pain-free by comparison. I took this as an indication that Tom's problem was infectious by nature—viral, bacterial, or both. Once again, Tom chose to ignore my opinion. He went to several doctors and a physical therapist, all of whom said the pain in Tom's left shoulder was due to a physical injury, most likely a torn rotator cuff. The doctors and the physical therapist concluded that an MRI was needed.

In the meantime, the pain became increasingly intense. Over the weekend, Tom started to feel as though the meningitis was coming on, so he called me and asked for help. Tom revealed that he had been trying to open the dorsal pathway ahead of schedule, which meant that he lacked the neurovascular capacity to put pressure on the virus/bacterium that had evolved over many years of conventional medical treatment into a determined adversary. As a result, he may have not only started an unwinnable war against the germs that had colonized him, but helped them migrate to new ground where they were pursuing their boosted drive to feed and reproduce.

Since the immediate threat was in his brain, getting immune-enhanced blood to that area seemed crucial, so I suggested that Tom lie prone and use the ventral pathway to self-treat his meningitis. I advised him that if this approach proved ineffective, he should get to his doctor or to an emergency room immediately. If he succeeded in calming the symptoms, he should try working on his inflamed shoulder via the ventral pathway.

The following Monday, Tom showed up for class with an amazing story. By following my advice, he had succeeded in stopping the meningitis from flaring up and had eliminated the pain from his shoulder. A few days later, Tom dropped by with more stunning news. He had just discussed the results of an MRI his physician had requested. There was no torn rotator cuff, but there were a couple of cysts (perhaps lipomas or fatty tumors) that were pressing on nerves in Tom's left shoulder. The physician theorized that the cysts had shrunk (perhaps, he conceded, because of Tom's "meditation practice") and thus no longer pressed on the nerves.

Of course another explanation is that Tom effectively focused his immune system on the site of an infection and brought it under control. The cysts may have been all that remained of the infection. If so, then so-called benign growths such as lipomas may be the aftermath of a battle between the body's immune system and an infectious agent.

## *Jane: A Cautionary Tale*

I met Jane before I went to China. She was in her mid-fifties at the time and worked as a psychotherapist for a major industry in the area. She lived with her husband, Frank, a bear of a man, in a cabin on a beautiful plot of land far from any signs of urbanization. Both Jane and Frank had grown up in New York City and wanted to live out their remaining years in Thoreauvian style. How Jane spent that remaining time was keenly important to her as she had been a breast cancer survivor for twenty years.

I have met few people as intense and talented as Jane and Frank, and I marveled at their courage and energy. It was only after I returned from China that I began to see a different side of them. Frank had injured his back working on the land and had given up building their dream house, which would have allowed them to move out of their one-room cabin. I tried to help him with acupressure massage techniques and liniments I had brought back from China, but the effects never lasted, and Frank turned to pills and dry martinis for relief. Jane, who previously had been cautious about alcohol, joined Frank in his evening libations. Given their state of affairs, I wouldn't have begrudged her a toddy or two, but there was one problem: her breast cancer had returned.

I offered to teach her reflective exercise and let her feel my lower abdominal pulse and how I could move it up my centerline, passing through the sternum, the place where the cancer had come back in her. She decided to try it, and I agreed to teach her under the condition that she stop drinking. This dismayed Frank, who was fond of the nightly ritual. I warned Jane that Frank might make trouble, but she assured me she would handle whatever he dished out.

Jane brought the same intensity to reflective exercise she applied to everything she did. In less than a month, she attained the abdominal pulse and brought it to bear on the site of the tumor. She was being treated at Duke University Hospital, and when she went for her regular visit, the doctors were astounded that the tumor had vanished.

Though as jubilant as Jane, I was cautious in my optimism and warned her that she would have to persist in her practice for the rest of her life. The news of this seemed to shock her, as though she had expected the exercise to work like chemotherapy, a regimen that could be dropped once the desired effects had been achieved. If she took this news badly, my insistence that she continue to completely avoid alcohol was untenable to her. At one point, I pressed her to talk about her relationship with Frank, who, she admitted, had degenerated into a shadow of his former self. When I remarked that if I were in her position I would be angry with Frank, she denied having any such feelings.

I decided to let the matter go, but she came back the next day and said she had thought over what I had said, and realized she was furious with Frank because he had welshed on his promise to build their dream house. This development came after she had spent many years as the breadwinner, enduring hardship as a result of her cancer and their minimalist living conditions. I urged Jane to talk things over with Frank and to insist that he stop drinking. If he refused, then she should move away and take care of herself.

Jane listened to my advice, which, though harsh, was reasonable from my perspective. She thanked me for my counsel and left. I never saw her again. I called her at work one day and she admitted that she hadn't been practicing and that she and Frank were drinking together again. A month or so later, her cancer returned, and she died within weeks.

I mourn the loss of Jane, but she taught me an important lesson that I might not otherwise have taken seriously. Reflective exercise represents a strong healing force, but like a tender bud poking from the ground in spring, it needs to be nurtured and protected until it becomes a viable plant capable of sustaining itself.

In all of these sixteen cases, reflective exercise posed difficulties for the people involved and the means of their triumph over their health problems. Those with more serious chronic disease required greater discipline and commitment than those with less threatening conditions to sustain their resolve against setbacks, shifting immunological reactions, and stealth psychosocial pathologies. Though Jane's situation posed the greatest difficulty out of the sixteen cases, I firmly believe that had she been able to keep practicing in an emotionally supportive environment, she would have lived longer and more happily. Even so, her efforts and those of the others illustrate the self-healing power of reflective exercise and its central place in the Unified Fitness approach.

## Amy Thwarts Metastatic Breast Cancer

Amy, a freelance journalist and homemaker, was diagnosed with metastatic breast cancer in her mid-thirties. She had already undergone a double mastectomy, radiation, and chemotherapy, so was horrified to learn when she went in for a follow-up exam that X rays had shown tumor sites in her lungs and hip. Amy tried a number of other therapies, such as a macrobiotic diet and hormone therapy, before a friend steered her toward Unified Fitness. Having achieved little sense of success with these other alternative therapies, she began her work with the program and reflective exercise under a cloud of gloom. The physician presiding over her chemotherapy treatments informed Amy that most people in her condition died between 10 and 18 months after diagnosis.

Within her third week, Amy began to feel results. During reflective exercise, she claimed to have had a vague sense of being able to feel inside her chest, near where the X rays had shown the tumor in her lungs. One day she felt something like turbulence near the tumor site and got a gentle bursting sensation as well. When she reported the incident to me, I suggested that she regard the experience as completely valid.

Two weeks later, she returned for an X ray of her tumor sites. Though the tumor on her hip showed no change, the one in her lung appeared to be dead, merely a mass of scar tissue. Exuberant, Amy contacted family members and me with what she thought was great news, but then came the letdown. Her physician doubted that the cancer was dead and urged Amy to resume chemo. Amy refused, over the stern warnings of the doctor.

Amy completed her 35-day class, but kept working on her own. She checked in every so often, reporting odd sensations and reactions to the exercises. When she said she had felt tremendous pain in her hip, around the tumor site, I speculated that the neurolymphocytes were working on the area, trying to separate healthy and carcinogenic tissue. Amy took my opinions with a grain of salt. She had been through a lot the previous year, and a number of wellness gurus had promised her pie-in-the-sky results and failed to deliver. Still, her experience with reflective exercise had been so encouraging that she kept up a twice-daily routine.

At the end of four months, she went back for a bone scan, fully prepared for a death sentence, even though she felt better than she had in years. The results were conclusive this time: both tumor sites were unquestionably dead.

Amy's case is fascinating because it leans toward affirming reflective exercise as an effective cancer treatment. If reflective exercise allowed Amy to neuro-charge, channel, and focus her immune system to tame her cancer, then it's reasonable to accept the possibility of Paul Ewald's theory that the genesis of many cancers is microbial. But more interestingly, Amy's case indicates that the immune system is a crucial player in overcoming cancer. Recent findings by Drs. John Nemaniatis and Lawrence Fong of Stanford University have come to a similar conclusion, suggesting that the immune system may play a vital role in *preventing* cancer, a view that runs contrary to the pervading medical consensus since the mid 1970s (Beasley). But the Stanford research is focused on the possibility of developing vaccines for the prevention of cancer, a possibility that Ewald's theories suggest must take into account the evolutionary nature of microorganisms, which are likely to develop counterstrategies in the face of such a widespread selective pressure. Thus, any creation of a vaccine without a deep understanding of the evolutionary tendencies of the infectious agent may generate another problem.

On this point, I'm reminded of the time that both Paul Ewald and Dr. Thomas Braciale, the immunologist at the University of Virginia School of Medicine, remarked to me that the immune system is the greatest defense against disease, bar none. According to Ewald, the best medical intervention constitutes two or three weapons in the war against germs, while the immune system constitutes over 100 such weapons. Braciale agrees with this assessment. Given those odds, I'll take the immune system over drugs. And Unified Fitness delivers the immune system in a uniquely conscious and highly focused way.

# Conclusion

## *The Health Benefits of Unified Fitness*

The Unified Fitness program consists of the best methods of traditional Chinese and conventional fitness rolled into a condensed package. It stretches and strengthens the musculoskeletal system, tones the cardiovascular system, activates and educates the immune system, and stabilizes the mind. It turns health into a sustainable resource, like air and water, and provides a means of efficient use and daily renewal. Its theoretical base combines traditional Chinese, conventional, and evolutionary medicine and adheres to the position that infectious disease poses a health threat that cannot be stemmed by antibiotic treatment or conventional exercise programs. Unified Fitness micromanages the threat within the body.

Unified Fitness delivers sustainable health through six exercise series, which, along with three optional exercises, are divided into three phases. Phase 1 covers Exercise Series 1, a stretching, cardiovascular, and dietary regimen designed to address mainstream physical fitness concerns. Phase 2 consists of Exercise Series 2 through 4, which collectively constitute reflective exercise, a method of making the immune system "smarter" in order to help tame infectious disease and its long-term degradation of health. Phase 3 introduces Exercise

# *The 35–Day Program at a Glance*

## Days 1–7. Learning Phase 1: Getting Physically Fit

**Exercise Series 1:**  1A Self-Mobilization

1B Lower Body Stretches

1C Cardiovascular Exercise

1D Advanced Stretching and Strengthening

Dietary regimen.

*Optimal time: 48 minutes; minimum time: 34 minutes.*

## Day 8. Learning Phase 2: Opening the Door to Immunological Fitness

**Exercise Series 2:**  2A Abdominal Breathing

2B Six Subtle Movements

*Time: approximately 25 minutes.*

## Day 9. Phase 2 Continued: The Door Opens Wider

**Exercise Series 3:**  3A Standing Reflective Meditation

3B Sensing the Middle Center

3C Closing Sculpt

3D Seated Reflective Meditation

*Optimal time: 35 minutes; minimum time: 19 minutes.*

## Days 10–15. Unifying Phases 1 and 2

Combine Exercise Series 1 with Exercise Series 2–3.

*Optimal time: 1 1/2 hours; minimum time: 34 minutes.*

Second Phase 2 Exercise

*Optimal time: 35 minutes; minimum time: 19 minutes.*

## Days 16–30. Deepening Phase 2: Going Through the Door

Exercise Series 4:   4A Gentle Chaosercise of the Low Center (Days 16–22)

4B Gentle Chaosercise of the Three Centers (Days 23–29)

4C 16-Step Acupressure Massage (Day 30)

*Unified Fitness (Phases 1 and 2 combined) optimal time: 1 1/2 hours; minimum time: 38 minutes.*

*Second daily practice (Phase 2 or reflective exercise only) optimal time: 41 minutes; minimum time: 26 minutes.*

## Days 31–32. Phase 2 Continued: Taming Germs

Exercise 4D (Rigorous Chaosercise), inserted in Phase 2, following Exercise 2B, Six Subtle Movements.

*Optimal time: 46 minutes; minimum time: 29 minutes.*

## Days 33–35. Phases 3 and 4: Prone Relaxation Meditation, Mapping and Using the Mind, Discovering the Spirit, Troubleshooting Unified Fitness

Optional Exercise 4E Prone Relaxation Meditation

*Optimal time: 20 minutes; minimum time: 5 minutes.*

Exercise Series 5:   5A Mapping the Mind

5B Using the Map

*Time: approximately 25 minutes.*

Exercise 6: Discovering the Spirit

*Time: approximately 20 minutes.*

Phase 4: Troubleshooting Unified Fitness

*Time: approximately 20 minutes.*

# Unified Fitness

Series 5 and 6 to identify psychological obstacles blocking the path to sustainable health. Phase 4 helps steer a course around fallacious notions of physical fitness and off-putting difficulties arising from reflective exercise. Followed with devotion, the program can produce stunning health benefits in thirty-five days.

Your thirty-five-day investment breaks down to the following commitment:

## Optimal

*A little over two hours a day, broken into two sessions:*
*Ninety minutes of Unified Fitness and forty-one minutes of Reflective Exercise.*

## Minimum

*A little more than an hour, also broken into two sessions:*
*Thirty-eight minutes of Unified Fitness and twenty-six minutes of Reflective Exercise.*

Once completed, the program can become a part of your life and yield even more satisfying benefits. When the good results start to accrue, there is plenty of room to experiment, especially with Phase 1. You may find that you don't need to do cardiovascular exercise every day, or you may find ways to make the suggested menu more appealing, based on the nutritional guidelines or on recipes you glean from other sources.

Phase 2, however, should remain a constant in your life, along with the lessons of Phase 3. Reflective exercise, unlike conventional forms of exercise, isn't bound absolutely to times, places, and conditions. You can practice certain aspects of reflective exercise, such as Exercise 2A, Reverse Breathing, or 3B, Sensing the Middle Center, while driving your car or sitting at your work desk. Similarly, the insight provided in Phase 3, Exercises 5A, Mapping the Mind; 5B, Using the Map; and 6, Discovering the Spirit, tends to sit at the forefront of your thoughts and actions, so that what you say and do contributes to helping you sustain, rather than waste, health.

# Reviewing the Theory behind Unified Fitness

Unified Fitness blends up-to-date conventional wisdom with a novel but plausible explanation for the seemingly miraculous results touted by advocates of traditional Chinese healing. Phase 1 consists of exercises that conform to boiler-plate medical ideas of the benefits of cardiovascular exercise, strength training, stretching, and nutrition. Unified Fitness distinguishes itself here by emphasizing contra-indications that should caution some people from doing them.

Phase 2 takes on the ambitious task of using a technical theory to account for the mechanisms by which traditional Chinese healing works its "magic." The theory reclassifies traditional Chinese exercises such as Qigong and Taiji as "reflective exercise," because they involve sensing "reflections," thermal, magnetic, acoustic, and electrostatic energy the body projects into the surrounding air. When the nerves in the hand detect these reflections, tactile centers in the brainstem, thalamus, and parietal lobe activate. Increasing sensitivity to reflections surrounding the pelvis, chest, and head (the Low, Middle, and High Centers) encourages the neurological chain to integrate with the deeper vagus nerve, which may gain tactile capacity. This allows the reflective exerciser to feel the internal sources of the reflections filling the air around the three Centers. Stroking the air a few inches from the body can elicit an internal reaction. This is known as "reflective skill."

The integration of the vagus nerve with the tactile centers in the brain leads to an ability to sense and manipulate portions of a venous pathway from the intestines to the heart. The vagus nerve's heightened capacity likely stimulates the flow of brain chemicals (neurotransmitters and neuropeptides) along this pathway and to the internal organs that the vagus nerve helps regulate. The increased flow of these substances probably encourages dense lymph glands in the intestines (Peyer's patches) to secrete lymphocytes, whose cell surfaces naturally bind to neurotransmitters and neuropeptides. The venous pathway carries these lymphocytes to the heart, which then pumps them into the arteries, one of which goes to the head.

Once there, the lymphocytes receive an even more thorough bath in neurotransmitters and neuropeptides. Thus, they become "smarter," capable of sharing chemical messages with other cells, including nerves and other lymphocytes. These intelligent lymphocytes can then rove the body's vascular and lymphatic channels, building extraordinary immunological ability.

Over time, these neurolymphocytes may build up in number and sophistication so as to make possible the development of an extraordinary "neurovascular" network of pathways, which eventually assumes a general structure. Reflective exercise builds this network of pathways, starting with the ventral pathway from the intestines to the head. These neurovascular pathways are likely the basis of traditional Chinese acupuncture channels, conceived empirically more than two thousand years ago without the benefit of microbiology. The theory of the neurovascular mechanisms behind reflective exercise explains this ancient concept in medically plausible terms.

The importance of reflective skill becomes clearer when considered along with some recent breakthroughs in evolutionary biology. This field of study has produced some startling suggestions about the influence of microorganic parasites on human health. According to compelling evidence gathered by Paul W. Ewald, microorganisms may be responsible for serious chronic illness long thought to have been genetic or multi-factoral in origin. Heart disease, cancer, stroke, and diabetes (both Types I and II) may be the result of cradle-to-grave infections that constantly wear us down. Moreover, these infections don't sit still. They evolve, sometimes rapidly, in response to environmental changes and opportunities, and they have been doing this longer than humans have been around.

Modern developments, such as air pollution and airtight buildings, represent opportunities to which evolutionary biology predicts microorganisms will respond. Health statistics back this prediction. Upper respiratory diseases, such as asthma, allergies, and nonspecific bronchitis, have seen a twenty-fold increase since the 1970s. Upper respiratory disease, even as a minor health threat, confronts anyone trying to achieve sustainable health. Strong evidence suggests that an airborne bacterium causes coronary artery disease, the biggest killer in the world. Other ordinary infections may prove to play major roles in the development of a host of serious, life-threatening diseases. From such a perspective, the situation seems daunting.

Great encouragement, however, lies in the ability of the reflective exerciser to fight, and perhaps even affect the evolution of low-grade infection. Such an ability is not simply a hopeful sign in an otherwise bleak scenario; it may provide science with a window on new approaches to treating disease, approaches first explored and mapped by cultures such as classical China. A serious, detailed examination of the mechanisms by which reflective exercise effects cures or improvements in people suffering from a broad range of illnesses may pave the way for a happy convergence between ancient Eastern medicine and modern medical science.

Perhaps the most convincing argument on behalf of the theory behind Unified Fitness lies in the fifty-one case studies presented in the book. The range of health problems illustrated by the case studies, along with the level of relief and cure the program helped bring about, suggest that Unified Fitness (especially the reflective exercise phase) operates on a set of immunological principles.

Based on this and other evidence I've seen or experienced first-hand, I suggest that Unified Fitness offers one of the best self-help approaches to sustainable health currently available. My hope is that this book will not only open more people's eyes to this self-healing program, but will also spark increased interest and research in Unified Fitness, reflective exercise, and traditional Chinese medicine. I hope that this may, in turn, widen our understanding of how we can best prevent and heal life-threatening disease and injury.

Such an understanding cannot help but lead us to greater fulfillment, but it also may be our best defense against the potential health threat of evolving infectious organisms hiding under our noses and in our backyards. New research suggests that some of these microbes may be possible causes of chronic, debilitating, and lethal disease. One day, practitioners of Unified Fitness may be considered pioneers who took steps to protect against this danger, and in so doing, established a globally accepted human value: sustainable health.

# References

Beasley, Deena. 2001. "Researchers Say Cancer Vaccines Hold Promise," Reuters 15:52, Mar. 13.

Braciale, Thomas. 2000. Interview by author. Nov. 9.

Ewald, Paul W. 1994. *The Evolution of Infectious Disease*. New York: Oxford University Press.

————. 2000. *Plague Time*. New York: The Free Press (Simon and Schuster).

Fox, Maggie. 2001. "Study: Infections Could Be Linked to Heart Disease," Reuters 15:48. Feb. 26.

Fukuyama, Francis. 1996. *The Great Disruption: Human Nature and the Reconstruction of Social Order.* New York: Doubleday.

Gaessar, Glenn. 1996. *Big Fat Lies.* New York: Fawcett Columbine.

Guyton, Arthur C., M.D., and John E. Hall, Ph.D. 2000. *The Textbook of Medical Physiology,* 10th ed., Philadelphia: W. B. Saunders.

Krause, William J., and J. Harry Cutts. 1981. *Concise Text of Histology.* Baltimore: Williams and Wilkins.

Luczak, Hania. 2000. "Neurology: How the Abdomen Governs the Head," *Geo Magazine* 11 (November), pp. 1–9.

Parham, Peter. 2000. *The Immune System*. New York: Garland.

Pert, Candace B. 1997. *Molecules of Emotion*. New York: Scribner.

Real, Terrance. 1998. *I Don't Want to Talk About It: Overcoming the Legacy of Male Depression.* New York: Scribner.

Sapolsky, Robert M. 1998. *Why Zebras Don't Get Ulcers*. New York: W. H. Freeman.

Schnatterly, Steve. 2000. Interview by author, November 7.

Sears, Barry. 1995. *The Zone*. New York: Regan Books.

Wheater, Paul Richard. 1993. *Wheater's Functional Histology*, 3d ed., edited by H. George Burkitt, Barbara Young, and John W. Heath. Edinburgh, United Kingdom: Churchill Livingstone.

# Index